PHILADELPHIA

HOW TO USE THIS GUIDE

The first section consists of useful general information—Facts at Your Fingertips—designed to help you plan your trip, as well as local facts that will be of use while you are traveling.

Next is an Introduction to help you with the background of the area that this Guide covers—the cultural scene, some historical insights, regional food and drink, and so on.

Following the Introduction comes the detailed breakdown of the area, geographically. Each chapter begins with a description of the place or region, broadly describing its attraction for the visitor; this is followed by Practical Information to help you explore the area—detailed descriptions, addresses, directions, phone numbers, and so forth for hotels, restaurants, tours, museums, historical sites, and more.

Two vital ways into this book are the Table of Contents at the beginning and the Index at the end.

FODOR'S TRAVEL GUIDES

are compiled, researched and edited by an international team of travel writers, field correspondents, and editors. The series, which now almost covers the globe, was founded by Eugene Fodor in 1936.

OFFICES
New York & London

FODOR'S PHILADELPHIA:

Area Editor: JOYCE EISENBERG

Editorial Contributors: MICHAEL ELKIN; PEARL GRIKA; POLLY HURST; BARBARA LEMPERT

Editor: DEBRA BERNARDI

Editorial Associate: AMIT SHAH

Illustrations: TED BURWELL; MICHAEL KAPLAN

Maps and Plans: PICTOGRAPH

FODOR'S
PHILADELPHIA

FODOR'S TRAVEL GUIDES
New York

All the following Guides are current (most of them also in
the Hodder and Stoughton British edition).

COUNTRY AND AREA GUIDES:

AUSTRALIA, NEW ZEALAND & THE SOUTH PACIFIC
AUSTRIA
BELGIUM AND LUXEMBOURG
BERMUDA
BRAZIL
CANADA
CANADA'S MARITIME PROVINCES
CARIBBEAN & THE BAHAMAS
CENTRAL AMERICA
EASTERN EUROPE
EGYPT
EUROPE
FRANCE
GERMANY
GREAT BRITAIN
GREECE
HOLLAND
HONG KONG
INDIA, NEPAL & SRI LANKA
IRELAND
ISRAEL
ITALY
JAPAN
JORDAN & THE HOLY LAND
KENYA
KOREA
MEXICO
NORTH AFRICA
PEOPLE'S REPUBLIC OF CHINA
PORTUGAL
SCANDINAVIA
SCOTLAND
SOUTH AMERICA
SOUTHEAST ASIA
SOVIET UNION
SPAIN
SWITZERLAND
TURKEY
YUGOSLAVIA

CITY GUIDES:

AMSTERDAM
BEIJING, GUANGZHOU, SHANGHAI
BOSTON
CHICAGO
DALLAS AND FORT WORTH
GREATER MIAMI & THE GOLD COAST
HOUSTON
LISBON
LONDON
LOS ANGELES
MADRID
MEXICO CITY AND ACAPULCO
MUNICH
NEW ORLEANS
NEW YORK CITY
PARIS
PHILADELPHIA
ROME
SAN DIEGO
SAN FRANCISCO
STOCKHOLM, COPENHAGEN, OSLO, HELSINKI, & REYKJAVIK
SYDNEY
TOKYO
TORONTO
VIENNA

WASHINGTON, D.C.

U.S.A. GUIDES:

ALASKA
CALIFORNIA
CAPE COD
COLORADO
FAR WEST
FLORIDA
HAWAII
NEW ENGLAND
NEW MEXICO
PACIFIC NORTH COAST
SOUTH
TEXAS
U.S.A.

BUDGET GUIDES:

AMERICAN CITIES
BRITAIN
CANADA
CARIBBEAN
EUROPE
FRANCE
GERMANY
HAWAII
ITALY
JAPAN
LONDON
MEXICO
SCANDINAVIA
SPAIN

FUN GUIDES:

ACAPULCO
BAHAMAS
LONDON
MONTREAL
PUERTO RICO
ST. MARTIN
SAN FRANCISCO
WAIKIKI

CONTENTS

FOREWORD

Philadelphia is more than the Liberty Bell. Though the city certainly has enough restored sites to satisfy any American history buff, it is also the location of world-famous art collections, fun ethnic neighborhoods, fine restaurants, beautiful parks—and so much more.

Fodor's Philadelphia is designed to help you plan your own trip to Philadelphia and the surrounding area—whether you're coming to see the Pennsylvania Ballet or eat a cheesesteak. We have, therefore, tried to offer you the widest possible *range* of activities and within that range *selections* that will be safe, worthwhile, and of good value to you. The descriptions we provide are designed to help you make your own intelligent choices from among our selections.

All selections and comments in *Fodor's Philadelphia* are based on personal experiences. We feel that our first responsibility is to inform and protect you, the reader. Errors are bound to creep into any travel guide, however. Much change can and will occur even while we are on press, and also during the succeeding twelve months or so that this edition is on sale. We sincerely welcome letters from our readers on these changes, or from those whose opinions differ from ours, and we are ready to revise our entries for next year's edition when the facts warrant it.

Send your letters to the editors at **Fodor's Travel Guides, 2 Park Avenue, New York, N.Y. 10016.** Continental or British Commonwealth readers may prefer to write to Fodor's Travel Guides, 9-10 Market Place, London W1N 7AG, England.

FACTS AT YOUR FINGERTIPS

 FACTS AND FIGURES. Philadelphia is the largest city in Pennsylvania and the fifth largest in the nation. According to the revised 1980 census, the population of Pennsylvania approaches 12 million; Philadelphia has approximately 1.69 million residents, the metropolitan area 4.72 million.

Location has always been an asset for the city and the state. Pennsylvania, nicknamed the Keystone State, was in the keystone position of the thirteen original colonies. Situated at the crossroads of the northern and southern colonies, Philadelphia was the birthplace of the nation. William Penn founded the city on a strip of land between the Schuylkill (skoo-kill) and Delaware rivers, 70 miles up the Delaware from the Atlantic Ocean. The city's location on the eastern seaboard, between New York and Washington, D.C., makes it easily accessible. New Jersey is at its eastern border; Delaware is to the south.

The metropolitan area loosely incorporates Philadelphia, Bucks, Chester, Delaware, and Montgomery counties, as well as three neighboring counties in southern New Jersey. This region (plus a few other counties) is known collectively as the Delaware Valley. Our guide concentrates on Philadelphia proper, but includes the major attractions nearby.

Philadelphia began as a thriving port city. Today, in the still-busy port, modern freighters have replaced sailing ships. Once predominantly a manufacturing city, Philadelphia is now a leader in the service industries of education, insurance, banking, government, medicine and health-related services. Other industry is still vital to the economy—particularly textiles, refining, chemicals and pharmaceuticals, printing, publishing, food processing, and the manufacturing of machinery and fabricated metals.

The ethnic mix here includes almost every European nationality, as well as Blacks, Hispanics, Chinese, and the more recent immigrants from Southeast Asia. Tourists are drawn to Philadelphia—they numbered 4 million in 1983—by the city's rich Colonial history and by its wealth of museums, lively arts, and beautiful parks.

 PLANNING YOUR TRIP. If you don't want to bother with reservations on your own, travel agents won't cost you a cent, except for specific charges like telegrams. They get their fees from the hotel or carrier they book for you. A travel agent can also be of help if you prefer to take your vacation on a "package tour"—thus keeping your own planning to a minimum. If you prefer the convenience of standardized accommodations, remember that the various hotel and motel chains publish free directories of their members, which enables you to plan and reserve everything ahead of time.

If you drive and don't belong to an auto club, now is the time to join one. These clubs can be very helpful with maps, routings, and providing emergency service on the road. Write to: *American Automobile Association*, 8111 Gatehouse Rd., Falls Church, VA 22047; or *Amoco Motor Club*, P.O. Box 9014, Des Moines, IA 50306. The *Texaco Oil Company* will send maps and mark preferred routes on them if you tell them what you have in mind. Write to *Goucha Chek Chart, Texaco Travel Service*, P.O. Box 381, Comfort, TX 78013. Most states have their own maps which pinpoint attractions. Convention and visitors bu-

1

reaus and chambers of commerce are also good sources of information. Specific addresses are given under "Tourist Information," below.

Look into the purchase of trip insurance (including baggage), and make certain your auto, fire, and other insurance policies are up-to-date. The American Automobile Association (AAA) offers both group personal accident insurance and bail bond protection as part of its annual membership fee. Flight insurance is often included in the price of the ticket when the fare is paid by major credit card. Before buying any separate travel insurance, check your regular policies carefully; many travelers unwittingly end up with redundant coverage. Several organizations offer coverage designed to supplement existing health insurance and to help defray costs not covered by many standard policies —emergency transportation, for example. Some of the more prominent of these organizations are: *NEAR* (Natonwide Emergency Ambulance Return), 1900 N. McArthur Blvd., Suite 210, Oklahoma City, OK 73127; (800) 654–6700. *Carefree Travel Insurance,* c/o ARM Coverage, Inc., 9 E. 37 St., New York, NY 10016; (212) 683–2622. *International SOS Assistance, Inc.,* P.O. Box 11568, Philadelphia, PA 19116; (800) 523–8930. *IAMAT* (International Association for Medical Assistance to Travelers), 736 Center St., Lewiston, NY 14092, in the U.S.; 188 Nicklin Rd., Guelph, Ontario N1H 7L5, in Canada. You may also want to investigate trip cancellation insurance, especially if you're flying a charter or APEX, where you might get stuck paying for a flight you are unable to be on. This insurance is usually available from travel agents. A valuable source of information on travel insurance is the *Travel Information Bureau,* 44 County Line Rd., Farmingdale, NY 11735; (516) 454–0880.

Today, most people who travel use credit cards for important expenses such as gas, repairs, lodgings, and some meals. Consider converting the greater portion of your trip money into traveler's checks. Since some hotel and motel chains give discounts (of 10 to 25 percent) to senior citizens, be sure to have some sort of identification along if you qualify. Usually AARP or NRTA membership is best. (See "Hotels and Motels," below.)

 TIPS FOR BRITISH VISITORS. Passports. You will need a valid passport (cost £15) and a U.S. Visitor's Visa (which can only be put in a passport of the 10-year kind). You can obtain the visa either through your travel agent or airline, or directly from the *United States Embassy,* Visa and Immigration Department, 24 Grosvenor Sq., London W1 (tel. 01–499 7010/3443). Allow four weeks if applying to the Embassy by mail; if you apply in person, your visa can be obtained in about three hours.

No vaccinations are required for entry into the U.S.

Customs. If you are 21 or over, you can take into the U.S.: 200 cigarettes, or 50 cigars, or 2 kilos of tobacco; 1 U.S. liter of alcohol. Everyone is entitled to take into the U.S. duty-free gifts to a value of $100. Be careful not to try to take in meat or meat products, seeds, plants, fruits, etc. And avoid narcotics like the plague.

Insurance. We heartily recommend that you insure yourself to cover health and motoring mishaps, with *Europ Assistance,* 252 High St., Croydon CRO INF (tel. 01–680 1234). Their excellent service is all the more valuable when you consider the possible costs of health care in the U.S.

Tour Operators. The price battle that has raged over transatlantic fares has meant that most tour operators now offer excellent budget packages to the U.S. Among those you might consider as you plan your trip are:

American Express, 6 Haymarket, London SW1.

Thomas Cook Ltd., P.O. Box 36, Thorpe Wood, Peterborough, PE 3 6SB.
Cosmos, Cosmos House, 1 Bromley Common, Bromley, Kent BR2 9LX.
Cunard, 8 Berkeley St., London W1.
Jetsave, Sussex House, London Rd., East Grinstead RH19 1LD.
Page and Moy, Z Hatfields, London SE1.
Speedbird, Alta House, 152 King St., London W6.

Air Fares. We suggest that you explore the current scene for budget flight possibilities. Unfortunately, there is no longer any standby service on any of the major airlines, but do check their APEX and other fares at a considerable saving over the full price. Quite frankly, only business travelers who don't have to watch the price of their tickets fly full-price these days—and find themselves sitting right beside an APEX passenger!

Hotels. You may have need of a fast-booking service to find a hotel room. One of the very best ways to do this is to contact *HBI-HOTAC,* Kingsgate House, Kingsgate Place, London NW6. They book rooms for most of the large chains (Holiday Inns, Hilton, Ramada, etc.), so you can have a multiple choice with only one contact. HBI-HOTAC specializes in booking for business firms, but also deals with the general public.

TOURIST INFORMATION. For Philadelphia proper, write or call the *Philadelphia Convention and Visitors Bureau* at Three Penn Center Plaza, Philadelphia, PA 19102; (215) 636–3300. Once you've arrived, visit or call the *Tourist Center,* 1525 John F. Kennedy Blvd., 568–6599. It is open every day except Christmas from 9 A.M. to 5 P.M. The *Visitor Center of Independence National Historical Park,* at 3rd and Chestnut sts., has information about the most important historic sites.

For the areas outside Philadelphia, see the specific addresses in the Practical Information sections of the appropriate chapters. For statewide information, contact the *Pennsylvania Bureau of Travel Development,* 416 Forum Bldg., Harrisburg, PA 17120, and request their "Best of Friends" kit of maps and brochures.

WHEN TO GO. In terms of weather, the best times to visit Philadelphia are in the mild, late spring and early fall. Like other northeastern American cities, Philadelphia can be uncomfortably hot and humid in the summer and freezing cold in the winter, although in recent years the weather has been too unpredictable to categorize.

Ultimately, anytime is right for a visit—for there are special pleasures to enjoy throughout the year. For sports fans, the schedule is packed with exciting competition year-round. In **summer,** the *Philadelphia Orchestra* gives free concerts at the Mann Music Center; there are also free performances at Penn's Landing and other outdoor plazas. The *Freedom Festival* celebrates the nation's birth and Philadelphia's prominent role in it with hot-air balloon races, restaurant extravaganzas, and special ceremonies. In **winter,** the highlight is the spectacular *Mummers Parade* on New Year's Day. The orchestra, theater, and ballet seasons are in full swing; and the *Philadelphia Flower and Garden Show* takes center stage.

In the **spring,** the city is at its most beautiful. The cherry blossoms come into bloom (Philadelphia has as many as Washington, D.C.), followed by the azaleas, tulips, and dogwoods. The city shows off with its *Easter Parade* and *Open House tours.* **Autumn** offers *Super Sunday,* a giant block party; numerous parades; and the *Army-Navy football classic.* Philadelphia has one of the most beautiful exurban regions of any American city. The rolling green hills and woodlands of the areas described in our "day-trip" sections are beautiful when the foliage changes in the fall.

PACKING. Travel wardrobes should be selected with an eye toward where you will be spending most of your time and the types of public places you will be frequenting. For sightseeing and daytime wear, almost anything goes in Philadelphia—from jeans, shorts, and T-shirts to conservative blue blazers and New Wave fashions. Select your clothes with comfort in mind.

For evenings (and for lunch in the finer restaurants) women may want to take along a casual skirt and top. Pants are acceptable almost anywhere. Men should take a sports jacket with an open collared-shirt, and a dress shirt and tie. Men might also wish to bring along a suit, and women, one or two dresses (which can be varied with a simple change of accessories) for special nights out.

The weather in Philadelphia is capricious and has been known to drop 40 degrees in 24 hours. Dressing in layers is the most practical option and good for going from overheated restaurants into the cold. Be prepared for all possibilities by packing a sweater and a light overcoat or raincoat. For late fall, early spring, and winter, substitute a warm outer coat. There are days when you'll want to wear that and your sweater. When it's really cold, you'll see plenty of parkas and heavy boots worn with the fanciest suits and dresses. You can be fairly certain of hot, humid summer days, so cottons are recommended over synthetics. But bring along a sweater for the many restaurants that are chilled by air conditioning.

An increasing number of in-town hotels have swimming pools, so be sure to pack a bathing suit if you're staying at a hotel or motel with such facilities.

WHAT WILL IT COST? The cost of a stay in the Philadelphia area can vary tremendously, depending on the accommodations you choose and your general style of travel. Lodging generally costs more in Philadelphia than it does in the areas outside the city, but if you stay in a Center City hotel, you can save on the cost of a rental car (and a daily parking fee) because so many attractions and restaurants are accessible by foot or taxi. From downtown, you may find it cheaper to take tours to the outlying areas than to rent a car and do it yourself. Whereas you might be charged $6 or $7 for a breakfast in your hotel, you can pay 50 percent less for similar fare in a restaurant just around the corner. (Add 9 percent tax to hotel bills; 6 percent to restaurant charges.)

Typical Expenses for Two People

Room at *moderate* hotel	$65
Breakfast at hotel or motel, including tip	$12
Lunch at *moderate* restaurant, including tip	$15
Dinner at *moderate* restaurant with wine, including tip	$40
Miscellaneous: drinks, admissions to museums and historic sites, bus or subway fares (taxis not included)	$15
	$147

A list such as this leaves a number of expenses that can be comfortably cut. You can cut hotel expenses by taking advantage of the reduced weekend package plans offered by even the city's most exclusive hotels. Budget-minded travelers can also find pleasant accommodations at less costly bed-and-breakfast-style tourist homes or at the city's inexpensive hostelries. The YMCA and International House (for the academically affiliated) offer basic budget accommodations. If you want a taste of the grandeur of the city's super-deluxe hotels, you can do so simply by lounging in their lobbies or having a drink at their bars.

After lodging, your next biggest expense will be food, and here you can have substantial savings if you are flexible. Plan to eat simply; buy the makings for a picnic and enjoy it in one of the city's parks or squares. You'll find that many businesspeople do the same at lunchtime. Instead of indulging in three meals a day, eat a big breakfast and skip lunch. You can enjoy a modest, but satisfying, dinner for two for under $25. Menus are often posted outside restaurants, or you can stop at the cash register and look over the menu before you sit down. Peruse the daily papers for good deals, such as "early bird" and *prix fixe* specials. Especially in the summer, when many Philadelphians head to the beaches, restaurants try to entice diners with such offers. Some establishments have happy hours with two-for-one cocktails and complimentary hors d'oeuvres.

Sightseeing expenses are minimal: most of the historic attractions are free, and museum admissions are reasonable. By using buses instead of taxis, you can greatly reduce your transportation costs.

 HINTS TO THE MOTORIST. Before you leave home, have your car thoroughly checked by your regular dealer or service station. You may find it wise to join an auto club that can provide you with trip planning information, insurance coverage, and emergency and repair service along the way. (Refer to "Planning Your Trip," above.) If you need to have your car serviced after you've left home, look for a repair shop that displays the National Institute for Automotive Service Excellence seal. This orange sign with a gear indicates that the mechanics have been tested and certified by NIASE. A blue-and-white sign with the AAA logo indicates an auto repair shop that has been approved by the American Automobile Association.

A right turn on a red light is permitted after a full stop unless prohibited by a sign.

During rush hours, it is best to avoid driving in and out of Philadelphia. During the 7 A.M. to 9:30 A.M. morning rush period, avoid the major arteries leading into the city, particularly I–95, U.S. 1, and the Schuylkill Expressway (I–76). Alternatives to the latter route are the often less crowded East or West River drives. The traffic pattern reverses during the 4 P.M. to 6:30 P.M. outgoing rush hours. During these periods, don't drive in downtown Philadelphia at all if you can possibly manage on foot or with public transportation. Even in the off hours, the narrow streets are congested.

A major reconstruction of the Schuylkill Expressway (nicknamed the "Surekill Expressway" by locals) is underway. Count on it to be either congested or closed in various sections. If you have to drive to Philadelphia International Airport from downtown Philadelphia, allow extra time for detours due to highway construction.

Whenever you drive, it's a good idea to tune into KYW news radio (1060 AM) for the frequent traffic reports. For alternative routings and information, AAA members can call 569–4321.

HOTELS AND MOTELS. If you are planning to stay in the Philadelphia area, especially in the spring or fall, reserve well in advance. Establishments may request a deposit.

A number of hotels and motels have one-day laundry and dry-cleaning services, and many motels have coin laundries. Most motels, but not all, have telephones in the rooms. If you want to be sure of room service, however, you'd better stay at a hotel. Many hotels and motels, even in the heart of the city, have swimming pools. Free parking is another advantage of motels.

Hotel and motel chains. In addition to the hundreds of excellent independent motels and hotels throughout the state, there are also many that belong to national or regional chains. A major advantage of the chains is the ease of making all reservations in advance or en route. If you are a guest at a member hotel or motel, the management will be delighted to secure a sure booking at one of its affiliated hotels—at no cost to you. Chains usually have toll-free WATS (800) lines to assist you in making reservations on your own. This, of course, saves you time, money, and worry. For directory information on (800) lines, dial 1 (800) 555–1212 to see if there is an (800) number for the hotel you want to reach. In the *Practical Information* sections of this book, under "Hotels and Motels," we've listed (800) numbers when available.

Since the single biggest expense of your whole trip is lodging, you may well be discouraged and angry at the prices of some hotel and motel rooms, particularly when you know you are paying for things you neither need nor want, such as a heated swimming pool, wall-to-wall carpeting, a color TV set, two huge double beds for only two people, meeting rooms, a cocktail lounge, maybe even a putting green. Nationwide, motel prices for two people now average $40 a night; hotel prices start at $45, with the average around $65. This explains the recent rapid spread of a number of budget motel chains with rates that average $20 for a single and $25 for a double.

The main national motel chains are *Holiday Inn, Howard Johnson's, Quality Inns, Ramada Inns, Sheraton Motor Inns,* and *TraveLodge.* Other popular family-type motel chains include *Best Western, Rodeway Inns,* and *Vagabond Motor Hotels.* Prices are uniform in some budget chains, but not in the case of all motel chains. They vary widely by area, location, and season. Thus, in the Philadelphia area alone, two adults may pay $25 more for a hotel room in Center City than in the airport area.

Travelers should be aware of the difference among *European Plan* (EP), *American Plan* (AP), and *Modified American Plan* (MAP). European Plan includes no meals. A full American Plan should include all meals and, often, other services as well. Hotels or resorts on the Modified American Plan generally offer one or two meals, usually dinner only or breakfast and dinner.

Senior citizens may in some cases receive special discounts on lodgings. Most Holiday Inns give a 10 percent discount to members of the NRTA (write to *National Retired Teachers Association,* Membership Division, 701 N. Montgomery St., Ojai, CA 93023), the AARP (write to *American Association of Retired Persons,* Membership Division, 215 Long Beach Blvd., Long Beach, CA 90801), and the *National Council of Senior Citizens* (1511 K St. NW, Washington, D.C. 20005). The Sheraton chain offers 25 percent off to members of AARP, NRTA, the *National Association of Retired Persons,* the *Catholic Golden Age of the United Societies of the U.S.A.,* the *Old Age Security Pensioners of Canada,* retired military personnel, and anyone 65 or older with an ID. Policies differ from hotel to hotel, so it is best to check with your organization or with the hotel, motel, or restaurant chain you plan to use.

Hotel chains in general are becoming more cognizant of the requirements of **women guests.** Inquire at reservation time if interested in "female" amenities such as skirt hangers or "women only" floors, which may require a special key. If security is a concern, it's often wise to take rooms above the first floor and to be sure that hotel personnel do not announce your room number at the front desk. Many women when traveling alone prefer to stay only in rooms that do not have direct access from the outside.

HOTEL AND MOTEL CATEGORIES

Hotels and motels in this guide are divided into five categories (*Super Deluxe, Deluxe, Expensive, Moderate,* and *Inexpensive*) arranged primarily by price but also taking into consideration the degree of comfort you can expect to enjoy, the amount of service you can anticipate, and the atmosphere that will surround you in the establishment of your choice. Space limitations make it impossible to include every establishment. We have, therefore, listed those that we recommend as the best within each price range. Our ratings are flexible and subject to change.

The dollar ranges listed under each category may vary from area to area. This variance is meant to reflect local price standards and take into account that what might be considered moderate in price in the city might be quite expensive in a rural area. In every case, however, the dollar ranges for each category are clearly stated.

Super Deluxe: This category is reserved for only a few hotels. In addition to giving the visitor all the amenities discussed under the deluxe category (below), the super-deluxe hotel has a special atmosphere of glamour, good taste, and dignity. It will probably be a favored meeting spot of local society. In short, super deluxe means the tops.

Deluxe: For a rough rule-of-thumb index, we suggest that the minimum facilities must include bath and shower in all rooms, valet and laundry service, suites available, a well-appointed restaurant and bar, room service, TV and telephone in room, air conditioning and heating, pleasing decor, ample and personalized service, and an atmosphere of luxury, calm, and elegance. In a deluxe motel, there may be less service rendered by employees and more by machine or automation (such as refrigerators and ice-making machines in your room), but there should be a minimum of do-it-yourself in a truly deluxe establishment.

Expensive: All rooms must have bath or shower, valet and laundry service, restaurant and bar, at least some room service, TV and telephone in room, attractive furnishings, heating and air conditioning. Although decor may be as good as that in deluxe establishments, hotels and motels in this category are frequently designed for commercial travelers or families in a hurry and are somewhat impersonal in terms of service. As for motels in this category, valet and laundry service will probably be lacking; the units will be outstanding primarily for their convenient location and functional character, not for their attractive or comfortable qualities.

Moderate: Each room should have an attached bath or shower, there should be a restaurant or coffee shop, TV available, a telephone in the room, heating and air conditioning, relatively convenient location, clean and comfortable rooms, and public rooms. Motels in this category may not have an attached bath or shower, may not have a restaurant or coffee shop (though one is usually nearby), and of course, may not have public rooms to speak of.

Inexpensive: Nearby bath or shower, telephone available, and clean rooms are the minimum.

Free parking is assumed at all motels and motor hotels. *Baby-sitter lists* are usually available in good hotels and motels, and cribs for children are always on hand—frequently at no cost, sometimes for $1 or $2. At many hotels, you can request two double beds, and the children can sleep in one of them at no extra cost. An extra bed, usually a rollaway, will cost about $10 per night in better hotels.

In Philadelphia and the surrounding areas, **bed-and-breakfast** accommodations are available in private homes that may also go by the various names of Tourist Home, Guest House, or Guest Home. Styles and standards vary widely, of course, and the main generalizations that one can make are that private baths will be less common, and rates will be pleasingly lower. In addition to economy, you get the personal flavor of a family atmosphere in a private home. In popular tourist areas, state or local tourist information offices or chambers of commerce usually have lists of homes that let out spare rooms to paying guests, and such a listing usually means that the places on it have been inspected and meet reliable standards of cleanliness, comfort, and reasonable pricing. (Refer to the end of the "Hotel and Motel" listings under *Practical Information* for the names of agencies that will arrange lodging in private homes for you.)

There are a number of guides to such accommodations. Comprehensive ones include *Bed & Breakfast USA: Guide to Tourist Homes and Guest Houses,* by Betty Rundback and Nancy Kramer (they've included Canada, too), published by E.P. Dutton, 2 Park Ave., New York, NY 10016; *Bed & Breakfast America: The Great American Guest House Book,* by John Thaxton, published by Burt Franklin & Co., 235 E. 44th St., New York, NY 10017; and *Sleep Cheap,* by Jon and Nancy Kugelman, who cover 44 states and 10 Canadian provinces, published by McBride/Publishers, 157 Sisson Ave., Hartford, CT. 06105.

Travelers who venture beyond the Philadelphia area to the surrounding counties will have no trouble discovering historic country inns and farmhouses that take in overnight guests. More information on these charming hostelries will be found in the various areas covered later in the book, including the sections on Bucks County, Lancaster County, and the Brandywine Valley.

 DINING OUT. For evening meals, the best advice is to make reservations in advance whenever possible anywhere in the Philadelphia area. Some restaurants are fussy about customers' dress, particularly in the evening, but a neatly dressed customer will usually experience no problem. If in doubt about acceptable dress at a particular establishment, call ahead.

If you're traveling with children, you may want to find out if a restaurant has a children's menu and commensurate prices—many do.

When figuring the tip on your check, base it on the charges for the meal, excluding the 6 percent state sales tax.

RESTAURANT CATEGORIES

Restaurants in the Philadelphia chapter are categorized in this volume by type of cuisine: Seafood, Chinese, French, etc.; and then broken down by price category: *Super Deluxe, Deluxe, Expensive, Moderate,* and *Inexpensive.* In the sections on areas outside the city, restaurants are divided by price category only. As a general rule, expect restaurants in the metropolitan area to be higher in price, although many restaurants that feature foreign cuisine are often surprisingly inexpensive. Price designations are for a complete meal (appetizer or soup, entree with vegetable, and dessert), but do not include cocktails, wines, cover or table charges, extravagant house specialties, tax, or tips.

Although the names of the various restaurant categories are standardized, the prices listed under each category may vary from area to area. In every case, however, the dollar ranges for each category are clearly stated before each listing. Limitations of space make it impossible to include every establishment. We have, therefore, included those which we consider the best within each category. We have chosen restaurants that are easily accessible, even for those visitors without a car.

In addition to indicating a price range, categories also imply certain qualities:

Super deluxe: This category is reserved for only a few restaurants in the metropolitan area. It indicates an outstanding restaurant that is handsomely decorated and which may take delight in the fear it inspires among the humble. It will have all the attributes of a deluxe establishment (described below) and more. And, you'll pay dearly for each delicious bite.

Deluxe: Many a fine restaurant in Philadelphia and the surrounding areas falls into this category. The price range here indicates a typical roast beef (prime rib) dinner. A restaurant in this category must have a superb wine list, excellent service, immaculate kitchen, and a large, well-trained staff. It will have its own well-deserved reputation for excellence, perhaps a house specialty or two for which it is famous, and an atmosphere of elegance or a unique decor.

Expensive: In addition to the expected dishes, it will offer one or two house specialties, a wine list and cocktails, air conditioning (unless locale makes it unnecessary), a general reputation for very good food and an adequate staff, elegant decor, and appropriately dressed clientele.

Moderate: Cocktails and/or beer, air conditioning (when needed), clean kitchen, adequate staff, better-than-average service. General reputation for good, wholesome food. In Philadelphia, a number of interesting, upbeat restaurants fall into this price category.

Inexpensive: The bargain place in town, it is clean, even if plain. It will have air conditioning when necessary, tables (not a counter), a clean kitchen, and it will attempt to provide adequate service.

 TIPPING. Tipping is supposed to be a personal way of thanking someone who has taken pleasure and pride in giving you attentive, efficient, and personal service. Because standards of service vary in the United States, you should reward genuinely good service when you receive it. However, if your service was slovenly, indifferent, or surly, don't hesitate to give less or withhold your tip. Remember that in most places the help are paid very little and depend on tips for the better part of their income. This is supposed to give them incentive to serve you well.

The going rate for tipping on restaurant service is 15 percent to 20 percent of the amount before taxes. A wine steward should receive 15 percent of the cost of the bottle ordered. Tipping at counters is not universal; however, most customers do leave 25 cents on anything up to a dollar and 10 percent on checks higher than that. There is no tipping in fast-food and take-out places.

For bellmen, 75 cents or $1 per bag is usual. If you weigh him down with cameras, coats, etc., you should give him an extra quarter or two. Because you may not have the same maid each day, it is most considerate to leave $1 on your pillow each day for the service. If you are staying at an American Plan hostelry (meals included), $2 per person per day for the waitress is considered sufficient and is left at the end of your stay. If you have been surrounded by an army of servants (one bringing relishes, another rolls, and such), add a few extra dollars and give the lump sum to the captain or maitre d'hotel when you leave and ask him to allocate it.

For the many other services you may encounter in a big hotel or resort, figure roughly as follows: doorman, 50 cents for taxi handling, $1 for help with baggage; parking attendant, 50 cents to $1; bartender, 15 percent; room service, 15 percent; laundry or valet service, drop $2 or $3 in the bag before it goes; pool attendant, 50 cents per day; snackbar waiter at pool, beach, or golf club, 15 percent of food and beverage bill; locker attendant, 50 cents per day; golf caddies, $2–$3 per bag or 15 percent of greens fee for an 18-hole course or $3 on a free course; masseurs and masseuses, 15 percent to 20 percent; barbers and hairdressers, 15 percent; shoeshine attendants, 50 cents; manicurists, $1. If you are uncertain of appropriate tips in a hotel, ask the concierge or front desk for advice.

Transportation: Give a 15 percent to 20 percent tip on taxi fares. Limousine service, 20 percent; car rental agencies, nothing. Bus porters are tipped 25 cents per bag; drivers nothing. On charters and package tours, conductors and drivers usually get $5 to $10 per day from the group as a whole, but be sure to ask whether this has already been figured into the package cost. On short local sightseeing runs, the driver-guide may get 25 cents per person, more if you think he has been especially helpful or personable. Airport bus drivers, nothing. Redcaps, 75 cents per bag; tipping at curbside check-in is unofficial, but same as above. On the plane, no tipping. Railroad sleeping car porters get about $1 per person per night. For railway baggage porters, 50 cents per bag is appropriate.

DRINKING LAWS. The legal age for purchase and consumption of alcoholic beverages is 21 in the state of Pennsylvania. In bars and restaurants, drinks may be ordered from 7 A.M. until 2 A.M. daily except Sundays; then, only establishments with a Sunday permit (available if food or nonalcoholic beverages account for at least 40 percent of the gross sales) may sell drinks from 11 A.M. to 2 A.M. Some restaurants have full liquor licenses; other have licenses for beer only. Some have no license but may let customers bring their own alcoholic beverages. Call first to check.

Stores where liquor can be bought for off-premises consumption are called "State Stores" and are operated by the Pennsylvania Liquor Control Board. As a result, prices are uniform in each store. Generally, hours are 11 A.M. to 7 P.M. Monday and Tuesday, 9 A.M. to 9 P.M. Wednesday through Saturday. Stores are closed Sunday and holidays. Half of the stores offer counter service only; the others are self-service.

Up to 144 fluid ounces of beer (two six-packs of 12-ounce cans) may be purchased over the counter in bars. Beer distributors can sell it by the case. No alcohol may be imported from other states.

Like much of the nation, Pennsylvania is involved in a campaign to reduce traffic fatalities due to drunken driving. Though the Motor Vehicle Code is too complex to discuss here, be assured that the penalties are severe.

BUSINESS HOURS, HOLIDAYS AND LOCAL TIME.
Pennsylvania, like the rest of the United States, is on
Standard Time from the last Sunday in October until the
last Sunday in April. In April the clock is advanced one
hour for Daylight Savings Time, and in October it is turned back an hour. The
entire state lies within the Eastern Time Zone, which is five hours earlier than
Greenwich Mean Time on local standard (winter) time.

Most businesses begin their day at 9:00 A.M. and end by 5:00 P.M., Monday
through Friday. Retail establishments generally open at 9:30 or 10 A.M. and close
at 5:30 or 6 P.M. daily except Sunday. On Wednesday evenings, many stores keep
later hours. You can shop several evenings and Sunday afternoons in some city
shopping malls and department stores. Between Thanksgiving and Christmas,
most stores stay open until 9 P.M.

Banks usually follow a 9 A.M. to 3 P.M. schedule except for Fridays, when they
have later closings. Although some buses run all night, their frequency is greatly
reduced after 6 P.M.

Downtown restaurants frequented by businesspeople may open at 7:00 or
7:30 A.M.; others don't open until 11:00 or 11:30 A.M. for the lunch trade. Business
lunches generally begin around 12:30 P.M. Few people dine before 6:00 P.M.; 7:30
or 8:00 P.M. are more popular times at better restaurants. However, most kitchens close by 10 or 11 P.M., except for the few places catering to an after-theater
crowd or the restaurants in Chinatown, which serve until the wee hours of the
morning. Always phone ahead to be sure of serving hours and to see if reservations are needed.

Many businesses and banks (but not necessarily restaurants) will be closed
on the following holidays in 1985: New Year's Day, January 1; Washington's
Birthday (observance), February 18; Easter Sunday, April 7; Memorial Day
(observance), May 27; Independence Day, July 4; Labor Day, September 2;
Thanksgiving Day, November 28; and Christmas Day, December 25.

In addition, banks and some businesses may be closed on Martin Luther
King's Birthday, January 15; Lincoln's Birthday, February 12; Good Friday,
from noon, April 5; Flag Day, June 14; Columbus Day (observance), October
14; Election Day, November 5; and Veterans Day (observance), November 11.
Tourist-oriented businesses often remain open on all important holidays, but
always phone ahead to be sure.

SENIOR CITIZEN AND STUDENT DISCOUNTS.
(For accommodation discounts, see "Hotels and Motels," above.) Many attractions throughout the Philadelphia area offer considerable discounts to senior
citizens and students. Always ask if there are special rates for you. A Medicare
card is the best identification for seniors; students may be asked to show high
school or college ID or an international student traveler card.

SEPTA, the public transportation system, offers free rides to seniors during
off-peak hours, and discounted fares of 40 cents from 6 A.M. to 9 A.M. and 3:30
P.M. to 6:30 P.M. *Yellow Cab Company* offers a 75 percent discount to seniors
who order a cab at least 24 hours in advance. Call 627–5100 between 8:30 A.M.
and 4 P.M. for reservations.

Although there are no special rates for seniors or students at movie theaters,
everyone can save money at the daily bargain matinees (usually $2.50 before 1
P.M.) offered by most theaters.

HINTS TO HANDICAPPED TRAVELERS. One of the newest and largest groups to enter the travel scene is the handicapped. Generally, their tours parallel those of the nonhandicapped traveler, but at a more leisurely pace and with all the logistics carefully planned out in advance. There have been some efforts to make Philadelphia more accessible for the handicapped. Newer SEPTA buses are equipped with lifts for passengers in wheelchairs. Handicapped people are issued license plates allowing special parking privileges.

One of the best sources of information about handicapped travel is based in Philadelphia. The *Travel Information Center, Moss Rehabilitation Hospital,* 12th St. and Tabor Rd., Philadelphia, PA 19141, is a free service which will send you information about sights, accommodations, transportation; the names of travel agencies which specialize in planning for the disabled; and the *International Directory of Access Guides.* A pertinent publication is the recently updated *Guide to Philadelphia for the Handicapped,* available free of charge from the *Mayor's Office for the Handicapped,* Room 143, City Hall, Philadelphia, PA 19107, or order by calling (215) MU6–2798.

A helpful book available at most bookstores is *Access to the World: A Travel Guide for the Handicapped,* by Louise Weiss, published by Chatham Square Press and available by mail from Facts on File, 460 Park Ave. S., New York, NY 10016. Although Douglass R. Annand's *Wheelchair Traveler* is out-of-print, you can write to him at Ball Hill Rd., Milford, NH 03055, for information on the topic. TWA publishes a free, 12-page pamphlet entitled *Consumer Information about Air Travel for the Handicapped.* Available at TWA offices, it explains the various arrangements that can be made. A free copy of *Access Amtrak,* a guide to their services for elderly and handicapped travelers, can be ordered by dialing (800) USA-RAIL or by writing to Amtrak Passenger Relations, 400 North Capitol St., N.W., Washington, DC 20001.

Many of the nation's national parks have special facilities and services for the physically disabled. These are described in *Access to the National Parks,* a handbook available from the U.S. Government Printing Office, Washington, DC 20402 for $6.50.

POSTAGE. At presstime, rates for international mail from the United States are as follows: letters to Canada and Mexico (they go by airmail carriage) are at the U.S. domestic rate of 22 cents for 1 ounce or under, 17 cents for each additional ounce up to 12. Surface letters to other foreign destinations are 37 cents for the first ounce and 57 cents for up to 2 ounces. Airmail letters to most foreign destinations are 44 cents, ½ ounce; 88 cents, 1 ounce; $1.32, 1½ ounces; $1.76, 2 ounces. Airmail rates to some Caribbean and South American countries begin at 39 cents for ½ ounce.

Postcards (except to Canada and Mexico, which, like domestic postcards, are 14 cents) are 25 cents for surface mail and 33 cents for airmail to any foreign destination. Standard international aerogram letters, good for any foreign destination, are 36 cents, but nothing can be enclosed in them. Postal rates are subject to inflation, so check before you mail, in case they have gone up.

METRIC CONVERSION. Although there is always talk about the U.S. going metric, it has yet to happen in most areas of American life. The following charts may prove helpful to foreign visitors in Philadelphia.

Converting Metric to U.S. Measurements

Multiply:	by:	to find:
Length		
millimeters (mm)	.039	inches (in)
meters (m)	3.28	feet (ft)
meters	1.09	yards (yd)
kilometers (km)	.62	miles (mi)
Area		
hectare (ha)	2.47	acres
Capacity		
liters (L)	1.06	quarts (qt)
liters	.26	gallons (gal)
liters	2.11	pints (pt)
Weight		
gram (g)	.04	ounce (oz)
kilogram (kg)	2.20	pounds (lb)
metric ton (MT)	.98	tons (t)
Power		
kilowatt (kw)	1.34	horsepower (hp)
Temperature		
degrees Celsius	9/5 (then add 32)	degrees Fahrenheit

Converting U.S. to Metric Measurements

Multiply:	by	to find:
Length		
inches (in)	25.40	millimeters (mm)
feet (ft)	.30	meters (m)
yards (yd)	.91	meters
miles (mi)	1.61	kilometers (km)
Area		
acres	.40	hectares (ha)
Capacity		
pints (pt)	.47	liters (L)
quarts (qt)	.95	liters
gallons (gal)	3.79	liters
Weight		
ounces (oz)	28.35	grams (g)
pounds (lb)	.45	kilograms (kg)
tons (t)	1.11	metric tons (MT)
Power		
horsepower (hp)	.75	kilowatts
Temperature		
degrees Fahrenheit	5/9 (after subtracting 32)	degrees Celsius

SECURITY. Like all big cities, Philadelphia has its share of crime. But, if you exercise common sense and follow some of these precautions, you won't be an easy target. It isn't hard to have a safe stay here. The neighborhoods described in the "Exploring" sections of the guide are heavily used and quite safe by day, with the possible exception of the more remote areas of Fairmount Park.

At night some of these areas are sparsely populated and unsavory, particularly the 13th St. "strip" between Spruce and Vine sts. Avoid walking down dark, deserted streets; women should not walk alone at night, except in the busiest areas. If you are uncertain of your route, take a cab. Extra security during rush hours makes the subway safe, but it can be dangerous at night, when you should avoid it unless traveling to the stadium complex for a sporting event—then you'll have lots of company. If your stop is not well lit, ride to a better-lit area. Try to park on the ground level of a parking lot or in a valet parking garage. Always lock your car and don't tempt thieves by leaving valuables in plain sight.

In any crowded area, watch out for pickpockets. Try not to succumb to the habit of slinging your purse over the back of the chair; place it on your lap or between your feet.

It's best to keep extra money, fine jewelry, and other valuables in the hotel safe, rather than in your room. Be sure to always lock your door, even when you are inside. At night, use the deadbolt and chain on the hotel-room door. Carry most of your funds in traveler's checks, and be sure to record numbers in a separate, secure place.

TELEPHONES. The area code for Philadelphia and the four surrounding counties (Bucks, Chester, Delaware, and Montgomery) is 215. You don't need to dial the area code if it is the same as the one from which you are calling. However, in the farther reaches of the counties, you must dial "1" (one) before the seven-digit number. If you are uncertain, dial the number without the "1"; if that is incorrect, a tape recording will tell you so. Information or directory assistance is 1–555–1212. When dialing long distance, dial "1" before the area code and the seven-digit number. For person-to-person, credit card, and collect calls, dial "0" for operator assistance. Pay telephones within the Philadelphia area are 25 cents.

EMERGENCY TELEPHONE NUMBERS. In the Philadelphia area, the emergency number for fire, police, ambulance, and paramedics is 911. Or dial "0" for operator and ask for help in connecting you immediately with the appropriate agency. The nonemergency police service number is 231–3131. Some other numbers:

Accidental poisoning: 922–5523 or 922–5524
Rape Hotline: 922–3434
Doctor (Philadelphia Medical Society): 563–5343
Dental Emergency: 925–6050
Travelers Aid Society: 546–0571.

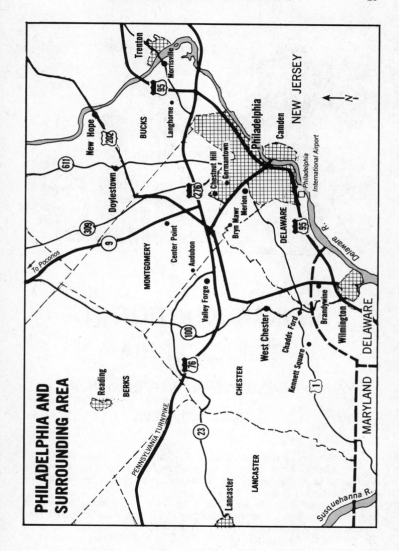

PHILADELPHIA AND SURROUNDING AREA

AN INTRODUCTION TO
PHILADELPHIA

William Penn, Old Ben, and Rocky Balboa

by **JOYCE EISENBERG**

Joyce Eisenberg is a free-lance writer and editor whose travel and feature articles have appeared in local and national publications. A Philadelphia native, she is editor of the Delaware Valley edition of Travelhost magazine.

Philadelphia is a city with character—and characters—a town of surprising contrasts. The world-renowned Philadelphia Orchestra performs at the Academy of Music, a dignified, opulent opera house on Broad Street. Along that same street 25,000 Mummers, dressed in sequins and feathers, pluck their banjos and strut their stuff on New Year's Day.

16

The city's residents include descendants of the staid Quaker founding fathers, the self-possessed socialites of the Main Line, and the unrestrained sports fans who are as vocal as they are loyal. (Some have been accused of booing the Easter Bunny and throwing snowballs at Santa Claus when their teams have failed them.)

The city's restaurant renaissance, and the sophisticated new cuisine which emerged, has garnered national acclaim. Philadelphia is also a junk-food capital; it's most famous cuisine may well be cheesesteaks, hoagies, and soft pretzels with mustard.

It is the dignified, but somewhat dull, image that has been associated with Philadelphia in the past. The city's conservatism inspired native son W. C. Fields to quip in 1946, when asked for a suitable epitaph for his tombstone: "On the whole, I'd rather be in Philadelphia."

If Fields were alive today, he'd probably eat his words. The inferiority complex he attributed to the city is out of date. There's a new, optimistic mood, aggressive leadership (Philadelphia elected its first black mayor in 1983), and national recognition of what the natives have long known: Philadelphia is a very pleasant place to live, a city with an impressive past and a promising future.

The Feel of the City

Situated on the Northeast corridor, between New York and Washington, D.C., Philadelphia is Pennsylvania's largest city and the nation's fifth largest—a classy, cosmopolitan place which has maintained the feel of a friendly small town. City planners have called Philadelphia a very livable city, and they are right. The population is less transient than in other large cities; people who are born here generally remain and many who leave home to study or work eventually return. Although the population is close to 1.7 million, residents are intricately connected; on any given day, a Philadelphian is likely to encounter someone with whom he grew up. The "it's a small world syndrome" makes people feel like they belong.

On the street, Philadelphians may appear reserved and businesslike, as in many big cities; but ask them for directions or information, let them know you're a visitor, and you'll find that they are friendly and proud of their city. Ask the cabdriver or storekeeper about Philadelphia; they'll be thrilled to talk to you.

The 1976 Bicentennial celebration put the finishing touches on the city's facelift, which has been underway for the last two decades—since young professionals began moving to the city and rediscovering decaying houses that had been abandoned in the post–World War II flight to the suburbs. The homes were lovingly restored, not razed. (Philadelphians receive a tax abatement for restoring an old house.) The preservation began in Society Hill, a neighborhood of Federal-style, brick row houses and quaint cobblestone streets stretching from the Delaware River to 6th Street. Because of its proximity to Independence National Historical Park—"America's most historic square mile," which contains national treasures such as the Liberty Bell and Independence Hall—property values in the area have escalated rapidly; a home that cost $68,000 in 1976 sold for $200,000 in 1982.

Just as the city originally expanded from the Delaware River westward, so has the restoration effort. A walk west on Spruce Street, from river to river, will show off three centuries of architecture: Colonial red brick, next to Victorian brownstones, alongside futuristic glass. There's a marked contrast between Society Hill's ornate, sumptuous Georgian homes, reminiscent of London (the Powel House is a fine example), and the austere, conservative buildings belonging to the Quakers, such as the Friends Meeting House north of Market Street. Elfreth's Alley, the oldest, continuously occupied street in America, provides an idea of how Colonial Philadelphia looked.

Philadelphia, which sprawls over 130 square miles, is divided into five sections: North, Northeast, South, West, and Center City. It is the latter area which has mostly benefited from the restoration dollars. The effort has not reached ghetto areas in North and West Philadelphia, where storefronts remain boarded up and the poor live in crowded public housing. But here, too, you can find evidence of civic pride, residents who band together to create a perfectly manicured, safe block for their children.

Philadelphia is a city of neighborhoods (109 by one count) and neighborhood loyalty. If you ask a native where he's from, he'll tell you Fairmount, Fishtown, or Frankford, rather than Philadelphia. These row-home neighborhoods are closely knit, self-contained ethnic enclaves where three generations of one family may live within a few blocks of each other. Though they live only a few miles from downtown, some of the older generation haven't been in Center City for years.

Natives use the nickname "Philly" with a neighborhood like North, West, or South Philly, but usually not alone as an abbreviation for Philadelphia. South Philly is the city's most colorful neighborhood: the bustling outdoor Italian Market, centered at 9th and Christian streets, is its heart. This is the neighborhood where Rocky, hero in the film of the same name, grew up, the area that the Mummers call home. It also produced famous stars like Mario Lanza, James Darren, Bobby Rydell, Joey Bishop, and Eddie Fisher.

Though its residential areas stretch for miles, the city's historic, artistic, and commercial center is just 24 blocks long (from the Delaware River on the east to the Schuylkill [pronounced skoo-kill] River on the West) and 12 blocks wide (Vine Street on the north to South Street). The streets are usually congested with traffic; walking is the best way for visitors to explore the city. If you tire, you can ride the SEPTA bus or subway system. Most routes are 85 cents (exact change required); the 50-cent Mid-City Loop provides convenient access to shopping and historical areas. Taxicabs are fairly expensive, but distances are short.

A Little History

William Penn founded the city in 1682 and named it for the Greek word meaning "city of brotherly love." He had secured the land from England's King Charles II when he went to collect a $50,000 debt owed to his father by the king. The king happily gave William, a Quaker and critic of the English establishment, land in the New World as long as William would leave and live on it. Penn brought with him English and Welsh Quakers who sought religious freedom.

By the time Penn arrived, there was already a thriving colony of Swedes, Dutch, English, Finns, and Irish. His Quakers settled on a tract of land, which Penn called his "greene countrie towne," between the two rivers. He designed a city with widely spaced streets, large building lots, parks, and a grid pattern of major thoroughfares and five pedestrian squares that still survive. The colony's large freshwater port and good docking facilities helped to sustain it. The port has remained vital to the city; in 1983 the Port of Philadelphia regained its first place among North Atlantic ports in terms of overall cargo tonnage.

Penn used the land for his "Holy Experiment"—the foundation of the Quaker religion. His vision was that men of all faiths could live in harmony and freedom. Penn guaranteed personal freedoms by allowing every taxpayer a vote, a prisoner the right to be heard, each man a trial by jury, and taxation only by law. Quakers, or Friends, believed in the abolition of war and slavery and equal rights for women. (The group still is antiwar; in 1947, the American Friends Service Committee, based in Philadelphia, shared the Nobel Peace Prize with London's Friends Service Council.)

One year after Penn arrived, thirteen German Quaker and Mennonite families settled in Germantown and founded the first German settlement in America. Their lifestyle and Philadelphia's Colonial history can be seen by touring this area.

Those who later came from England were the well-off younger sons of country gentlemen and yeoman farmers—Anglicans and Presbyterians who had a running conflict with the "stiff Quakers" who frowned upon music and dancing. The new arrivals built summer palaces outside of the city in Chestnut Hill and Germantown and named them after their father's estates in England. They maintained their traditions of horse and hound breeding and wearing English tweeds, and they also propagated traditions which remain strong in Philadelphia to this day: united families, comfortable houses, handsome furniture, good education, and well-defined standards of morality.

From these early years came the attitudes which Mark Twain summed up as: "In Boston they ask: What does he know? In New York, How much does he make? In Philadelphia, Who were his parents?" Wealth was never a social passport in Philadelphia; in fact, showy, gaudy riches were frowned upon. What was important was to be wellborn and well-bred. As expected, however, many of the wellborn and well-bred also became wealthy as leaders in the businesses that sustained Philadelphia's economy: education, medicine, insurance, banking, money management, and law.

The city was the queen of the English-speaking New World from the late 1600s to early 1800s. In the last half of the 1700s, Philadelphia was the largest city in the Colonies, a great and glorious city second only to London in the British Empire.

When the delegates from the Colonies wanted to meet, they chose this centrally located, thriving city. The rebellious colonists united against King George when the First Continental Congress met in 1774 at Carpenters' Hall. The rest, as they say, is history. It is here that the Declaration of Independence was written and adopted, the Constitution was framed, the capital of the United States was established, the Liberty Bell was clanged, the nation's flag was sewn by Betsy Ross (some say this is a myth), and George Washington served most of his presidency.

Much of this history was made in the area now known as Independence National Historical Park, Philadelphia's number one tourist attraction. Just around the corner is the museum which honors Philadelphia's number one favorite son; Franklin Court, an imaginative, fun presentation, is a fitting tribute to Benjamin Franklin's interests as a scientist, inventor, statesman, and printer. Franklin is often dramatized as Old Ben; he was indeed elderly when he signed the Declaration of Independence. However, it was the youthful Ben who came to the city from Boston at the age of seventeen and was responsible for many items on Philadelphia's impressive list of firsts: he founded the first public library in the country (the Library Company of Philadelphia), the nation's first hospital (Pennsylvania Hospital), fire insurance company (Philadelphia Contributorship), and learned and scientific society (the American Philosophical Society). He also invented the Franklin Stove, bifocals, and the lightning rod.

The Main Line

When in the mid-nineteenth century the Pennsylvania Railroad opened a commuter route—the Paoli local—from the city to the western suburbs, many of the wellborn and well-bred, the city's "establishment," made an exodus to the string of towns along the line. The area was called the Main Line and the towns, made famous by novelist John O'Hara (*Butterfield 8, A Philadelphian's Story*), were named for the train's stops: Bryn Mawr, Rosemont, Villanova, Devon, etc. This is where Philadelphia society found the genteel life; from here they sent their sons and daughters to private schools and prestigious colleges like Haverford and Bryn Mawr, socialized at debutante parties and the Merion Cricket Club, and groomed their horses for the Devon Horse Show. The WASP Main Line social life has been depicted in films like *The Philadelphia Story* and *The Young Philadelphians*.

The late Grace Kelly was perhaps Philadelphia's biggest celebrity. She was probably the most loved as well. In Hollywood, and later as the Princess of Monaco, she exemplified for the world the traits that Philadelphians hold dear: she was well-mannered, well-bred, and always a gentlewoman. She starred in *High Society,* but ironically, she didn't belong to this city's; she was the daughter of an Irish-Catholic bricklayer and contractor and grew up in East Falls, a middle-class Philadelphia neighborhood.

The Look of Today's City

The city's modern look finds its roots firmly in its past. Ben Franklin's most famous achievement has been immortalized by Isamu Noguchi's 30-ton, 96-foot bolt of lightning, which sits on a plaza at the foot of the Benjamin Franklin Bridge. The sculpture is one of the newest additions to the city's public art. As a result of a unique law passed in 1958, 1 percent of the cost of all new buildings, public and private, is to be used to purchase art for the city. That ruling has added more than 400 pieces of art to public places, from whimsical bears that stand in city playgrounds to Claes Oldenburg's 45-foot Clothespin which faces City Hall. Denounced as "obscene" when it was first erected, the sculpture is now a landmark of sorts. All this sculpture led Frank Lloyd Wright to dub Philadelphia "The Florence of America."

The city's most famous sculpture is the bronze statue of William Penn atop City Hall, at Broad and Market streets. Billy Penn reaches to 40 stories and is the tallest structure in the metropolis—for now. No law prohibits taller buildings; the tradition springs from a gentleman's agreement.

In May 1984, when a developer proposed building two office towers that would break the 491-foot barrier, it became evident how much Philadelphians cared about their city—and how entrenched this tradition was. The proposal provoked a public outcry. The traditionalists contended that the height limitation had made Philadelphia a city of human scale, given its streets and public places intimacy, and showed respect for tradition. The opposing camp thought that a dramatic new skyline would shatter the city's conservative image and encourage economic growth. After painstaking debate, the go-ahead was granted. Expect Philadelphia's skyline to take on a new look in the years to come.

The midtown area, with City Hall as its focus, is the hub of the city's commercial center. As businesses returned to the city, Market Street west of City Hall became a district of high-rise office buildings. Investments totalling about $1 billion are planned for this strip, a symbol of the city's transformation from a dying industrial town to a major center of service industries. Along Broad Street, which as the widest of the city's north-south thoroughfares is aptly named, and farther west near fashionable Rittenhouse Square, are some of the city's finest hotels, restaurants, and stores. Most of the theaters are in the midtown area east of Broad Street.

The Cultural Institutions

The view from City Hall's observation deck northwest along the Benjamin Franklin Parkway is probably the city's finest. From here you can see the Greco-Roman temple on a hilltop that is the Philadelphia Museum of Art. The parkway is the city's Champs-Elysées, a boulevard designed by French architects and alive with flowers, trees, and fountains. Three generations of the Calder family are represented by the sculptures along the avenue: Alexander Milne Calder's statue of William Penn, Alexander Stirling Calder's Swann Memorial Fountain at Logan Circle, and the works of Alexander Calder (the mobile- and stabile-maker) in and around the Museum of Art.

Here are many of the city's finest cultural institutions. The Academy of Natural Sciences is another of the city's firsts and oldest: it's been exhibiting natural history since 1812. Its dinosaurs and stuffed animals in natural settings are a favorite with children. The Franklin Institute, the country's oldest science museum, isn't just for kids. Like its namesake, it cleverly presents basic and applied sciences. Farther up the parkway is the Rodin Museum, which houses the largest collection of works outside of Paris by sculptor Auguste Rodin.

But the crowning glory is the Museum of Art, with its long, sweeping steps that were made famous when Sylvestor Stallone jubilantly scaled them in the film *Rocky*. The museum has an outstanding collection of paintings and decorative arts. Thomas Eakins, a native son and one of America's greatest 19th-century realist painters, is well represented at the museum; one of his most famous paintings is of a solitary oarsman on the Schuylkill River.

Though it's not on the parkway, don't miss the Pennsylvania Academy of the Fine Arts. The building itself is a work of art, the masterpiece of architects George Hewitt and the innovative (and sometimes eccentric) Frank Furness, who designed more than 400 Philadelphia buildings, including many of the banks, hospitals, libraries, university buildings, and private homes. Inside are more than 4,000 works spanning three centuries. Many of America's greats, including Charles Willson Peale (he founded the Academy as a teaching institution), Edward Hopper, and Andrew Wyeth are represented here.

It is worth a trip to Philadelphia just to see the masterpieces at the Barnes Foundation in Merion, on the Main Line. The monumental private collection of Impressionist, post-Impressionist, and other European as well as American art is never loaned to museums.

Philadelphia's art consciousness began to bud in the mid-1700s. Benjamin West, a Quaker portrait painter, rose from humble roots to become the favorite painter of King George III and president of the Royal Academy. Under his tutelage in London, many local artists blossomed and then returned home to find fame. At the end of the century, artists flocked to the city to paint George Washington during his presidency. At one point, the president was giving sittings to no less than four members of the Peale family at one time.

Mary Cassatt, a contemporary of Eakins, is another local girl who "made good." She trained at the Academy of the Fine Arts and then moved to Europe and to the forefront of the French Impressionist movement.

Philadelphia Music and Dance

Of all the arts, it is music for which the city is most renowned and the Philadelphia Orchestra of which the people are most proud. Considered one of the world's best symphony orchestras, it rose to fame under the batons of former conductors Leopold Stokowski and Eugene Ormandy. Riccardo Muti, who also serves as conductor-laureate of the London Philharmonic, is the current musical director. The orchestra's home is the Academy of Music, an acoustically superb concert hall; the interior, stage, and auditorium were modeled after the La Scala Opera House in Milan. The Academy opened with a lavish ball in 1857; attending an orchestra concert during the September-to-May season is still one of the city's premier social events. If you can get tickets, go. You'll see one of the city's finest groups in an opulent setting and Philadelphians dressed to match the occasion.

The Opera Company of Philadelphia also performs at the Academy. They've gained national prominence with their performance of *La Boheme,* which was one of PBS's Great Performances. It was the most widely watched opera in the history of public television.

The Pennsylvania Ballet also calls the Academy home. The highlight of their season is the annual Christmas week performance of *The Nutcracker Suite.*

There is no shortage of live entertainment. The Philly Pops, led by Peter Nero, is popular. Local theaters, notably the Forrest, Shubert, and Walnut Street, stage Broadway-bound and original plays. There are summer concerts of popular and classical music at the Robin Hood Dell East and the Mann Music Center in Fairmount Park.

Rock music is as dear to Philadelphians as is classical. The Spectrum, Tower Theater, and sometimes the Academy schedule frequent concerts by popular entertainers. Many rock groups include Philadelphia as a stop on their national tours. Not only is the city's Electric Factory Concerts one of the biggest promoters of rocks concerts nationally, but Philadelphia music fans, like the sports fans, are loyal and enthusiastic. Billy Joel and David Bowie, among others, have said that the constancy of Philadelphia's fans has won them a special place in their hearts. Elton John immortalized the city in his hit "Philadelphia Freedom."

Philadelphia holds a special place in pop music history. *American Bandstand,* hosted by Dick Clark, began as a local dance show. When it went national in 1957, it gave a boost to many hometown boys, including Fabian, Bobby Rydell, Frankie Avalon, and Chubby Checker. The city's rock-and-roll tradition began in 1955 with Bill Haley and the Comets' "Rock Around the Clock." In the '70s, the local rhythm-and-blues songwriting team of Kenny Gamble and Leon Huff wrote their sexy soul sound for Harold Melvin and the Blue Notes and for the O'Jays, among others. The South of Philadelphia, a polished blend of disco, pop, and rhythm and blues, became nationally recognized. Today, that sound is alive with Hall and Oates, another local duo who made it to the top.

Sports

Philadelphia sports fans have lots to cheer about. Their professional teams—the Eagles, football; Phillies, baseball; Flyers, ice hockey; and 76ers, basketball—frequently make it to the playoffs. The Phillies took the World Series in 1980; the 76ers the national championship in 1983. Games are played at the Spectrum or Veterans Stadium in the South Philadelphia sports complex. There is always a crowd: Philadelphians buy more tickets to pro sporting events than do residents of any other U.S. city.

The Army-Navy football classic is a Philadelphia Thanksgiving tradition. College basketball teams—Villanova, LaSalle, Saint Joseph's, Temple, and Penn—known as the "Big Five," are regularly national contenders. For those who prefer to participate, there are boats and bicycles available for rent, skating rinks, trout-stocked streams, public golf courses, and health clubs.

Today, on the Schuylkill River, you can see scores of Eakins's oarsmen. The sculls are launched from Boat House Row, a string of Victorian houses along the East River Drive, now home to the city's many rowing clubs. The West River Drive affords the best nighttime view of the city; the boathouses are strung with little lights which flicker like diamonds; alongside them are the Greek Revival Water Works, and overhead is the Art Museum looking as grand as the Parthenon.

The boathouses are at the foot of Fairmount Park, the largest landscaped city park in the world. With more than 8,500 acres and two million trees (someone claims to have counted), the park winds along the banks of the Schuylkill River and through parts of the city. The park contains not only nature trails, jogging paths, and tennis courts, but also concert halls, a zoo, a Japanese teahouse, and Early American houses dating from the Colonial to the Federal period.

Fairmount Park, like the city, can be enjoyed throughout the year. Philadelphia has four distinct seasons with temperatures ranging from the 80s and higher to below freezing. In spring and fall, the city is at its finest: trees are in bloom, temperatures range from the fifties to the seventies, and there is a comfortable breeze. Summers can be hot and sticky, but air-conditioned attractions offer a respite. Winter snowfall is variable.

"University City"

The city is second only to Boston in its concentration of colleges and universities; there are six medical schools in town. Two of the larger institutions, Drexel University and the University of Pennsylvania, are located in an area dubbed "University City" in West Philadelphia, near 34th and Walnut streets. The primary cultural attraction here is Penn's University Museum, one of the country's best archaeological and anthropological collections. Quite a few of the artifacts were uncovered on digs by members of the university's renowned archaeology department. University City is buzzing with activity. There are frequent shows at Penn's Annenberg Center, named after Philadelphian Walter H. Annenberg, multimillionaire, publisher, philanthropist, and founder of the School of Communications at the university. University City is a good place to eat or catch a movie. Because of the large student population, movie theaters and restaurants here are generally less expensive than those in Center City.

The Food

Philadelphia's restaurant renaissance has made it one of the four or five most exciting restaurant cities in the country. You can find restaurants to please all budgets and tastes—a classic French meal at Le Bec-Fin, a dim sum lunch in Chinatown, or a hot dog and fish cake at Levis' Hot Dogs, a Philadelphia favorite since 1895. Since 1978, more than 400 restaurants have opened. The "Philadelphia Cuisine" which has emerged is an artful combination of American, French, and Oriental cooking. On the whole, the city's restaurants are casually elegant and pleasantly creative. You are likely to receive better service and pay less for a comparable meal than in New York City. It's a good idea to call the restaurant to see if jackets are required for men and reservations needed. Philadelphia has an East Coast dress code and a history of conservative forefathers: people are usually well dressed. Although informality has its place, it is not the rule.

There are no dress codes on South Street, the city's eclectic, artsy, Greenwich Village-like area. Along the strip from Front Street to about 8th Street, and on the side streets, are art galleries, antique shops, avant-garde clothing stores, and many good restaurants; this is actually the neighborhood where the restaurant renaissance began. You'll find people on the streets and in the restaurants and clubs until late at night. It's one of the city's liveliest spots.

The Night Life

Philadelphia has been the butt of disparaging remarks, particularly about its sidewalks rolling up at sundown. Things have changed. True, there is no night life as it is known in New York City; there is no central entertainment district, no throngs of partying people, or rows of neon lights. In fact, if you walk the streets after a leisurely dinner, you might believe the cynics.

But enter any one of the city's comedy clubs, piano bars, small cabarets, discos, jazz clubs, or popular pubs, and you'll see crowds of people who know how to have a good time. You simply need to be in the know to find out where to go. (To find out what's happening where, refer to this guide, to the monthly listings in *Philadelphia* magazine, and weekend sections of the local papers. Or, call the Philly Fun Phone at 568–7255.) In the summer months, there are concerts, many of them free, in Fairmount Park, at Penn's Landing (along the Delaware River), and at the Museum of Art.

The city is in the midst of a hotel boom. Three newly-constructed first-class hotels opened in 1983, as did a luxury apartment building that was converted to a suite hotel. These added about 1,500 hotel rooms to the city's census. Other hotels are undergoing restoration, new complexes are opening by the airport—and soon in the historic area—and more are proposed for the future convention center site near the Reading Terminal Market at 12th and Filbert streets.

Shopping

Philadelphia is a shopper's paradise. Even here, tradition runs strong. The leading department stores are city institutions: John Wanamaker has been at its current Chestnut Street location since 1877; Strawbridge & Clothier has been a family-run business since 1868. Both are full-service stores in which one could happily get lost for a day. Strawbridge & Clothier marks one end of the three-city-block-long urban mall known as The Gallery at Market East, which houses more than 250 restaurants and stores under its glass roof.

The Bourse, a restored grand Victorian building opposite Independence National Historical Park, has exclusive designer boutiques and restaurants. In Society Hill, overlooking the Delaware River, is New-Market, a wood and glass village with specialty shops and restaurants in its nooks and crannies. Antique Row stretches along Pine Street, a pedestrian mall lines Chestnut Street, and Walnut Street is home to the most exclusive shops.

Philadelphia is an exciting but not overwhelming city, a town that's easy to explore but big enough to keep surprising even those most familiar with it. The same features that make a vacation here so pleasant for a tourist also keep the native-born in residence. Philadelphia is no longer a "well-kept secret." The word is out.

Beyond the City

Several one-day outings and longer trips are easily arranged from Philadelphia. Valley Forge's showplace is the National Historical Park, which has been restored to demonstrate how it looked during the bitterly cold winter of 1777–78 when Washington and his Continental Army were camped there. You can continue on to Reading, whose number one claim to fame is as the "outlet capital of the world." It's a must for bargain hunters.

The Brandywine Valley was once the kingdom of the wealthy Du Pont family. Much of their splendor is shared with the public at Longwood Gardens, Pierre Du Pont's former country home, and at the Winterthur Museum and Gardens, a 200-room Du Pont mansion that houses America's best collection of native decorative arts dating from 1640 to 1840. This is also Wyeth Country. The Brandywine River Museum highlights three generations of the painting family: N. C., Andrew, and James.

New Hope, in Bucks County, is an artists' colony with restaurants, specialty stores, and art galleries. You can take a barge trip on the Delaware Canal, sort through "antiques" in Lahaska, and dine and stay overnight in charming country inns along this northern section of the Delaware River. Of historical interest is Pennsbury Manor, a reconstruction of the mansion that William Penn built in the late 1600s.

Lancaster County's main attractions are the farms, shops, and restaurants of Pennsylvania Dutch Country. Guided tours give visitors a closer look at one of the groups of "plain people," the Old Order Amish sect who still use horse-drawn buggies and shun modern conveniences. Be sure to sample the food: family-style restaurants feature local cooking with the traditional seven sweets and seven sours. Hershey is Chocolate Town, USA; even the streetlights are shaped like Hershey Kisses. Hershey Park, open May to September, resembles a small Disneyland with lightning-fast rides for the stout-hearted.

EXPLORING PHILADELPHIA

by JOYCE EISENBERG

Philadelphia was the birthplace of the U.S., the home of the first government. Nowhere is the spirit of the early days—the boldness of conceiving a brand new nation—more palpable than along the cobbled streets and in the red-brick Georgian buildings in the city's historic district. Many of the important structures along what's been dubbed "the most historic square mile in America" are part of Independence National Historical Park. The park, which covers forty-two acres and close to forty buildings, has been administered and maintained by the National Park Service since 1951.

In the late 1940s, before civic-minded citizens banded together to save the area and before the Park Service stepped in, Independence Hall was crowded by factories and warehouses. Then, city, state, and federal governments took interest. Some buildings were restored, others were reconstructed on their original sites. Some attractions were built for the 1976 Bicentennial celebration. The several-block-long Independence Mall plaza and a fine urban renewal effort in Washington

Square East (Society Hill) ensured that Independence Hall would never again keep unsightly company. Today, besides being the city's most historic area, it is also one of the loveliest.

Independence National Historical Park

Whether this is your first day or your only day in Philadelphia, it should be savored in Independence National Historical Park. Admission is free; most buildings are open daily from 9:00 A.M. to 5:00 P.M. In the summer, the hours are often extended. Like most of the city, this area is best explored by foot. You can leave your car at the garage on 2nd Street between Walnut and Chestnut. From the Center City hotels, take any bus going east along the Chestnut Street Transitway.

The best place to orient yourself is at the Visitor Center at 3rd and Chestnut streets, where you can get a map of the park's important sites and see the founding fathers come to life in the 30-minute film *Independence*, narrated by John Huston. The bell atop the tower, cast at the same foundry as the Liberty Bell, was a Bicentennial birthday gift from Queen Elizabeth II. Pick up free tickets and reserve a spot on one of the frequent tours of two Colonial homes: the Bishop White House, where the wealthy first Episcopal Bishop of Pennsylvania lived in grand style, and the modest home of Quaker John Todd, from whence Todd's widow, Dolley Payne, emerged to become the first lady of President James Madison.

The walking tour in these pages covers many of the more important historic sights in the park. The Visitor Center also offers suggestions for half-day and full-day do-it-yourself tours. For a complete listing of the city's historic sites, refer to the *Practical Information* section in this guide.

From the Visitor Center, walk west into the park to Carpenters' Hall, built as the meeting place of the Carpenters' Company, which in 1770 designed and constructed this guild hall as well as many distinguished buildings in the area. The same group, an organization of master builders and architects, still owns and maintains the building. This is where the First Continental Congress met in September 1774 to air their grievances against King George III. Some delegates talked treasonously of independence, others sought a less radical solution. Locked in debate, they voted to reconvene. Some early carpentry tools, the beautiful woodworking wrought with them, and furnishings from the period are on display.

Hurry over to Independence Hall to get a place at the head of the classes of schoolchildren who've come to see one of our nation's most precious gems. After 10 A.M. from April through October you can expect to wait in line for the thirty-minute tour. The hall, built in 1732 as the State House, the provincial government building of Pennsylvania, became the birthplace of the United States. The delegates to the Second Continental Congress met in the hall's Assembly Room in May 1776, united in anger over the blood that had been shed when British

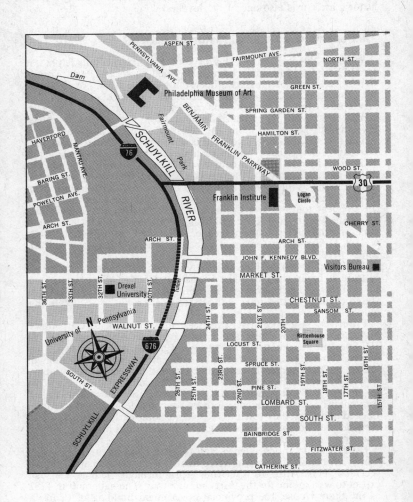

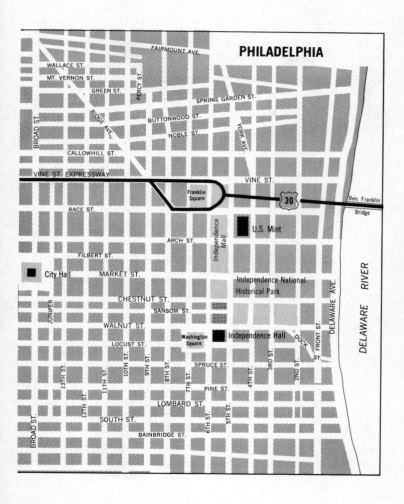

troops fired on citizens in Concord. In this same room, George Washington was appointed Commander-in-Chief of the Continental Army, Thomas Jefferson's eloquent Declaration of Independence was signed, and later the Constitution of the United States was adopted. Before and after the British occupation, the national government was centered at Independence Hall. Here, the first foreign minister to visit the United States was welcomed, the news of Cornwallis's defeat was announced signaling the end of the Revolutionary War, and John Adams and Abraham Lincoln lay in state. The memories that this building holds linger in the collection of polished muskets, the silver inkstand that was used by delegates to sign the Declaration of Independence, and the "Rising Sun" chair in which George Washington sat during the Constitutional Convention.

Independence Hall is bordered by Congress Hall—where the newly formed U.S. Congress met from 1790 to 1800 and where Washington and Adams were inaugurated—and Old City Hall, the first home of the U.S. Supreme Court.

The Liberty Bell, which had hung in the belfry of Independence Hall since 1753, was moved to a glass pavilion on the mall north of the Hall in 1976. The bell, originally cast in Whitechapel, London, was cracked by its clapper during the test run, but two Philadelphia foundrymen ingeniously recast it. The bell fulfilled the words of its inscription when it rang to "proclaim liberty throughout all the land unto all the inhabitants thereof," beckoning Philadelphians to the State House Yard to hear the first reading of the Declaration of Independence. The crack you see today occurred when the bell tolled for its last time at the funeral of Chief Justice John Marshall.

From the Liberty Bell Pavilion, it's a short walk west on Market Street to the Graff House, where Jefferson drafted the Declaration of Independence. The upstairs rooms in which he labored have been re-created; you can see Jefferson's original version—which would have abolished slavery had the passage not been stricken by the committee that included Benjamin Franklin and John Adams.

Though they are not part of Independence National Historical Park, you may want to visit two adjacent sites while you are in the neighborhood: the Atwater Kent Museum, which focuses on the city's growth and its municipal services, and the Balch Institute for Ethnic Studies, dedicated to the history of immigration and ethnic cultures in the United States.

Chestnut Street, between Fifth and Third, is lined with museums. The Parthenon lookalike is the Second Bank of the United States, which under the direction of Nicolas Biddle became one of the largest and most influential financial institutions in the world. Built by William Strickland, it is one of the finest examples of Greek-Revivial architecture in the United States. Many of the distinguished gentlemen in the second-floor portrait gallery were painted by Charles Willson Peale and members of his family. Military buffs will enjoy the Army-Navy Museum (in the Pemberton House) and Marine Corps Memorial Museum (in New Hall).

If you have time to see just one site other than Independence Hall and the Liberty Bell, make it Franklin Court. The Chestnut Street entrance is a narrow walkway alongside the Philadelphia Maritime Museum. The underground museum at Franklin Court, which once held the home of Franklin, is an imaginative tribute to the Renaissance man. Dial-a-quote to hear his thoughts, pick up a telephone and call his contemporaries to find out what they really thought of him. At the Market Street side are several houses, now exhibit halls, that Ben had rented. In one, visitors can see how Franklin fireproofed the building. (His interest led him to start the Philadelphia Contributionship, the first fire insurance company, and to experiment with kite flying and lightning.) In other houses are a demonstration of Colonial printing techniques and a display of original copies of Franklin's *Pennsylvania Gazette*.

Outside of Independence Hall you'll find a line of guides waiting to whisk you away for a horse and carriage ride through the district. Tours range from 15-minute trips around the square (for about $10) to 45-minute excursions over to Head House Square in neighboring Society Hill (for about $20).

Many visitors opt for lunch or dinner at the reconstructed eighteenth-century City Tavern at 2nd and Walnut streets. Authentically costumed waiters and waitresses serve hearty beef pies, roasts, pheasant, and other Early American specialties. The tavern was the center of the city's social and political life, a genteel club where delegates to the Continental Congresses engaged in fiery debate and indulged in rum toddies.

Enter The Bourse (5th Street between Market and Chestnut) and you're in another century. The skylit Great Hall, with its Corinthian columns, marble and wrought-iron stairways, and Victorian gingerbread details, has been restored. Built as a commodities exchange in 1893, The Bourse is now home to 50 stores and restaurants, including the exclusive boutiques of Saint Laurent, Cacharel, and Howard Heartsfield. The cafes along the uppermost balcony offer ethnic specialties, salads, cheesesteaks, pastries, and more.

Old City

Old City, the neighborhood north of Market Street, has always been "the other side of the tracks." Its earliest residents were a strict sect of Penn's followers called "stiff Quakers." South of Market lived the "World's People," the wealthier Anglicans who arrived after Penn and who loved music, dancing, and partying—pursuits the Quakers shunned. Society Hill's poorer neighbors—Old City to the north and Southwark to the south—remained modest neighborhoods of artisans and craftsmen involved in trades like printing and stone masonry. Many people who lived in Old City worked in the thriving shipping

Points of Interest

1) Afro-American Cultural House
2) American Jewish History Museum
3) Arch St. Friends Meeting House
4) Atwater Kent Museum
5) Balch Institute of Ethnic Studies
6) Betsy Ross House
7) Bourse Building
8) Carpenters' Hall
9) Christ Church
10) Franklin Court
11) Graff House
12) Horticultural Society of Pennsylvania
13) Independence Hall
14) Independence National Historical Park Visitors Center
15) Liberty Bell Pavilion
16) Library Hall
17) Marine Corps Museum
18) Old City Hall
19) Pemberton House
20) Philadelphia Contributorship
21) Second Bank of the United States
22) U.S. Mint
23) Washington Square

industry that grew with Philadelphia's prominence as an important Atlantic seaport. The community became a melting pot of Jews, blacks, Germans, and Welsh; 2nd Street was one of the city's major north-south arteries. Some of the Victorian cast-iron warehouses still remain; urban renewal efforts have transformed other vast, empty spaces into airy lofts. Artists and craftsmen—and numerous young professionals—call this neighborhood home.

A few sights in this area complete the picture of Colonial Philadelphia. From the Visitor Center, head east to 2nd Street, and then walk north. Just above Market is Christ Church, which was the only Anglican church in the city for at least half a century. For close to sixty years, Bishop White was the rector; fifteen signers of the Declaration of Independence worshiped here. The church is a gem of Colonial architecture; its bells and slender white steeple were financed in part by lotteries organized by Ben Franklin. It is still an active Episcopalian parish.

A few blocks north is Elfreth's Alley, said to be the oldest continuously occupied residential street in the United States. Much of Colonial Philadelphia resembled this: cobblestone streets and narrow two-story houses. Numbers 122 and 124 are thought to be the oldest houses, dating from around 1725. Though the facades are original, some interiors are ultramodern. The houses are open to the public once a year on Elfreth's Alley Day, the first weekend in June. Otherwise, you'll have to be content with visiting Number 126, the Mantua Maker's House, a small museum maintained by the Elfreth's Alley Association.

A little farther north, at Quarry Street, is Fireman's Hall, an authentic firehouse-turned-museum with a rare collection of hand- and horse-drawn pumpers and steamers, parade hats, a fireboat, and uniforms from the 1800s.

One of the most famous residents of this Quaker neighborhood was Betsy Ross, who worked in her family's flag-making and upholstery business. Whether she actually lived in the little brick house on Arch Street, and whether or not she really made the first Stars and Stripes, is debatable. Nonetheless, the house is a splendid example of a Colonial Philadelphia home and is fun to visit. You may have to wait in line here, as this is one of the city's most popular tourist attractions. Between 321 and 323 Arch Street is Loxley Court. The court's claim to fame, according to its residents, is as the spot where Benjamin Franklin flew his kite; the key tied to it was the key to carpenter Benjamin Loxley's front door. Across the street is the Friends Meeting House, a Quaker building of simple lines, in keeping with their faith. Penn's life and achievements are depicted in the exhibit area. The simplicity of the meeting room gives an insight into this peaceful group. If your timing is right, attend a meeting for worship on Thursdays at 10 A.M. or Sundays at 10:30 A.M. Visitors are always welcome.

The grave of Benjamin Franklin lies in the Christ Church Burial Ground at Fifth and Arch streets. The weathered stones in this hallowed place mark the graves of many celebrated Colonial and Revolutionary War heroes.

At the U.S. Mint, across the street, you can take a self-guided tour and watch coins being made. On Fifth Street is the Museum of American Jewish History, chronicling the roles of Jews in the nation's development. Attached is Congregation Mikveh Israel, dating from 1740. Two blocks west is the Afro-American Historical and Cultural Museum. The special exhibits change; in 1984 they focused on the achievements of black women and on South Africa. The museum sponsors an annual jazz festival.

During the six years that Edgar Allan Poe lived in Philadelphia, he published some of his most famous stories, including "The Gold Bug," "The Tell-Tale Heart," and the "Fall of the House of Usher." The small home at the Edgar Allan Poe National Historic Site is the only one of his Philadelphia residences that still exists. To get there, take the #50 bus north on Fifth Street to Spring Garden Street. The house is two blocks west at the corner of Seventh Street.

Penn's Landing

Penn's Landing, the thirty-seven acres that stretch along the Delaware River from Market Street to South Street, is the largest piece of undeveloped land remaining in the city. The urban development projects that have transformed waterfronts into dramatic public spaces—like Baltimore's Inner Harbor and New York's South Street Seaport—have not yet changed the character of Philadelphia's harbor. This, one of the world's largest freshwater ports, is a working port: it generates about $1 billion a year in revenue and more than 90,000 related jobs.

There has been some progress: construction has begun on residential developments at Piers Three and Five and the Chart House Restaurant. And glorious plans are in the works to make the riverfront, which one urban planner called "the jewel in the belly button of Philadelphia," shine.

Still, Penn's Landing deserves a visit today. To get there, head east on Chestnut Street or Spruce Street until the street dead-ends at the river. In the warmer months, the "Down by the Riverside" program brings free concerts and festivals to the waterfront. Four ships, open for tours, are docked where Spruce Street meets the river. The U.S.S. *Olympia* was Commodore George Dewey's flagship during the Spanish-American War. From its bridge, Dewey launched the Battle of Manila Bay with the famous words: "You may fire when you are ready, Gridley." A single entry fee also allows you to clamber through the U.S.S. *Becuna*, a guppy-class submarine that "searched and destroyed" in South Pacific waters during World War II. At the admission booth, you can buy a ticket for a twenty-minute narrated excursion along the riverfront in a Penn's Landing Trolley.

In the same basin are the *Gazela of Philadelphia,* the world's oldest wooden square-rigger still in sailing condition, and the *Barnegat Iron*

Lightship. Along the waterfront promenade to the north is the Port of History Museum and the *Moshulu,* the world's largest steel sailing ship, which has been converted into a maritime museum and restaurant. The *Moshulu*'s floating Victorian bar is a novel place for before- or after-dinner drinks.

For a view of harbor lights and Navy warships, you can board the *Spirit of Philadelphia,* a 600-passenger luxury liner, for a lunch, buffet dinner, or moonlight-dance cruise, all with live entertainment.

Society Hill

Society Hill, the area south of Independence Hall between Sixth and Front and Walnut and South streets, took its name from the Free Society of Traders, the group of British investors to whom William Penn granted the land. In Colonial times, political leaders, foreign notables, and citizens of wealth lived here. As the city grew, the wealthy moved ever westward to bigger houses. By the end of World War I, the area was becoming a slum. It took the combined will of federal, civic, and private agencies to renew Society Hill. They were eminently successful: Society Hill has become not just a showcase for historic churches and mansions, but a living, breathing urban neighborhood. From May to October, guides in Colonial dress lead Candlelight Strolls through Society Hill. They depart at 6:30 P.M. from City Tavern at Second and Walnut streets on Saturday evenings.

Along these streets are charming hidden courtyards, delightful decorative touches like odd chimney tops and brass door knockers. You'll stumble upon an occasional hitching post, a wrought-iron foot-scraper, or a marble stepping stone, remnants from the days of horse-drawn carriages and muddy, unpaved streets. Notice the exquisite ironwork on railings and balconies: much of New Orleans' famed ironwork was done by Philadelphia craftsmen. You'll see the narrow Trinity houses, with just one room on each of the three floors; and the 2½-story Colonial houses, generally dating from before 1750, with their gabled roofs, shed dormers, paneled shutters, and hoods over the entrances and first-story windows. The more elaborate three- or four-story houses were built after the 1750s.

The area is well marked for self-guided tours. From Penn's Landing, walk west on Spruce Street to Society Hill. In the shadow of the I.M. Pei-designed Society Hill Towers is the Man Full of Trouble Tavern, a colorful Revolutionary-era tavern (restored as a museum) where sailors and dock workers caroused. Leon Perelman's personal collection of American tin and cast-iron toys from the Victorian era fills three floors of the Perelman Antique Toy Museum. This, the world's largest collection of mechanical banks, attests to the Quaker and Victorian passions for savings. (And it was Ben Franklin who said, "A penny saved is a penny earned.")

On the southeast corner of Third and Spruce streets is a small hexagonal structure. The city said that the owners of the adjacent house couldn't have just a garden on the corner; they needed a house on the lot as well. In a stroke of ingenuity that would have made Ben Franklin proud, they built the small structure, put in a mail slot to meet the requirements, and planted their garden!

Head north on Third Street. The brownstones on your left were called Bouvier Row, as a few of them were once owned by Jacqueline Kennedy Onassis's family. A guide will take you through the grand salons of the Georgian-style Powel House and regale you with stories of how Samuel Powel, last mayor before and first mayor after the Revolution, entertained luminaries like Washington and Lafayette.

Proceed west on Walnut Street past the Horticultural Society's Colonial garden, and then walk south on Fourth Street. Here is the Philadelphia Contributionship, the oldest fire insurance company in America, another Franklin institution. (The building is open for tours.) When there was a fire, all fire companies would run to it, but if the Contributionship's crossed-hand symbol was displayed on the facade of the building, only they would put it out. The Contributionship wouldn't insure houses with trees in front, so the Mutual Assurance Company filled the void. Their motif, a green tree, can be seen on many Society Hill homes.

Hidden in Willings Alley is Old St. Joseph's National Shrine, the oldest Roman Catholic parish in the country (founded by Jesuit fathers in 1733), and the only place in the English-speaking world where mass could be celebrated at that time. Franklin suggested they put up the iron gate at the entranceway in case religious tolerance ever ran out. Nearby, Old St. Mary's Church, the most important Catholic church during the Revolutionary era, was built by the Jesuits of St. Joseph's as the more ornamental "Sunday" church. Commodore John Barry, father of the American Navy, is buried in the churchyard.

On the east side of Fourth Street, past Delancey, is the Hill-Physick-Keith House, the only freestanding house in Society Hill, and a handsome example of Federal architecture. Its second owner was Philip Syng Physick, the father of American surgery who pioneered new techniques, like the stomach pump, at nearby Pennsylvania Hospital. One of Dr. Physick's most famous patients was Chief Justice John Marshall, for whom the Liberty Bell last tolled.

"Old Pine," the Third Presbyterian Church at Fourth and Pine streets, looks more like a Greek temple than a Colonial church; it is the only Presbyterian church of that era still standing. Farther east on Pine is St. Peter's Protestant Episcopalian Church, reminiscent of those in England. Many congregants who didn't want to tramp through the mud to Christ Church, prayed in this elegant, pristine Georgian chapel with its cedar box pews painted white. In the graveyards of both St. Peter's and the Third Presbyterian, beneath ivy-wreathed tombstones, lie many American heroes.

At Second and Pine is Head House Square, a Colonial marketplace that is the site of the Head House Crafts Fair on summer weekends. Artisans exhibit and sell their jewelry, quilts, stained glass, and more;

street entertainers woo the crowds. Head House, topped by a cupola and weathervane, was the home and office of the Market Master; fire engines were kept under the arch. Between Head House and the river is NewMarket, an indoor-outdoor mall with landscaped courtyards and fancy shops and restaurants. Many of the restaurants have outdoor terraces for dining. This is a good place to stop for lunch, dinner, an ice cream cone, or a snack from the new, upscale farmer's market.

Southwark

Southwark, a modest, older neighborhood similar to Old City, is buzzing with the sounds of restoration. Directly south of Society Hill, Southwark is neither as glamorous nor as historically renowned as its neighbor. Chiseled in stone on one facade are these words: "On this site in 1897, nothing happened!"

Southwark was settled by the Swedes in 1638, years before Penn landed. It didn't get its current name until the middle of the eighteenth century when wealthy Englishmen invested in the area and named it Southwark after the London borough of the same name. The neighborhood, which stretches from Front to Sixth Street and from South Street to Washington Avenue, was the center of the commercial and shipbuilding activity that made Philadelphia the biggest port in the Colonies and in the young United States. It was a working-class neighborhood of artisans, merchants, carpenters, and shipbuilders.

In later years, Southwark was home to the waves of European immigrants who flooded our shores from the mid-1800s until well after the turn of the century. Today, this is an area in transition. Young professionals have restored many of the homes in Queen Village, the area between Front and Second, Bainbridge and Fitzwater streets, and the rents are now almost as steep as in Society Hill. But quite a few abandoned houses still wait for developers.

A leisurely stroll through Southwark, South Philadelphia, and along South Street is a fun day's outing. Begin your tour with breakfast at Famous Delicatessen (Fourth and Bainbridge, one block south of South Street), one of the city's most popular culinary institutions and a holdover from the era when this was a Jewish neighborhood, when immigrants hawked their wares from pushcarts.

Walk east on Bainbridge and then proceed south on Second Street, which the oldtimers call "Two Street." The homes along these streets are the oldest in the city. Even when their construction dates are not chiseled on the facades, the ravages of settlement—wavy lines of bricks above the overhangs, crooked windows and shutters that don't hang straight—attest to their vintage. The stars or circles on the facades aren't simply decorations, they are the ends of iron rods that are inserted in the floors for added structural support. If you get a late start and miss breakfast, have lunch at Walt's King of Crabs, a casual bar with fresh, inexpensive seafood.

Turn east on Catherine Street and then south on Hancock. This is one of the most charming streets in the city. The tiny clapboard houses at 813 and 815 were built by a shipwright and are the last of their type. Detour onto Queen Street to see the old firehouse with the gas lamps at 117. It has been converted to a single home, and you'll be awed by the beautiful restoration.

Continue down Hancock to Christian Street; go east about one block (under the I–95 overpass) to Swanson Street. Here is Gloria Dei, the Old Swedes' Church, the oldest church building (circa 1700) in the state. The church sits in the center of its graveyard; it is pleasing in its toylike simplicity and tranquility. Models of the ships which brought the first Swedish settlers to shore hang from the ceiling inside. Back on Second Street walk south. You'll see a neighborhood landmark, the Shot Tower, where lead shot was made during the War of 1812.

At Washington Avenue is the Mummers Museum. If you aren't lucky enought to see the January 1 extravaganza known as the Mummers Parade—in which feathered and sequined string bands, fancy brigades, and comics prance, strut, and carry on along Broad Street (the string band anthem is "O' Dem Golden Slippers")—don't miss the Mummers Museum. Mummers' costumes, which take as long as a year to make, are on display, as are other exhibits glorifying a century of Mummer folklore. Beginning in early May and continuing through the summer, there are String Band concerts each Tuesday night in the parking lot behind the museum. Bring your own chair (or blanket) and come before 7:30 for a place to put it.

South Philadelphia

The city's "Little Italy," a huge neighborhood of identical row homes with gleaming white marble steps, is its most colorful section. From the Mummers Museum, walk west on Washington Avenue to Ninth Street and then proceed north.

The five-block-long, open-air Italian Market (open daily except Mondays) at South Philly's heart is more Naples than Philadelphia; vendors crowd the sidewalks and spill onto the streets; live crabs and caged chickens wait for the kill; picture-perfect produce is piled high. Italians and some Asians, the city's newest immigrants, sell designer handbags and T-shirts from their stalls. The shops behind are brimming with ricotta cheese-filled cannoli, imported Parmesan, sweet sausages, and exotic olives. Be sure to look in the barrels at Claudio King of Cheese.

Although there are chic eateries in South Philadelphia, the majority of the neighborhood restaurants are not fancy (decor such as red-checked vinyl tableclothes and plastic grapes hanging from plastic vines is not uncommon), but the food is terrific and authentic. Most likely Mama is in the kitchen preparing a Southern-Italian specialty for you. (See our restaurant listing for suggestions.) Restaurant owners proudly display the gold records of neighborhood celebrities like Bobby

Rydell, Frankie Avalon, James Darren, and Fabian. A neighborhood park was dedicated to tenor Mario Lanza, who was supposedly moving a piano into the Academy of Music when he seized the opportunity to sing from its stage—and was first discovered.

Though its restaurants are crowded, South Philadelphia's streets are quiet at night. If you eat a late dinner, have the waiter call a cab for you about thirty minutes before you're finished. It's often hard to get taxis on the street.

You'll have to stand at a counter or lean against a car to eat what many would say is the best meal in South Philly: a cheesesteak from Pat's King of Steaks at Ninth and Passyunk. These may be the original. Ask anyone for directions. Cheesesteaks are one of Philadelphia's native foods: very thinly sliced beef is fried in lots of oil, layered on an Italian roll, and spread with sticky Cheddar spread.

When you've had enough food, walk north on Ninth, turn east on Catherine, and wander by the Samuel S. Fleisher Art Memorial at 719, an art school that offers free instruction. Ask to be shown the interior of the nineteenth-century Romanesque basilica next door. The church was bought by Fleisher, a German Jew, to prevent it from being made into a warehouse. He then commissioned altar scenes of the life of Moses. Modeled after basilicas in Italy, the inside is eerily beautiful. This is a fabulous treasure that few Philadelphians have ever seen. (Open temporarily by appointment only. Regular hours will resume September 1985.)

At the southern end of South Philadelphia is the city's sports complex, including the Spectrum, Veterans Stadium, and John F. Kennedy Stadium. The easiest way to get to a game is on the Broad Street Subway which takes you from City Hall Station to Pattison Avenue in ten minutes. That's also the best way to reach the American Swedish Museum, which documents the Swedish presence in the area since 1638. At the far end of South Broad Street, where the Schuylkill River meets the Delaware, is the Philadelphia Naval Base. Here, on a fascinating tour of this city within a city, you'll see battleships, cruisers and other carriers, the drydocks, and the land facilities.

South Street

South Street, the dividing line between Society Hill and Southwark, is where you'll see Philadelphia at its funkiest.

According to the original plans that Thomas Holmes drew up for William Penn, South Street was the city's southern boundary. For hundreds of years, it was a shopping street; but by the 1950s, like much of the city, it was a decaying ghost town. A decade later, a group of artists and businesspeople, lured by the low rents and possessing lots of imagination, moved into the neighborhood. They opened galleries, restaurants, coffee houses, and theaters and began the South Street Renaissance—and the city's restaurant renaissance. South Street, from Front to about 8th Street, and blossoming westward, is the city's

Greenwich Village, an eclectic, lively, artsy strip. There is activity here any time of day.

From South Philadelphia, walk north on Seventh Street until you reach South Street. Then, head east. You'll pass bookstores with rare books, antique shops (detour to 512 South Third to see Gargoyles Ltd.), galleries of exquisite crafts (don't miss The Works at 319 South), hand-carved furniture, vintage and new-wave clothing stores, European-style cafes, and natural food outlets.

You'll probably want to return to experience the bizarre fun of South Street after dark. The atmosphere spills into the restaurants. Lickety Split, which calls itself "the longest-running dinner party on South Street," Cafe Nola, featuring New Orleans Creole cooking, and MARS, with its far-out decor and imaginative menu, are very popular. Many shops remain open until 11 P.M., especially on weekends. The TLA Cinema has an almost daily change in schedule of art films and fine movies you might have missed the first time around. Grendel's Lair features a cabaret show, dance parties, and live rock. "Let My People Come," a risqué musical, has played on and off for eight years. The best show, however, is on the street, where orange-haired punkers, leather-jacketed South Philly toughs, blue-jeaned hippy holdovers, and decked-out suburban folks (who come to watch the scene, but become part of the show) promenade along the strip.

Washington Square West

The section of the city that reaches from Independence National Historical Park west to Broad Street and from Market to South Street was developed primarily in the Nineteenth century as the city expanded westward. Though many of the homes surrounding Washington Square have been restored, the area hasn't yet regained the reputation it held in the 1840s as Philadelphia's most fashionable and affluent neighborhood.

Today, Washington Square West is a mix of residential enclaves and businesses. (You'll find the stores along Walnut Street and north.) Much of the activity here is medicine-related with the Thomas Jefferson University and Hospital complex at Eleventh and Walnut, and Pennsylvania Hospital at Eighth and Spruce.

Several vestiges of the neighborhood's earlier glory remain. The Musical Fund Hall at 806 Locust Street, now in disrepair, was the scene of cultural and political events until the Academy of Music opened in 1857. The first Republican Party National Convention met here and nominated John Charles Fremont as their presidential candidate; Ralph Waldo Emerson and Charles Dickens lectured here; P. T. Barnum introduced soprano Jenny Lind, "The Swedish Nightingale," to the city from this stage. The Walnut Street Theatre, whose first play was staged in 1812, is the oldest playhouse in the English-speaking world. Edwin Forrest debuted here; John and Ethel Barrymore and Edwin Booth, brother of John Wilkes, starred in performances on its stage. It is alleged that Sarah Bernhardt took seriously ill and died (in France) soon after she caught a cold in one of the theater's drafty dressing rooms. The Walnut, still one of the city's main stages, is now a performing arts center for music, drama, and dance.

Washington Square, one of the five squares in Penn's original plan, has remained the heart of the neighborhood. The wide paths and tall shade trees are reminiscent of a London park. Fittingly, it's a tranquil place in an otherwise busy area: the square is actually a cemetery. Until after the Revolutionary War it was a burial ground for Colonial and British soldiers and for prisoners from the old Walnut Street penitentiary. The square's tomb to Unknown Soldiers of the Revolution is its only memorial.

Surrounding the square are the establishments which made Philadelphia an important publishing center. On the south corner is Lea and Febiger, America's oldest publishing house. Founded in 1785 as Carey, Lea and Blanchard, they've published Dickens, Poe, Washington Irving, and Thackeray. On the east is J.B. Lippincott, on the west W.B. Saunders, the world's largest medical publisher. The Curtis Publishing Company building, a block north at Sixth and Walnut, was once the home of *The Saturday Evening Post* and *The Ladies' Home Journal.* Don't miss the treasure in its lobby—a fifteen-by-fifty foot glass mosaic mural based on a painting entitled "The Dream Garden" by Maxfield Parrish, a renowned early-twentieth-century painter/illustrator and a Philadelphian. Executed by the Louis C. Tiffany Studios in 1916, it is the world's second largest mosaic of its sort, with 260 different colors of glass. Curtis also houses the Norman Rockwell Museum whose collection includes the painter's *Saturday Evening Post* covers.

The Athenaeum on East Washington Square is a private library that was founded in 1814 by members of the American Philosophical Society as a sort of clubhouse for people of literary, artistic, and scientific merit. One can inherit membership in the library—the 1,000 stockholders can will their shares to succeeding generations—or subscribe by paying an annual fee. The building, open for tours, is as distinguished as its collection of material relating to nineteenth-century social and cultural history. Inside are marble columns, rich woodwork, and Empire furnishings.

From the square, walk west on Locust to Eighth Street and turn left. Between Spruce and Pine is Pennsylvania Hospital, the oldest hospital in the United States, founded by Benjamin Franklin and Dr. Thomas Bond in 1751. Pass the modern buildings until you reach the old Colonial structures, fine examples of eighteenth-century public buildings. Inside is Benjamin West's masterpiece, *Christ Healing the Sick.* The original buildings house the first medical library and the first surgical amphitheater with a skylight (this dates from the days before gas lamps). In 1867, when women came to attend a clinical lecture here, they were spat upon and stoned by the interns who were disgraced because a male patient's buttocks were exposed. But women were not excluded from medical education. The Female Medical College of

Pennsylvania, the nation's first medical school for women, graduated its first class in 1851 from a facility on Arch Street. (The college later changed its named to Women's Medical College. Today, it is the co-ed Medical College of Pennsylvania, and it has a new location outside of Center City.)

Opposite the modern annex of the hospital (on Spruce Street) is the brick-walled Mikveh Israel Cemetery. It was built in 1740 as the old burial ground of the city's Spanish-Portuguese Jewish community. Among the notables buried here are Nathan Levy, whose ship brought the Liberty Bell to America; Haym Solomon, the Pole who helped finance the Revolution; and Rebecca Gratz, the inspiration for Sir Walter Scott's heroine Rebecca in *Ivanhoe.*

Continue south on Eighth Street to Pine and turn right. Here is the city's Antique Row, offering a fine collection of American and English antiques and good reproductions. Intersecting with Pine are two streets worth exploring. Walk north on Quince Street, between Eleventh and Twelfth; the cobblestone alley and the little side streets are lined with charming houses from the Federal period. Between Twelfth and Thirteenth streets is Camac. Along here are some of the small private clubs that played an important part in the city's history: The Sketch Club, the oldest professional artists club in the country; the Charlotte Cushman Club, a private club for actresses; and the Plastic Club, for women painters and sculptors.

Continue north on Camac to Locust and walk west to Thirteenth Street. At the corner is the Historical Society of Pennsylvania, an important repository for the study of Colonial and Revolutionary history. Almost all of the city's notables are represented in the collection of artifacts, silver, furniture, and paintings in its museum. At 1314 Locust is America's first public library—The Library Company of Philadelphia, founded by Franklin in 1731. It has an outstanding collection of rare books, photographs, and prints.

Walking north on Thirteenth Street will bring you to John Wanamaker's, as prominent a Philadelphia landmark as the Liberty Bell—almost. The department store was dedicated by President Taft in 1911. The focal point of the twelve-story building is the splendid five-story Grand Court. Here, each day at 11:15 A.M. and 5:15 P.M., an organist plays the world's largest organ with its more than 30,000 pipes. During the Christmas season, there's a spectacular sound and light show. Shoppers and businesspeople still meet for lunch in the elegant Crystal Room, named for its ornate chandeliers, as they have since the store first opened.

The area around Thirteenth and Locust streets has a long history of after-dark activity. When Washington Square was in its heyday, this was a strip of fashionable restaurants, taverns, and illicit pleasures: The Library Company possesses a document from 1849 entitled *A Guide to the Stranger: Or Pocket Companion for the Fancy, Containing a List of Gay Houses and Ladies of Pleasure in the City of Brotherly Love and Sisterly Affection.*

During Prohibition, high-class clubs and speakeasies flourished here. Later, when Prohibition was repealed, the area "went legit"; supper clubs and theaters drew top entertainers such as Dean Martin, Louis Armstrong, and Frank Sinatra. Until about twenty-five years ago, this was the city's hottest entertainment district.

In the sixties, clubs closed their doors and Thirteenth Street, from about Spruce to Arch, became the city's vice strip. It maintains that reputation today. City planners anticipate that the sprucing up of Broad Street and investment interest in the area will shut down the "red light" district and close many of the X-rated movie houses and adult book stores. Till then, it's wise to avoid the blocks just east of Broad Street after dark.

Chinatown and Market Street East

A few blocks west of Old City is Philadelphia's Chinatown. The entrance to the community is marked by a dazzling, ornamental, Chinese gate that spans Tenth Street just north of Arch. It was made by a team of artisans from China; the tile and other materials were contributed by Philadelphia's sister city of Tianjin in the People's Republic of China.

There are 80,000 Asian residents in the Greater Philadelphia area; the largest concentration live in the area defined by Eighth and Eleventh, Arch and Vine. You will know you're in Chinatown not just by the groceries, souvenir shops, and scores of restaurants featuring Mandarin, Szechuan, Cantonese, and Hunan specialties, but also by the bilingual street signs and the red and green phone booths with pagoda tops.

Several restaurants serve a dim sum tea lunch—a Chinese smorgasbord of mostly steamed and bite-sized foods which are stacked on carts and rolled around the room. (Try Joy Tsin Lau, 1026 Race; or Golden Inn, 134 N. Tenth). Chinatown is also your best bet for a late dinner. The Chinese New Year (February to April) is celebrated with ten-course banquets at the Chinese Cultural Center. Dinner is by advance reservation only. If you'll be here during those months, call 923–6767 for reservations.

Just southwest of Chinatown is the Reading Terminal Market, which affords another opportunity for a food orgy. The still-active nineteenth-century European-style markethouse is lined with meat, fish, and produce stands, plus more than twenty stalls that serve ready-to-eat treats. Here, amidst the local color, you can sample Bassetts ice cream, Philadelphia's best; down a cheesesteak at Olivieri's or a bowl of chowder at Pearl's Oyster Bar; or nibble Greek, Mexican, and Indian specialties. On Saturdays, the Amish from Lancaster County cart their goodies, including Lebanon bologna, shoofly pie, and scrapple, to the market. The city is planning to build a new convention facility adjacent to the Reading Terminal Market and predicts that the development will enliven the otherwise drab area that surrounds it.

On Market between Eighth and Eleventh streets is The Gallery at Market East, a four-level urban mall. Sunlight streams through the glass atrium and makes browsing through the 250 shops and restaurants a pleasant diversion, especially on a cold day. In addition to the ground-floor international eateries, Strawbridge & Clothier, Gimbels, and J. C. Penney department stores are big draws. Below the mall, at Eleventh and Market streets, lining the walls of the new Market Street East commuter station, is a brilliantly colored mural of 250,000 German ceramic tiles that form an impressionistic landscape. The mural was executed from a design by architect David Beck.

Midtown and Rittenhouse Square

Philadelphians first settled by the Delaware River and then continued to move ever westward as their fortunes grew. After the Academy of Music opened in 1857, the section of Center City from Broad Street west to the Schuylkill River became a fashionable address. Rittenhouse Square replaced Washington Square as the center of high society, and remained so until the 1920s when many city dwellers fled even farther west to suburbs on the Main Line. Today, this midtown area is a mix of residential, business, and cultural institutions. Here are some of the city's finest hotels and restaurants, most exclusive stores, and private clubs.

City Hall, at the intersection of Broad and Market streets, is a good place to start a tour of this part of the city. An elevator will take you to the base of Alexander Milne Calder's bronze statue of William Penn for a panoramic view of the city. Enter the building on its northeast or northwest side, take the elevator to the seventh floor and follow the red lines. Until 1908, this was the tallest building in America; for now, it still dominates Philadelphia's skyline. You can tour the interior of this French-style Victorian structure, patterned after the New Louvre in Paris. Amidst the splendor of mahogany paneling, gold-leaf ceilings, and marble pillars are the Mayor's Reception Room, the City Council Chambers, and the Supreme Court of Pennsylvania.

From City Hall, walk south on Broad Street. At 140 South Broad is the French Renaissance-style Union League, the oldest Republican club in continuous existence. Its two neighbors, the Bellevue Stratford Hotel and the Academy of Music, share the title of the "grand dames of Broad Street." Both have hosted balls and galas as opulent as their interiors. The Bellevue, a fine example of French Renaissance architecture, opened in 1904. Its $25-million revitalization in 1979 brought new life to the hotel and the neighborhood. Walk through the lobby and stay for afternoon tea in the Stratford Court. The Academy, modeled after the La Scala Opera House in Milan, is acoustically perfect and visually grand. Twelve presidents have spoken from its stage; once a football game was played here. The only way to see its interior (other than on a once-a-month tour arranged through its office) is by attending a performance of the resident Philadelphia Orchestra, Pennsylvania Bal-

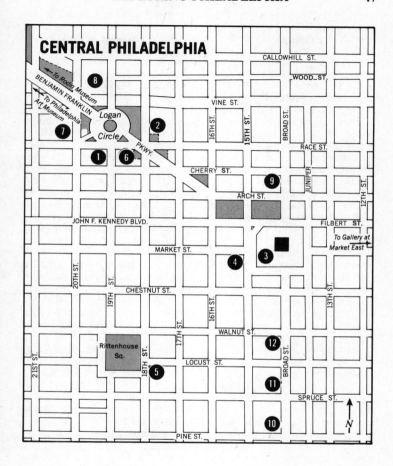

Points of Interest

1) Academy of Natural Sciences
2) Cathedral Basilica of Saints Peter & Paul
3) City Hall
4) Convention & Visitors Bureau
5) Curtis Institute of Music
6) Four Seasons Hotel
7) Franklin Institute Science Museum
8) Free Library
9) Pennsylvania Academy of the Fine Arts
10) Philadelphia College of Art
11) Shubert Theater
12) Westin Bellevue Stratford Hotel

let, Opera Company of Philadelphia, or the All-Star Forum. If you can't get tickets in advance for the Orchestra, you can buy general admission tickets to the amphitheater for $2 each. These are sold before each Friday afternoon, Friday evening, and Saturday evening concert. You'll need to line up about two hours in advance for the big-name concerts, an hour before for other ones. A block south of the Academy is the Shubert Theater, one of the city's leading stages, and the Philadelphia College of Art, which displays student works in its galleries.

Head back to Walnut Street and walk west. Along Walnut and the intersecting Seventeenth and Eighteenth streets near Rittenhouse Square are some of the city's most exclusive men's and women's clothing boutiques. Art galleries, where you can find old masters and contemporary crafts, are scattered throughout the neighborhood. (See *Practical Information,* "Shopping" for suggestions.) At the corner of Eighteenth and Walnut streets is Urban Outfitters. Formerly the Fell-Van Rensselaer House, it is one of the last nineteenth-century mansions remaining on Rittenhouse Square. Built in 1896, it's a shining example of the Beaux Arts style. Be sure to look inside. As you enter, walk into the room on the far right for a glimpse of its spectacular ceiling and moldings.

Rittenhouse Square was a grazing ground for sheep and cattle before it was transformed into the city's most elegant square designed after a Parisian park. Another of Penn's originals, this square was named in honor of David Rittenhouse, astronomer, clockmaker, and first director of the United States Mint. Many of Philadelphia's movers, shakers, and celebrities have lived here. Extra paths were made for Dr. William White, a leader in beautifying the square, so that he could walk directly from his home to the exclusive Rittenhouse Club across the square and lunch with the likes of Henry James. Swank high-rise apartment buildings have replaced the townhouses that bordered the square until thirty-five years ago. At least one private residence remains: on the southwest corner (1914 Rittenhouse Square) are three townhouses belonging to one of the city's leading socialities, Henry P. McIlhenny of the Tabasco fortune. In the Philadelphia telephone directory there is a separate listing for Mr. McIlhenny's servants quarters.

Today, the good life continues in Rittenhouse Square: annual events include the Easter Parade, the Mozart on the Square festival, the Rittenhouse Square Flower Market, and the Fine Arts Annual, a clothesline art festival. You may want to join the office workers who have lunch-hour picnics in the park. You'll find scores of restaurants and sandwich shops with take-out service along Walnut, Sansom, and Chestnut streets, east of the square.

Along the east side of the square are the dignified Barclay Hotel and the Philadelphia Art Alliance, a gay-nineties mansion with galleries open to the public. The Curtis Institute of Music, the Italian Renaissance palazzo at Eighteenth and Locust streets, is a tuition-free school for select musicians. Efrem Zimbalist and Rudolf Serkin were directors of the Institute; famous graduates include Leonard Bernstein and Gian-Carlo Menotti.

Walk south on Eighteenth Street past Spruce to Delancey. Delancey is an urban residential showcase; its homes are grand. At the corner (320 South Eighteenth) is an interesting old sea captain's house. However, the 2000 block wins the prize. At 2010 is the Rosenbach Museum and Library, an extraordinary collection amassed by two bachelor brothers. The collection includes James Joyce's original, handwritten manuscript of *Ulysses,* Chaucer's *Canterbury Tales,* Maurice Sendak drawings, Daumier prints, furniture, silver, and an entire living room that once belonged to poet Marianne Moore. You may recognize the entrance of 2014 Delancey from the film *Trading Places* with Eddie Murphy. Pearl Buck once lived at 2019; Rudolf Serkin at 2020. 2026 and 2034 are noteworthy for their gorgeous, beveled leaded glass. While you're in this area, explore the 1900 block of Panama (one block south of Delancey.) The homes here make this one of the city's most interesting streets.

Follow any numbered street north to Chestnut Street; at Eighteenth Street, Chestnut becomes a pedestrian mall. Many of the city's first-run movie theaters are here. At the street level are rows of glass storefronts, but the second- and third-story architecture is wildly divergent and interesting.

At 1622 Chestnut is the Art and Fashion Institutes of Philadelphia. You'll need to cross the street to see its top. Built in 1932 as the original WCAU Building for radio broadcasting and restored fifty years later, this building, now housing a school, is one of the city's great Art Deco structures.

If you continue east on Chestnut to Broad, you'll see City Hall once again. Four blocks north, at Broad and Cherry streets, is the Pennsylvania Academy of the Fine Arts. Whether you see its collection now or before you begin your tour of museums along the Benjamin Franklin Parkway, plan to spend at least one hour here. Founded in 1805 by Charles Willson Peale, the Academy was the nation's first art museum and school. Both the museum and school are still in operation. The building, by Philadelphia-architects Frank Furness and George Hewitt, is an imaginative, detailed work, a Victorian masterpiece studded with Moorish and Greek columns, Art Deco, and Italianate touches. America's finest nineteenth- and twentieth-century painters, many of whom worked in this city, are represented: Benjamin West, Gilbert Stuart, Thomas Sully, Andrew Wyeth, and the Peale family.

Benjamin Franklin Parkway

This mile-long boulevard, which begins a block northwest of City Hall and ends at the Philadelphia Museum of Art, is the city's "museum row." There may be more cultural attractions per square foot here than along any boulevard in the world.

The tree-lined parkway wasn't part of Penn's original plan. It was designed in 1926 by French architects on the occasion of the country's 150th birthday. The cultural palaces that opened soon after competed with each other in grandeur. The Museum of Art is a beautifully proportioned Greco-Roman temple. The Free Library of Philadelphia and the Family Court are copies from Paris's Place de la Concorde. The newest addition to the parkway is the luxurious Four Seasons Hotel on the south side of Logan Circle. Though built in 1983, its dignified design and granite facade made it look like a local institution from the day it opened. It completes the circle which is surrounded by the classical forms (counterclockwise) of the Cathedral Basilica of Saints Peter and Paul, the Family Court, the Free Library, the Franklin Institute, and the Academy of Natural Sciences. In the center of the circle is the Swann Fountain, a water ballet sculpture by Alexander Stirling Calder. This is a place befitting pomp and ceremony: in October 1979, Pope John Paul II celebrated a mass for about 150,000 people in Logan Circle.

Occasionally, the parkway lets down its hair. Each October, on "Super Sunday," there is a giant block party with games, rides, entertainment, and food. There's an annual restaurant festival, July 4th fireworks, foot races, free concerts, and the Gimbels Thanksgiving Day Parade.

Begin your tour of the parkway at the Tourist Center at Sixteenth Street and John F. Kennedy Boulevard. Here, Wednesday through Sunday, from April 1 until November 30, you can board a Victorian-replica Fairmount Park Trolley Bus for a guided tour of the parkway and adjacent Fairmount Park. The single fare includes the all-day privilege of getting off at any stop and reboarding whenever you are ready to move on. If it's off season, the folks at the Tourist Center can tell you about alternative transportation. Don't forget about your feet; it's a beautiful walk.

The Academy of Natural Sciences sits at Nineteenth Street and the Parkway. Founded in 1812, this is America's first natural history museum. The Academy has achieved fame for its collections of animals, birds, and insects. Stuffed animals, such as giant buffalo, antelopes, and brown bears from Alaska, are exhibited in lifelike settings that depict their natural habitats. A two-story dinosaur skeleton and daily live-animal nature programs are favorite features. A block away, the Franklin Institute Science Museum makes science and technology understandable through fun and games. The exhibits and experiments beg to be touched—by kids and adults. There is a room-sized walk-through model of a human heart and a Boeing 707 parked in the backyard ready for boarding. Daily shows are presented in the Fels Planetarium. In the event that hunger strikes, you'll find vending machines in these museums. However, your best bet for lunch is the cafeteria or restaurant at the Philadelphia Museum of Art.

Across Logan Circle is the Free Library of Philadelphia with its impressive collection of rare books. There's a tour of the rare books department Monday through Friday at 11 A.M. In addition to cuneiform tablets and European and Oriental manuscripts, there is a fine collection of Pennsylvania German Fraktur (folk art on paper) and works by Charles Dickens and Edgar Allan Poe.

On the north side of the parkway at Twenty-Second Street is the Rodin Museum. The French Renaissance exterior is highlighted by an original casting of *The Thinker.* You'll pass through Auguste Rodin's awesome *Gates of Hell* into an exhibition hall; here the largest collection outside of Paris of the sculptor's works are made even more dazzling by the use of light and space.

The Philadelphia Museum of Art is the city's premier cultural attraction and one of the country's leading art museums. Most noteworthy are the crafts, furniture, and glass in the American Wing, the paintings by realist Thomas Eakins (the nation's largest collection), Van Gogh's *Sunflowers,* Marcel Duchamp's *Nude Descending a Staircase,* and the upstairs gallery that includes a Hindu temple, a Chinese Buddhist temple hall, a medieval cloister, a Japanese teahouse and period rooms, all of which are originals—they were removed from their original homes and reassembled inside the museum.

When your feet give out and you're ready to be pampered, return to the Four Seasons or The Palace Hotel across the street for afternoon tea. The pastries, which are served from about 3 P.M. to 5 P.M., and the lobbies are as lovely as the masterpieces you've just seen.

Fairmount Park

Through private bequest and public purchase, Fairmount Park grew gradually from 5 acres to its current status as the world's largest landscaped municipal park, containing more than 8,500 acres.

In 1812, there was a reservoir atop the hill known as Faire Mount—the present site of the Philadelphia Museum of Art. The city bought the 5 acres west of the reservoir for a Water Works and public gardens. You can still see the Greek Revival architecture of the mill housings along the banks of the Schuylkill; the Water Works have been designated a National Historic Engineering Landmark, and plans are underway for restoration.

The city snatched up more land as the opportunity arose; the park eventually came to include several of the country homes built by wealthy citizens in the eighteenth century. These outposts were safe ground for those who fled from the city during the yellow fever epidemic of 1793. When it opened in 1836, the terracing and romantic monuments at the Gothic Laurel Hill Cemetery became a popular attraction, the place to stroll on a lazy afternoon. In the 1850s, Boathouse Row, a group of Victorian homes along the East River Drive, was developed for crew and racing sculls. The park, which is on both sides of the Schuylkill River, was officially named in 1867.

Fairmount Park won national attention as the site of the nation's Centennial Exposition. For the event, the Zoological Gardens were landscaped and more than a hundred buildings were constructed. Two of the original structures remain today: Memorial Hall and the Ohio House.

The twentieth century saw the addition of statues (thanks to the Fairmount Park Art Commission); the Robin Hood Dell East, where top stars from the world of music and dance perform in July and August; the Mann Music Center, where the Philadelphia Orchestra and guest stars give free summertime concerts (tickets available on the day of the performance at the Tourist Center at Sixteenth Street and John F. Kennedy Boulevard); the opening of eight of the restored historic mansions to the public; and the construction of recreation facilities like tennis and basketball courts.

The city and the park often intertwine. Many of Philadelphia's little neighborhood parks are part of the Fairmount Park system. Quite a few city dwellers consider the park to be their backyard. On weekends, the four-mile stretch along the East River Drive is crowded with joggers, bicycling moms and dads with children strapped into kiddie seats atop the back wheel, hand-holding senior citizens out for some fresh air, budding artists trying to capture the magic as Thomas Eakins did, hopeful fishermen with homemade rods, and sculls filled with collegiate crew teams trying to synchronize their strokes.

The easiest way to see the park is on the Fairmount Park Trolley Bus, the same bus that stops at museums along the parkway. If you've walked to the Art Museum and want to get to destinations in the park, board the bus outside the west entrance.

If you plan to spend a day in the park, pack a lunch. The zoo is about the only munching oasis. The Market at the Commissary, at 130 South Seventeenth Street, sells the makings for a gourmet picnic. Viking Pastries and The Fruit Lady Charcuterie, both at 1717 Walnut Street, offer Belgian chocolates, beautiful cakes, and a variety of other ready-to-eat goodies.

The trolley driver, who serves as a narrator, will deliver you into the capable hands of the well-informed guides at the Fairmount Park mansions: Federal-style Lemon Hill; Mount Pleasant; Laurel Hill; Woodford with its outstanding collection of Colonial gadgets and housewares; Strawberry Mansion; Cedar Grove, a Quaker farmhouse; and Sweetbriar, home of a congressman and site of many lavish parties. The houses are furnished with antiques and decorative objects from the appropriate period. Many of the antiques are on loan from the Philadelphia Museum of Art. Each December, special tours show off the houses, which are lit up with old-fashioned Christmas decorations. The trolley also stops at the Japanese House, patterned after a seventeenth-century Japanese home and teahouse. The building was originally on display in the Museum of Modern Art in New York but was moved to a more appropriate setting in Fairmount Park.

The zoo could very well be a separate trip. At the very least, try to visit the Hummingbird, Monkey and Ape, and Reptile houses. The habitats for the animals are remarkably natural, especially considering that the zoo is in a city, not a jungle. The many indoor exhibit halls make a zoo visit possible even on a rainy day.

A pleasant alternative to the bus is an independent tour of the park by car. (A map, available from the Tourist Center, will keep you from getting lost.) It's not advisable to wander through many parts of the park on foot. In spots, the park borders high-crime areas; because of its size, sections can be deserted and the police aren't always visible. If you'd like to stroll or picnic, do so along the East and West River Drives or, in late summer and early spring, in the colorful azalea garden behind the Art Museum. On weekdays, when most Philadelphians are behind their desks, you'll have the park pretty much to yourself.

Nighttime Views

For the best nighttime views of the city, head to the West River Drive just behind the Art Museum. The Boathouses are strung with little white lights that are reflected in the river. The museum and city are illuminated in the background. From the top of the Art Museum steps, you get a majestic view of the city, most notably the tree-lined Benjamin Franklin Parkway and City Hall. The Chestnut Street Transitway from Broad to Sixth Street is often draped with flags and makes a grand entranceway to Independence Hall which stands quiet and dignified in the night.

University City

University City is the portion of West Philadelphia that includes the campuses of the University of Pennsylvania, Drexel University, and the Philadelphia College of Pharmacy and Science. The neighborhood caters to its more than 32,000 students with moderately priced restaurants, movie theaters, and lively bars. The universities add to these offerings with film series, exhibition galleries, live performances at Penn's Annenberg Center and Drexel's Mandell Theater, and sporting events at Franklin Field and the Palestra.

The Route D and 42 buses travel along Walnut Street from Society Hill to University City; Thirty-fourth and Walnut is the stop for Penn. Follow Locust Walk through this charming, Ivy-League campus. (Ivy really does cling to the stately stone buildings.) The Palladium Restaurant, on Locust Walk, is a lovely spot for lunch or dinner; they have a cafeteria, too.

The University Museum at Thirty-third and Spruce has a stunning collection of ancient artifacts, many gathered on excavations by the university's renowned archaeology and anthropology departments. There is a crystal ball from the dowager Empress of China, fascinating Egyptian and Peruvian mummies, carved ivories from Africa, and tools from tribes of North American Indians. In a special gallery, funded by the Nevil Foundation for the Blind, visitors have a rare opportunity to touch some of the small treasures.

Three blocks west is the Wistar Institute Museum where exhibits of anatomy and biology are popular with students, high-school age and above, who are interested in science—and who are not squeamish. The city's convention facility is at the nearby Civic Center. The most popular annual event here is the Philadelphia Flower and Garden show in March. The Pennsylvania Horticultural Society sponsors this, the nation's largest indoor flower show.

Germantown

About six miles northwest of Center City is Germantown, which has been an integrated, progressive community since thirteen German Quaker and Mennonite families settled here in 1683 and soon after welcomed English, French, and other Europeans seeking religious freedom. Germantown has a tradition of free thinking—the first written protest against slavery came from its residents. During the Civil War, the Johnson House was a stop on the Underground Railroad.

Along Germantown Avenue, which has been designated a National Historic Landmark, are Revolutionary battlefields and simple farmhouses, the nation's first summer White House, and other landmarks that can tell you much about life in Colonial Philadelphia.

Battle-scarred Cliveden, a mid-Georgian country house that was occupied by the British, was attacked by General Washington and his troops in the 1777 Battle of Germantown. Other relics from this era are Stenton, James Logan's fine Georgian country manor; the one-room stone Concord Schoolhouse; the Germantown Mennonite Meetinghouse, home of the oldest Mennonite congregation in America; and Wyck, one of the oldest houses in Philadelphia, graced with magnificent gardens and its original furnishings.

After the Revolutionary War, Germantown became a rural retreat for the city's wealthy residents who wanted to escape summer heat and disease. The Deshler Morris House was the summer White House where President Washington and his family resided in 1793 and 1794 when the yellow-fever epidemic drove them from the city. The Germantown Historical Society Museum Complex has several houses from the Federal period, as well as displays of agricultural and domestic tools.

Years later, a commuter railroad made Germantown one of the first suburbs. By the 1850s, flamboyant Victorian villas with gingerbread architecture were the rage; the Ebenezer Maxwell Mansion is a great example of the style.

The historic district covers a hilly three-mile stretch of Germantown Avenue from about 4500 to 6600. Before you set out, pick up a do-it-yourself tour brochure and map from the Visitor Center at Sixteenth Street and John F. Kennedy Boulevard. If you don't have a car, take the Chestnut Hill West commuter line from Suburban Station (right across the street from the Visitor Center) to either Upsal or Tulpehocken station. The Visitor Center suggests thirteen stops, beginning at the top of the hill and walking down. Before you begin, check the opening dates and times as they vary widely; most of the houses are closed Monday and many are open only in the afternoons.

At the "top" of Germantown Avenue is Chestnut Hill; though it is part of the city, it is more a classy, Main Line-like suburb. If you have a whole day, you might want to spend the morning wandering in Chestnut Hill's quaint shops and lunching in one of the many fine restaurants. To do so, take the Chestnut Hill West line to its final stop; it will drop you in the heart of Chestnut Hill. Later, you can ride the trolley about two miles south on Germantown Avenue to the historic area.

The Barnes Foundation on the Main Line

The Barnes Foundation houses one of the world's greatest collections of Impressionist art—175 Renoirs, sixty-six Cezannes including his *Card Players,* sixty-five Matisses, plus the work of Van Gogh, Rousseau, Degas, Picasso, and others—estimated by some authorities to be worth $500 million, by others to be incalculable.

The foundation is in Merion, about eight miles west of Center City. If you are in Philadelphia, don't miss the collection, because you won't see it anywhere else: the paintings are never loaned for exhibit; no glossy catalogues or postcards document the holdings.

Dr. Albert Barnes, the son of a Philadelphia butcher, grew up poor in South Philadelphia. Fortunately for art lovers, he changed careers from medicine to chemistry. His discovery of the miracle-drug Argyrol, a silver compound used chiefly as an eye disinfectant for newborns, earned him the millions that he spent on art.

Barnes considered art an educational tool to be appreciated by the masses, not just the rich. He thought art could be studied objectively and scientifically. In his factory, he hung paintings and gave seminars to his workers, wanting to teach them a way of looking at life through art. He collected European Impressionists before they were favored by most art critics; he allegedly bought a Henri Rousseau painting for $10 in a Paris jewelry shop. In 1923, he exhibited some of his treasures at the Pennsylvania Academy of the Fine Arts and the collection was scorned.

By the time Philadelphia's establishment came to appreciate his collection, Barnes wanted no part of them. He refused to loan any of the paintings and granted admission only to those he favored. In 1961, after his death, the collection was opened to the public.

More than 1,000 works are hung—exactly where Barnes originally placed them—in the French Renaissance-style mansion at 300 North Latches Lane. They are shown by natural light and hang three tiers high, over doorways, alongside Pennsylvania Dutch chests and iron hinges. They are neither grouped by painter or period, nor labeled. The stunning collection and its unconventional display make a visit to the Barnes an unparalleled museum experience.

The SEPTA Route 44 bus from Center City, or the Paoli local train to Merion Station will leave you off within walking distance. On Friday and Saturday, one hundred guests are admitted by reservation (667–0290), another hundred without; only half as many people get in on Sunday afternoon. Children under 12 are not admitted.

PRACTICAL INFORMATION FOR PHILADELPHIA

HOW TO GET THERE. Philadelphia, in the past ten years, has dramatically improved its airport and train terminals and is in the process of getting the road systems up to par. Because of the many difficulties in getting into the city via the main arteries, tourists are advised to use air, train, or bus travel when possible.

By bus. The two major bus lines that have coast-to-coast service both have terminals in Philadelphia. *Trailways,* 13th and Arch sts. (215–569–3100), and *Greyhound,* 17th and Market sts. (215–568–4800) both arrive in the heart of Center City Philadelphia. *New Jersey Transit* (215–569–3752) runs a bus line from Philadelphia to Atlantic City with eleven stops in New Jersey along the way. New Jersey Transit stops at the Trailways and Greyhound terminals, and at 30th and Market sts. *Carl Bieber Tourways* (call either the Trailways or Greyhound Terminal) also departs from the two bus terminals to interesting tourist spots near Philadelphia such as Reading, Kutztown, Allentown, and Quakertown.

By air. Philadelphia International Airport, located in the southwest section of Philadelphia, is served by most major airlines: *American, Capitol, Continental, Delta, Eastern, TWA, United, Pan Am, Braniff,* and *Northwest.* International carriers are: *Air Jamaica, British Airways, Frontier, Lufthansa, Mexicana,* and *American International.* Regional airlines include: *Ransome, Jetstream, Colgon, Ozark, Piedmont, Wing, Pegasus, Air North, Precision, Midway, New Air, Republic, Air Florida, Air Virginia, Allegheny, Atlantic Air,* and *U.S. Air.*

The airport, approximately 8 miles from Center City, has over 8,000 parking spaces available at $5.00 to $10.00 per day. (For information about transportation from the airport to the city, see "How to Get Around," below.)

By train. Philadelphia is, of course, a major stop on *Amtrak*'s Northeast corridor, less than 90 minutes from New York City and 2 hours from Washington, DC. Amtrak pulls into 30th Street Station at 30th and Market sts. To get to Center City, you must board a local train which will take you to either the Suburban Station at 16th St. and John F. Kennedy Blvd. (close to the major hotels), or through the new commuter tunnel to the Market Street East Station at 10th and Market sts. (closer to the historical area). Phone (215) 824–1600 for Amtrak information. Locally, Philadelphia's transit line, the *Southeastern Pennsylvania Transportation Authority* (SEPTA), has commuter lines that stretch about 60 miles into the four surrounding counties—Bucks, Chester Delaware, and Montgomery. Phone (215) 574–7800 for times and prices. The *PATCO High Speed Line,* or what is known around Philadelphia as *The Lindenwold,* is a computer-operated train that makes four stops in Center City Philadelphia, then speeds at 75 miles per hour over the Benjamin Franklin Bridge, making nine stops in New Jersey and terminating in Lindenwold. The train leaves Philadelphia from 16th, 13th, and 10th and Locust sts., and from 8th and Market sts.; phone 922–4600 for information.

By car. The Philadelphia area has two major expressways: the Schuylkill (I–76) and the Delaware (I–95). The Schuylkill is currently under repair and completion is not expected until 1987. Needless to say, it is a good place to avoid during rush hours. The major route into Philadelphia from the north or the south is I–95. The expressway is not quite completed within the city, and you may find yourself unable to exit where you wish. AAA clubs can give you details; call Philadelphia's *Keystone Auto Club* at (215) 864–5000.

From the west, the Pennsylvania Turnpike runs from Pittsburgh to Valley Forge and enters Philadelphia as the Schuylkill Expressway, which has several exits in the downtown area. The turnpike also has a Northeast Extension from Scranton to Norristown, north of the city. From the east, the New Jersey Turnpike and I–295 provide easy access to either U.S. 30, which enters the city via the Benjamin Franklin Bridge, or to New Jersey S.R. 42 (The Atlantic City Expressway or North-South Freeway) leading to the Walt Whitman Bridge and South Philadelphia.

 HOTELS AND MOTELS. In Center City and the surrounding area, there are more than 10,000 rooms to satisfy a variety of budgets and tastes, though most hotels are clustered in the expensive and deluxe categories.

Unlike Florida and other resort areas, there are no off-season rates in Philadelphia; the best time to get a good deal at a downtown hotel is on the weekend, when business travelers and conventioneers have gone home. To attract guests, many hotels offer appealing weekend packages with significantly reduced rates or extras such as Sunday brunch, museum tickets, and champagne.

Summer is traditionally the peak travel time for families, fall and spring the seasons for business travel. No matter when you plan your visit, it is wise to have reservations. When you call, don't hesitate to ask for the lowest possible price, weekend specials, or family rates. If a member of your party is disabled, ask about special facilities for the handicapped. There is a wide range of policies regarding pets and children; the latter can sometimes stay in their parents' room for free. Inquire about specifics.

Hotels are listed by geographical area. There are many moderately priced accommodations in the vicinity of the Philadelphia International Airport, about a 20-minute ride south of the downtown area. These hotels provide complimentary limo service to the airport and free parking. You'll need a car or taxi to get to Center City as there is little to interest tourists in the airport area.

The city's super deluxe and deluxe properties are concentrated in the downtown area. Some are set on Broad St. near the theaters and the Academy of Music. Others are clustered west of that major artery in the vicinity of fashionable, treelined Rittenhouse Square. You'll find other hotels in the historic area not far from the Delaware River and in the commercial district north of 16th and Market sts. Two luxury hotels grace beautiful Logan Circle and are very close to the major museums on the Benjamin Franklin Parkway. Because Center City is relatively small, all the hotels are within walking distance (or a short bus or taxi ride) of theaters, shopping, and historic sites. Most Center City hotels provide parking facilities, although there is usually a daily charge.

Some visitors with cars prefer to stay in one of the hotels clustered at the City Avenue exit of the Schuylkill Expressway, about five miles west of the downtown area. These hotels, listed under the City Line heading, offer easy access to the greater metropolitan area. The hotels have several restaurants and lively lounges with entertainment, which have become popular meeting places. They are also close to shopping and dinner theater.

There is just one offering in Chestnut Hill, a lovely residential area northwest of the city lined with fine shops and restaurants. The hotels in University City, near the Civic Center—the city's current convention facility—and the campuses of University of Pennsylvania and Drexel University, provide another option. This area, just two miles from downtown, is loaded with movie theaters, moderately priced restaurants, and more greenery than you'll find in Center City.

Within the geographical listings, hotels are in alphabetical order within a price category. Price categories are based on double occupancy. The rates are *Super Deluxe,* $130 and up; *Deluxe,* $95 to $130; *Expensive,* $75 to $95; *Moderate,* $55 to $75; *Inexpensive,* under $55. (Most of the deluxe hotels fall at the lower end of that category. The inexpensive hotels cost about $35. In this latter category, ask to see a room before you decide to stay.) Six percent state sales tax and 3 percent occupancy tax are added to each bill. Prices are subject to change. Major credit cards are accepted unless otherwise noted. For a more complete explanation of hotel and motel categories, see *Facts at Your Fingertips* at the front of this volume. Because of space limitations, we can offer only a sampling of the city's accommodations.

CENTER CITY

Super Deluxe

The Bellevue Stratford. Broad and Walnut sts, near the Academy of Music and theaters; (215) 893–1776, (800) 228–3000. A Westin Hotel. The grandest hotel in the city has regained much of its former glory since its $25-million restoration. The Bellevue has been a local landmark, an enclave of tradition and elegance, since the turn of the century. Every president since Teddy Roosevelt has stayed here; the city's movers, shakers, and socialites have met in its ballrooms. Opulent French Renaissance lobby with stately marble columns and spiral staircases, elegantly appointed guest rooms with Chippendale-style furnishings, many modern comforts and amenities. French-Continental *Versailles* restaurant; *O'Brien's Restaurant, Pub, and Sporting Emporium* with seventy-six imported beers and large-screen TV; *Hunt Room* for clubby lunches and evening cabarets; and *Stratford Court* for afternoon tea, raw bar, and piano music.

Four Seasons. One Logan Square, near the major museums; (215) 963–1500, (800) 828–1188. The Four Seasons group brought their experience and reputation to this hotel which opened in 1983 on the Ben Franklin Parkway. Good taste and class predominate here, from the breathtaking, expansive marble lobby to the rooms furnished in the Federal style. Extraordinary service and every imaginable amenity—including robes and fresh flowers in the bathrooms, transcription services to and from any language, and a staff that remembers your favorite cognac—make this the first choice of many American and foreign corporate travelers. The international menu changes daily in the superb *Fountain Restaurant;* the *Swann Café* offers lighter fare. Afternoon tea, piano bar. Health spa with indoor pool, Jacuzzi, masseuse, exercise equipment, and personalized instruction. One hour pressing. Pets accepted.

Deluxe

The Barclay. Rittenhouse Square East; (215) 545–0300, (800) 421–6662. Old World elegance, a fashionable location, and a long-established reputation (since 1929) distinguish this quiet, dignified, service-oriented hotel. With the refurbishing in 1981 came a more contemporary image. Rooms appointed with Oriental armoirs, traditional furnishings, and modern comforts. Popular with business and leisure travelers. Award-winning Continental cuisine in *Le Beau Lieu,* piano bar.

Hershey Philadelphia Hotel. Broad and Locust sts., across from the Academy of Music; (215) 893–1600, (800) 533–3131. New, ultramodern glass-faced tower with a four-story atrium lobby. Popular with conventioneers and families. (This is the Hershey of chocolate fame.) Bustling and impersonal. Centrally located, good family plans available. Indoor pool, racquetball, health spa. Gourmet and family-style restaurants, live entertainment.

The Latham. 17th at Walnut, near Rittenhouse Square; (215) 563–7474, (800) 228–0808. Charming, intimate 144-room hostelry with a European flavor, known for personal attention and excellent service. The soothing ambiance and thoughtful extras—*Wall Street Journal*s and flowers in the hallways, safes in the closets—make this home away from home for many corporate travelers. Rooms exquisitely furnished with French writing desks, marble-topped bureaus. The Fine Casablanca-inspired *Bogart's* restaurant and popular *Not Quite Crickett* lounge are off the beautifully appointed lobby.

The Palace Hotel. 18th and Ben Franklin Pkwy., near major museums; (215) 963–2222, (800) 223–5672. Trusthouse Forte's management lends well-bred British style to this circular apartment-house-turned-hotel with spectacular views. Tasteful, sophisticated but warm. Rates are at the low end of the deluxe price scale for super deluxe service and accommodations. Accommodations are one or two-bedroom suites furnished with antiques and wet bars. *Café Royal,* featuring French nouvelle cuisine, is one of the city's top-ranked restaurants; afternoon tea; outdoor pool.

The Warwick. 17th and Locust sts., near Rittenhouse Square; (215) 735–6000, (800) 523–4210. Luxurious, stylish hotel built in 1926, popular with young business and leisure travelers. *Elan,* a restaurant and private club that is one of the city's hottest nightspots, is open to hotel guests. The *Brasserie* is one of the few all-night eateries in town. French Renaissance decor, attentive service, good security. Complimentary HBO, pets accepted.

Wyndham Franklin Plaza. 17th and Race sts., between Logan Circle (by major museums) and Suburban Station; (215) 448–2000; call collect for reservations. A busy, modern convention hotel that is the biggest in town. Dramatic, glass-roofed lobby is an architectural award-winner. 800 rooms, four restaurants, an indoor pool, running track, health club, tennis, racquetball, and squash courts. Comfortable, contemporary rooms. *Horizons,* rooftop supper club with entertainment and a great view.

Expensive

Holiday Inn—Center City. 1800 Market St.; (215) 561–7500, (800) HOLI-DAY. Popular with conventioneers and tourists for its central location and better-than-usual Holiday Inn amenities. *Reflections* offers fine dining, live entertainment nightly. Also *Bull & Bear* restaurant and coffee shop. Movie theater, outdoor pool, free valet parking garage.

Holiday Inn—Independence Mall. 4th and Arch sts., historic area; (215) 923–8660, (800) HOLIDAY. Comfortable high-rise closest to major sightseeing attractions. A good choice for families on vacation. Two restaurants, lounge with entertainment, outdoor pool, free parking, free HBO, pets accepted. Children under 18 free in parents' room.

Moderate

Franklin Towne Econo Lodge. 22nd and the Parkway, walking distance from major museums and Fairmount Park; (215) 568–8300, (800) 446–6900. Excellent value and location. Popular with small groups, tourists, businesspeople. Totally remodeled in California style. Restaurant, outdoor cafe, nightly entertainment in *Gertie's Saloon.* Outdoor pool, car rental, courtesy van, children under 18 free.

Holiday Inn—Midtown. 1305 Walnut St.; (215) 735–9300, (800) HOLI-DAY. Within easy walking distance of theaters, though walking alone in the immediate vicinity at night is not recommended. Less expensive than other downtown Holiday Inns. Restaurant and lounge with entertainment, outdoor pool, free parking, children under 16 free in parents' room. Pets accepted.

Penn Center Inn. 20th and Market sts., in the commercial district; (215) 569–3000, (800) 523–0909. This neighborhood is quiet and safe at night, though the hotel shares the block with some X-rated establishments which have withstood the revitalization of the area. The hotel offers good value and is within a few blocks of movie theaters and restaurants. Clean, comfortable accommodations, restaurant, outdoor pool, sauna, minigym, free parking. No charge for children under 16 in parents' room. Car rental and ticket agency in lobby.

Philadelphia Centre Hotel. 1725 John F. Kennedy Blvd.; (215) 568–3300 (800) 523–4033. Extensive meeting facilities and direct underground connections to Suburban Station and the Greyhound Bus Terminal make this popular with conventioneers and businesspeople. Offers conveniences rather than luxuries. Two restaurants and take-out service, beauty salon, pharmacy, airline offices, etc., off the large, attractive lobby. Rooms are basic and compact. Facilities at Philadelphia Athletic Club free to guests.

Inexpensive

Apollo Hotel. 1918 Arch St., a few blocks from major museums; (215) 567–8925. Clean budget hotel popular with young travelers; in a convenient, safe location. Rooms with private baths available. Air conditioning, color TV with HBO, elevator. Caring, helpful management. No credit cards.

Chamounix Mansion. Chamounix Drive, west Fairmount Park; (215) 878–3676. Philadelphia's youth hostel in a renovated Quaker farmhouse. Dorm style; sleeping sack rentals. Check in between 4:30 and 8 P.M.; lock up at 11 P.M. Nonmembers admitted at slightly higher price. Kitchen facilities available; it is wise to bring food with you. No credit cards.

St. Charles Hotel. 1935 Arch St., (215) 567–5651. Across the street from the Apollo is another clean, basic budget hotel. Private baths available, air conditioning, color TV. No elevator. Coffee shop and restaurant adjacent. No credit cards.

AIRPORT

Expensive

Embassy Suites. Gateway Center; (215) 365–6600. The newest hotel in Philadelphia. Slated to open Spring 1985. 250 comfortable suites with living room, bedroom, wet bar, refrigerator, and two televisions; rooms look onto an eight-story atrium lobby. Restaurant and cocktail lounge, indoor pool, sauna, whirlpool.

Philadelphia Airport Hilton. 10th St. and Packer Ave.; (215) 755–9500. The location, across the street from the stadium complex, draws sports teams and fans as well as those seeking a convenient midpoint between the airport and Center City. Spacious rooms, outdoor pool, and nightly entertainment. Pets accepted.

Philadelphia Marriott Hotel Airport. 4509 Island Ave.; (215) 365–4150, (800) 228–9290. A fine airport hotel with many amenities. Attractive lobby and cocktail lounge built around an indoor pool. Disc jockey and dancing nightly in *Sigi's.* Two gourmet restaurants, Jacuzzi, saunas.

Moderate

Airport Ramada Inn., Philadelphia International Airport, 76 Industrial Hwy.; (215) 521–9600, (800) 2–RAMADA. *Reflections* disco/nightclub, outdoor pool, dining room, and 24-hour coffee shop.

Best Western Airport Inn. At International Airport; (215) 365–7000, (800) 528–1234. You can't get any closer to the terminal. Restaurant and cocktail lounge, outdoor pool.

Holiday Inn—Airport. 45 Industrial Hwy; (215) 521–2400, (800) HOLIDAY. Live entertainment, outdoor pool. Pets accepted. Children under 19 free in parents' room.

Quality Inn Airport. 20th St. and Penrose Ave.; (215) 755–6500, (800) 228–5151. Circular high-rise. Restaurant, lounge, outdoor pool, baby-sitting and valet services. Pets accepted.

Inexpensive

Days Inn. Two Gateway Center; (215) 492–0400. A recently opened four-story budget property. Guests can use recreational facilities at Embassy Suites, just 200 feet away. Restaurant, outdoor pool. Children under 12 free.

CHESTNUT HILL

Moderate

Chestnut Hill Hotel. 8229 Germantown Ave., in the heart of Chestnut Hill; (215) 242–5905. 19 cozy, well-appointed rooms in a restored Colonial country inn. Charming and comfortable. 18th-century reproduction furnishings. Adjacent are the *Cheese Cellar* and *Chautauqua,* which is one of the city's best restaurants, serving nouvelle Philadelphia cuisine.

CITY LINE

Expensive

Adam's Mark. City Ave. and Monument Rd.; (215) 581–5000, (800) 231–5858. 515 guest rooms in newly remodeled high-rise hotel. Impressive public areas and much to do. Two restaurants; dancing at *Quincy's* (an "in" place with young professionals); jazz in the intimate *Pierre's;* an indoor and outdoor pool, racquetball, and health club with nautilus. Free in-room movies, car rental on premises.

Philadelphia Marriott Hotel City Line. City Ave. and Monument Rd.; (215) 667–0200, (800) 228–9290. A low-rise hotel which sprawls over 22 acres. Less formal, more suitable for children than the Adam's Mark across the street. Lots of choices here. Coffee shop and three restaurants, several lively lounges with dancing and entertainment, indoor and outdoor pool, platform tennis, and whirlpool. Some rooms designed specifically for the handicapped. Pets allowed.

Moderate

Philadelphia Best Western Hotel. 4100 Presidential Blvd.; (215) 477–0200, (800) 528–1234. Hotel restaurant serves breakfast only, though several other eateries are just steps away. Indoor pool, whirlpool, game room. Children free, pets accepted.

UNIVERSITY CITY

Expensive

The Hilton of Philadelphia. Civic Center Blvd. and 34th St.; (215) 387–8333. Adjacent to Civic Center and on University of Pennsylvania campus. Popular with businesspeople and academics. Pretty, peaceful lobby; good views from rooms. Indoor pool and sundeck, restaurant, coffee shop and lounge. Parking garage. Pets accepted.

Sheraton University City. 36th and Chestnut; (215) 387–8000, (800) 325–3535. A high-rise midway between Penn and Drexel campuses. A giant-screen TV, music, and dancing nightly in *Smart Alex*, a popular watering hole and restaurant. Outdoor pool, access to local gymnasiums. Complimentary parking.

Inexpensive

International House. 3701 Chestnut St.; 387–5125. Anyone with an academic affiliation may reserve a room. Foreign and American students from the University of Pennsylvania reside on the lower floors. A good value—not fancy but fun. Small, pleasant, air-conditioned rooms, some with private baths. Only towels and linens provided. No children allowed. Gourmet cafeteria. Visa and MasterCard accepted; no personal checks.

BED AND BREAKFASTS. A new option in Philadelphia is bed and breakfast, the European tradition of overnight lodging in a private residence or small hotel, with (obviously) breakfast included. Two agencies will match visitors with hosts in homes that meet price and location specifications. This option is becoming increasingly popular with people looking for a personal, inexpensive way to travel.

Bed & Breakfast, Center City. 1908 Spruce St.; (215) 735–1137 or 923–5459. This agency will place you in a home in the city, from a restored townhouse to an elegant high-rise, according to your stipulations. Doubles range from $35 to $65. Deposit required; no personal checks or credit cards accepted for the balance.

Bed & Breakfast of Philadelphia. P.O. Box 680, Devon, PA 19333; (215) 688–1633. A reservation service for B&B accommodations in private homes in Center City, suburbs, Bucks County, Lancaster, and Brandywine Valley. Doubles $35 and up. Deposit required; balance in cash or travelers checks.

Society Hill Hotel. 3rd and Chestnut sts., in the historic area; 925–1394. The city's only bed and breakfast establishment—an urban inn. The 12 rooms here include brass double beds, antiques, fresh flowers, handmade chocolates, and private baths. Six are two-room suites. Continental breakfast served in bed. Piano bar and restaurant, featuring Philadelphia cheesesteaks. Rooms average about $75.

HOW TO GET AROUND. Whether you take advantage of the city's public transportation system or decide to explore on foot, it helps to first orient yourself. William Penn's Philadelphia was laid out in a grid pattern, 24 blocks long (from the Delaware River on the east to the Schuylkill River on the west) and 12 blocks wide (Vine St. on the north to South St. on the south). This is the area that we now refer to as Center City. The major north-south streets are numbered, beginning with Front St. (1st), a block west of the Delaware

River, and running up to about 24th St., along the Schuylkill River. Broad St., the major north-south artery, is the equivalent of 14th St. From Market Street, the principal east-west artery, the city runs four miles south through South Philadelphia to the Naval Base and eight miles north past Temple University in North Philadelphia.

All downtown north-south streets alternate one-way traffic with the exception of Broad, which has three lanes in each direction. The east-west streets also alternate one-way traffic but in no regular pattern. The Chestnut Street Transit-way between 6th and 18th sts. is closed to all traffic except buses from 6 A.M. to 7 P.M. daily. North and south numbering begins at Market St. For example, 532 S. 8th St. is between five and six blocks south of Market St. Westward numbering begins at Front St. Addresses on these streets add 100 for every block; therefore, 1620 Chestnut St. is between 16th and 17th sts. From City Hall, the broad Benjamin Franklin Parkway sweeps northwest to the Philadelphia Museum of Art. Beyond is Fairmount Park.

To and from the airport. Allow at least 20 minutes travel time, more during rush hours, for the eight-mile trip between Center City and Philadelphia International Airport. By car, the airport is accessible via I–95 south or I–76 east (follow detour signs to airport). Taxis are plentiful, but the most expensive option: fares average $13, without tip. *SEPTA's Airport Express* offers bus service from 6 A.M. to 11 P.M. daily between downtown and the airport for $2.25. You can pick up the bus at several stops along Market St., John F. Kennedy Blvd., and at the 30th St. Station. The ride averages 35 to 40 minutes. For information, phone 574–7800. *Yellow Limousine Service* travels between the airport and all major Center City hotels, railroad stations, and bus terminals for a $4.75 fare. The limos operate daily from 6:30 A.M. to 6 P.M. They also service the hotels in the City Line area for $7.50. Phone 744–2100. Several other companies also provide limo service. Refer to the Yellow Pages. A high-speed rail line connecting the airport to 30th St., Suburban, and Market East train stations is slated to begin operation this year. The trip will take just eight minutes. Inquire at the airport information desk (492–3333) for prices and location.

By bus, trolley, subway. The *Southeastern Pennsylvania Transportation Authority (SEPTA)* operates an extensive system of buses, trolleys, subways, and commuter trains. Their information number is 574–7800. Be patient; the line is often busy. You can pick up timetables, routes, and the official street and transit map at SEPTA information centers in the underground concourse at 15th and Market sts. (take the down escalator across the street from City Hall and turn right) and at the new Market Street East Station. Be sure to enter this concourse to see the brilliantly colored 880-foot-long mosaic mural that lines the walls. Transit information is also available at the Tourist Center at 1525 John F. Kennedy Blvd. The fares are uniform: 85 cents for the base fare; 15 cents additional for a transfer. Senior citizens ride free during off-peak hours (9 A.M. to 3:30 P.M.; after 6:30 P.M., and on weekends); they pay 40 cents during peak hours. Exact change is required. At the information centers, you can buy tokens (10 for $7) or a weekly Transpass for $10 which entitles you to unlimited rides on most routes. Many routes operate in the evenings, some all night, but the frequency is greatly reduced. The 50-cent *Mid-City Loop,* which runs on Market and Chestnut sts. between Independence Mall and 19th St., will drop you off close to shopping and many historic attractions. The only north-south trolley line still in operation is the #23 which runs north on 11th St. and south on 12th. The whole trip takes several hours and covers 23 miles, from the Italian Market area in South Philadelphia to Germantown and Chestnut Hill. The *Subway-Surface Line* includes five trolley cars which service the west and southwest sectors (above ground) after tunneling under the city. These locals connect City Hall and 30th St. Station, stopping at 19th and 22nd sts. along the way. The city's two high-speed subway lines intersect at City Hall. The *Broad Street Line* runs north and south, passing through Center City to the South Philadelphia sports complex (at Pattison Ave.). It's a 10-minute ride from City Hall. The *Market Frankford Line* runs east and west beneath Market Street, with stops at 2nd, 5th, 8th, 11th, 13th, 15th, and 30th sts. Subways run all night, but caution is advised.

By Fairmount Park Trolley Bus. Reproductions of Victorian trolleys take visitors from the Tourist Center at 1525 John F. Kennedy Blvd. along the Benjamin Franklin Parkway and into Fairmount Park for a guided tour. The $2 fee ($1 for seniors, 50 cents for children) for the *Fairmount Park Trolley Bus* includes on/off privileges at any of the cultural or historic sites along the way. Call 568–6599 for information.

By commuter train. Philadelphia has a fine commuter rail network serving its suburban regions. In fact, the well-known Main Line communities evolved when the Penn Central Railroad opened up a commuter line from Philadelphia westward to Harrisburg. All trains, now operated by SEPTA, service 30th St. Station (30th and Market sts.), where you can connect with Amtrak; the Suburban Station (16th St. and John F. Kennedy Blvd.), across from the Tourist Center; and the brand-new Market Street East Station (10th and Market), beneath the Gallery at Market East shopping complex. The information number is 574–7800. These commuter trains are your best bet for reaching Germantown, Chestnut Hill, and Merion (location of the Barnes Foundation).

By taxi. Taxis are relatively plentiful in the downtown area, especially near City Hall, hotels, and train stations. At night, if you've strayed from the Center City area, let's say toward South Philadelphia, taxis may be scarce. The major cab companies are *Yellow Cab,* 922–8400; *United Cab,* 625–2881; *Quaker City,* 728–8000; and *Mid-City,* 222–2223. Rates are competitive and the cabs are metered: they average $2 to $2.10 for the first mile; $1.20 to $1.32 for each additional mile. Standard tip is 15 to 20 percent. Yellow Cab offers 75 percent discounts to senior citizens who reserve a cab up to 24 hours in advance. Call 627–5100.

By foot. The best way to see the city is on foot. Most of the historic and cultural attractions are easy walks from midtown or from available public transit. For suggested routes, refer to the Exploring Philadelphia chapter of this guide. The Tourist Center at 1525 John F. Kennedy Blvd. has "Philly Walk" brochures with maps of five downtown "walkercise"/sightseeing routes; all are well-marked.

By car. If possible, avoid using a car in the downtown area. Narrow streets and congestion, especially during rush hours (7–9:30 A.M.; 4–6:30 P.M.), make driving difficult. On-street parking is often forbidden during rush hours. At other times, there is a slim chance of finding parking on clogged downtown streets, but some metered parking is permitted on side streets and less traveled avenues. Parking meters are 25 cents for 20 minutes, 75 cents for an hour, and meters register for up to two hours. On-street parking is sometimes free after 6:30 P.M. Be sure to read signs as the regulations vary from street to street, and the meter maids are vigilant.

There are no on-street parking spaces specifically marked for use by handicapped drivers. However, cars with handicapped plates don't have to feed the meters. Read the warning signs carefully; illegally parked cars will be ticketed or towed away. Parking lots and garages range from about $2.25 an hour to around $7 for 24 hours.

Rental cars. The major car rental agencies, including *Avis, Budget, Dollar, Hertz,* and *National,* have offices at Philadelphia International Airport at convenient downtown locations. (Smaller companies are listed in the Yellow Pages.) Most agencies will allow you to pick up at the airport and drop off downtown, or vice versa. Reservations are usually necessary. You'll find it slightly cheaper to rent cars at the airport. If your schedule is flexible, rent a car on the weekend when rates are half as much as the weekday prices. There are also a number of limousine rental services available. For specific companies, it's best to consult the Yellow Pages.

 TOURIST INFORMATION. If you have a question, need information, or have any other tourist-related problem, the *Philadelphia Convention and Visitors Bureau's Tourist Center* is the place to contact: they know everything about Philadelphia. The Center offers information on events around town, group tour assistance, personalized itineraries, information for the disabled including braille maps and free guides for wheelchair users, tickets for various events such as those at the Mann Music Center, and special services for foreign visitors. It is housed in a round building on the northeast corner of 16th St. and John F. Kennedy Blvd., next to J.F.K. Plaza. Hours are 9:00 A.M. to 5:00 P.M. (until 6:00 P.M. in the summer), every day except Christmas; phone (215) 568–6599. They also provide the *Philly Fun Phone* 24 hours a day: the two minute taped message, updated three times a week, lists happenings in the city. Call (215) 568–7255.

The *National Park Service* runs a *Visitor Center* at 3rd and Chestnut sts. strictly for Independence National Historical Park. There, too, you can pick up brochures and pamphlets about historical Philadelphia and in addition, see a movie and obtain free tickets to events in the park. The Center is open daily from 9:00 A.M. to 5:00 P.M.: phone (215) 597–8974, or 627–1776 for a recorded message.

The *Council for International Visitors* is a programming and hospitality center for international visitors. They arrange professional appointments, tours, seminars, personal sightseeing and shopping tours. They also have a program for visiting "Philadelphians at Home." The main telephone number is (215) 823–7261; the 24-hour emergency telephone number is (215) 879–5248.

The *Greater Philadelphia Cultural Alliance* provides information and printed materials about Philadelphia's diverse cultural community. By late May 1985 their discount ticket booth on the northwest corner of 15th and Market sts. (across from the Clothespin) will offer half-price tickets on the day of scheduled arts performances and full-price advance tickets. The Alliance prefers that you phone first and not just drop by their office. For information, phone (215) 735–0570.

Philadelphia Magazine, published monthly, has an excellent calendar of Philadelphia events, and the city's daily newspapers—the *Philadelphia Inquirer* and *Philadelphia Daily News*—publish weekend pullout sections every Friday listing shows, movies, artistic, historic, and other events going on in the city, the surrounding four counties, and Atlantic City. The *Welcomat* is also a good guide to what's happening. It's free, published Wednesdays, and available at the Tourist Center and 1816 Ludlow St. The papers' entertainment sections are free at the Tourist Center on Friday.

Foreign Currency Exchange: *American Express Travel Service,* Two Penn Center Plaza, 587–2300; *Central Penn National Bank,* 1700 Arch St., 854–3608/09; *Continental Bank,* 1201 Chestnut St., 564–7188; *Fidelity Bank,* Broad and Walnut sts., 985–7068/7729; *First Pennsylvania Bank,* 786–8865/66; *Girard*

Bank, Broad and Chestnut sts., 585–2145; and *Philadelphia National Bank,* 5th and Market sts., 629–4402.

 RECOMMENDED READING. There are plenty of book stores all over Center City, as well as three libraries, at which you might find these books. Libraries are at 10th and Chestnut sts., 19th and Locust sts., and the Central Library at Logan Circle.

Walking Tours of Historic Philadelphia, John Francis Marion. ISHI Publications, Philadelphia, PA; 1984.
Country Walks Near Philadelphia, Alan Fisher. Appalachian Mountain Press, Boston, MA; 1983.
Hexcursions, Sally and David Keehn. Hastings House Publishers, New York, NY; 1982
Country Inns, Lodges and Historic Hotels of the Mid-Atlantic States, Anthony Hitchcock and Jean Lindgren. Burt Franklin & Co., New York, NY; 1983–84.
Philadelphia Preserved, Richard Webster. Temple University Press, Philadelphia, PA; 1976.
Philadelphia—A Dream for the Keeping, John Guinther. Colonial Heritage Press, Tulsa, OK; 1982.
Best Restaurants: Philadelphia and Environs, Elaine Tait. 101 Productions Inc., San Francisco, CA; 1981.

 SEASONAL EVENTS. January. Philadelphia's favorite tradition, the Mummers, celebrate on New Year's Day by strutting up Broad St. for the annual *Mummers Parade.* More than 30,000 members of the string bands, fancies, and comic divisions don their feathers and glitter to perform in front of City Hall for judges who award a series of prizes. Later in the month, the top-ranking men in the world of tennis meet head to head at the *U.S. Pro Indoor Tennis Championships* at the Spectrum, Broad St. and Pattison Ave.

February. *Black History Month* and black contributions to America are commemorated with exhibitions, lectures, and music at the Afro-American Historical and Cultural Museum, 7th and Arch sts. On the other side of the city, the *Philadelphia Boat Show* will display more than 500 yachts, sailboats, and power boats at the Philadelphia Civic Center, 34th St. and Civic Center Blvd. This month, the Mummers are at it again in the *Mummers String Band Show of Shows,* also at the Civic Center. From February through April, the Chinese Cultural Center, 125 N. 10th St., celebrates the *Chinese New Year* with a 10-course festival banquet every Tuesday through Sunday night at 6:30 P.M. Chefs come from Mainland China to prepare the feast. Call 923–6767 for reservations.

March. The month is welcomed by the *Philadelphia Flower and Garden Show,* touted as the nation's largest indoor flower show. Acres of flowers, landscapes, and exhibits transform the Civic Center. The *St. Patrick's Day Parade* is usually held on the Sunday closest to March 17. The parade starts at 20th St. and Benjamin Franklin Pkwy. and ends at Independence Mall, 6th and Chestnut sts.

April. The *University Hospital Antiques Show* features museum-quality antiques, gallery tours, lectures, and appraisals to benefit the University Hospital. It is held at the 103rd Engineers Armory, 33rd St. near Market. The *Easter Promenade* celebrates the holy day with a stroll down Walnut Street, music, entertainment, celebrity guests, and a fashion contest at Rittenhouse Square,

18th and Walnut sts. A funkier version enlivens South St. near 5th. The *University of Pennsylvania Spring Regatta* features rowers from eight area colleges competing on the Delaware River near Penn's Landing. And don't forget that the *Phillies,* the championship baseball team, start their season at Veterans Stadium.

May. Selected private homes, gardens, and historic buildings in 10 different neighborhoods open their homes to the public during *Philadelphia Open House Week.* At least 10 organized tours are conducted by the Friends of Independence National Historical Park. They cost from $10 to $30, depending on whether they are by foot, bus, trolley, or boat; phone 928–1188 or 597–7919. The *Rittenhouse Square Flower Market* offers plants, flowers, snacks, and a children's amusement corner all at Rittenhouse Square. Farther west is the world famous *Devon Horse Show and Country Fair,* at the Devon Fairgrounds on Rt. 30; phone 964–0550. Back in Philadelphia, the *Philadelphia Restaurant Festival* on the Benjamin Franklin Pkwy. has booths from the city's finest restaurants. *Israel's Independence Day* is in May, and it inspires the city to have another parade beginning on the Benjamin Franklin Pkwy. and ending at Independence Mall. Finally, *University Citiweek,* in the vicinity of the University of Pennsylvania, is a weeklong celebration with art exhibits, plays, recitals, concerts, dances, and bazaars.

June. America's oldest outdoor exhibit of fine art, the *Rittenhouse Square Fine Arts Annual,* will mark its 54th year at Rittenhouse Square. It features the works of over 100 Delaware Valley artists representing just about every creative medium. *Elfreth's Alley,* America's oldest continuously occupied street, opens its homes to the public in June. The Museum House at 126 Elfreth's Alley hosts a *Colonial Crafts and Bake Sale* that week. The *Kool Jazz Festival,* featuring jazz greats, will hold week-long concerts at the Mann Music Center in Fairmount Park and at the Academy of Music, Broad and Locust sts. If you prefer your music classical, the sixth annual *Mozart on the Square Festival,* at locations around Rittenhouse Square, spends a week celebrating the music of Mozart, Beethoven, Bach, and others.

June–July. The *American Music Theater Festival,* devoted entirely to American music theater, includes a repertory of opera, musical comedy, cabaret-style revues, children's programs, and experimental works at indoor and outdoor theaters across the city.

June–August. More than 40 artisans exhibit jewelry, stained glass, leather, quilts, and other items on summer weekends during the *Head House Crafts Fair* at the Head House Market, 2nd and Pine sts. The Mann Music Center features the *Philadelphia Orchestra's free concerts* in an outdoor setting in the heart of Fairmount Park. The Music Center also has special concerts by classical, popular, and jazz artists. There's more music at the *Dockside Concert Series* at Penn's Landing, covering the musical spectrum from bluegrass to gospel. Also at Penn's Landing, every Thursday evening, is *folk dancing* from around the world.

July. Philadelphia was the birthplace of the nation; the city goes all out in celebration of America's birth. If you can choose one week to visit Philadelphia, this should be it. The week-long *Freedom Festival* culminates in a July 4th fireworks display. In the days preceding are free concerts, parades (including a summer Mummers procession), hot-air-balloon races, a drum-and-bugle competition, Independence Day ceremonies at Independence Hall, and the Olde City Outdoor Restaurant Festival (near Front and Chestnut sts.).

July–August. The *Robin Hood Dell East* in Fairmount Park features top stars from the world of music and dance in a series of low-cost concerts.

August. The *Philadelphia Folk Festival* is actually not in Philadelphia, but at the Olde Poole Farm in Schwenksville, PA. Lots of people choose to camp out on the grounds for this Woodstock-like event. If you like folk music, it might be worth the trip to see these top performers at workshops and in concert.

September. In the early part of the month is the *International In-Water Boat Show* with yachts and boats floating into the Delaware River at Penn's Landing. The *Hero Scholarship Thrill Show,* which benefits children of police and firemen who were injured or died in the line of duty, features top stars and motorcycle and firefighting feats. The NFL football season starts with the *Eagles* at Veterans Stadium.

October. *Super Sunday,* a giant block part on Philadelphia's Champs-Elysées, the Benjamin Franklin Pkwy., will have games, rides, entertainment, crafts, antiques, food, and exhibits. The *Pulaski Day Parade* in early October honors the Polish patriot. It begins at 20th St. and the Benjamin Franklin Pkwy. and ends at Independence Hall. A second parade, the *Columbus Day Parade,* begins at Broad and Washington sts. and ends at Marconi Plaza in South Philadelphia. Yet another procession, the *Von Steuben Day Parade,* honors the German General who served in the Revolutionary War. This is the month the *Flyers,* Philadelphia's hockey team, and the *76ers,* the basketball champs, open their seasons.

November. The annual *Thanksgiving Day Parade* includes thousands of marchers, plenty of floats, television, and radio personalities and the real star—Santa Claus himself. The parade begins at 16th St. and the Benjamin Franklin Pkwy. and ends at Gimbels Department Store at 9th and Market sts. The *Philadelphia Marathon* will have leading runners from around the world dashing through the city's more scenic and historic spots.

December. The most traditional of football games, the *Army–Navy Game,* takes place at Veterans Stadium the weekend after Thanksgiving. Later in the month, the *Christmas Tours of the Historic Houses* takes visitors in re-created Victorian trolley buses to the holiday-adorned Colonial mansions in Fairmount Park. Also for the Christmas season, *John Wanamaker's stages its spectacular light show* (with pipe organ music) hourly in the Grand Court of their department store at 13th and Market sts. Finally, don't miss the Pennsylvania Ballet's annual production of the *Nutcracker.*

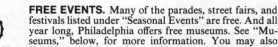 **FREE EVENTS.** Many of the parades, street fairs, and festivals listed under "Seasonal Events" are free. And all year long, Philadelphia offers free museums. See "Museums," below, for more information. You may also want to visit the *Historical Society of Pennsylvania,* 1300 Locust St., dedicated to Pennsylvania history, or the *Pennsylvania Hospital Museum,* 8th and Spruce sts., with a library and displays of works by famous American artists. The *Philadelphia Museum of Art,* on the Benjamin Franklin Pkwy., is a real bargain on Sundays until 1:00 P.M.: it's free. A number of galleries, many featuring work of local artists, are free. (See "Galleries," below.)

All attractions in Independence National Historical Park are free and quite close together, so there's not much walking involved. (See "Historic Sites and Houses.") The Betsy Ross House, 239 Arch St., is free, too.

Tickets for *Philadelphia Orchestra* concerts at the Mann Music Center in Fairmount Park are available for free on the day of the concert at the Tourist Center, 1525 John F. Kennedy Blvd. During the summer months, there is a *Phillyfest* at JFK Plaza adjacent to the Tourist Center, with music, dance tournaments, and entertainers, daily from noon to 1:00 P.M. (See "Seasonal Events" for other free musical events.) The Philadelphia Actors' Theater presents *A Visit to 1784* during the summer months at 1:00 and 3:00 P.M. at the Second Bank of the U.S., 4th and Chestnut Sts.

Finally, there are many free guided and self-guided tours through interesting sights in the city. (See "Special Interest Sightseeing," below.) *Boathouse Row,* along the Schuylkill River at the East River Drive, is full of classic Tudor structures that are especially beautiful at night outlined by hundreds of white lights. *Philadelphia's City Hall* is an interesting array of hundreds of statues, relief, and other embellishments honoring many ethnic Americans. A self-guided tour through the building up to William Penn's statue, currently the highest point in Philadelphia, is free. The *United States Mint,* 5th and Arch sts., offers self-guided audio-visual tours, including coinage operations, viewed from a glass-enclosed gallery. Finally, the *Tinicum National Environmental Center,* 86th St. and Lindbergh Blvd., with its mammals, birds, foot trails, observation platform, and boardwalk, is free and open daily.

 TOURS. *Gray Line* (568–6111) offers a variety of tours. For example: a three-hour tour through historic Philadelphia happens twice a day in the fall and winter, and three times a day during the summer; phone 569–3666 or 569–3173. Costumed drivers in antique horse-drawn carriages guide you on tours of either Old City or Society Hill year-round; call *Philadelphia Carriage Company* at 922–6840. From May to October, *Centipede Tours* supplies guides in Colonial dress who lead 1½ hour Candlelight Strolls through Colonial City (Wednesday and Friday) or Society Hill (Saturdays). Groups leave at 6:30 P.M. from City Tavern, 2nd and Walnut Sts.; phone 564–2246. Centipede will also arrange private tours any time of year; to make arrangements, contact them at the same number.

The *Penn's Landing Trolley* uses an authentic turn-of-the-century trolley car for a ride along the historic Delaware River waterfront; the conductor serves as tour guide. The 20-minute trip leaves from Delaware Ave. at Dock or Spruce sts., Thursday through Sunday during the summer months and weekends only the rest of the year; phone 627–0807. The *Fairmount Park Trolley Bus,* a re-creation of a Victorian trolley, departs about every 30 minutes from the Tourist Center, 1525 John F. Kennedy Blvd., Wednesday to Sunday, from April through December. It stops at attractions in the park, including museums and historic houses. The tour takes 90 minutes and includes on–off privileges for the day; phone 568–6599. Throughout the winter, and Monday and Tuesday only the rest of the year, the *"Town and Country Tour"* takes a 2½-hour trolley bus trip through Society Hill and into Fairmount Park. For information, call 568–6599. *Black History Tours* offers several strolls and bus excursions that focus on black history. (See "Special Interest Sightseeing," below.) The *Lively Arts Group* sponsors a different tour every week; it can be a visit to historic Philadelphia, museums, or spots outside the city—always concentrating on the artistic, cultural or historic. For a schedule of tours, call 877–7788 or write 3900 Ford Rd., Philadelphia, PA 19131.

DELAWARE RIVER TOURS

Combine lunch or dinner with a sightseeing cruise on the Delaware River on the *Spirit of Philadelphia,* a new luxury ship that sails every day from Penn's Landing, Delaware Ave. and Spruce St. Lunch cruises are from noon to 2 P.M.; dinner excursions from 7 P.M. to 10 P.M. In addition to the food, there is live entertainment. Moonlight dance cruises are from 11 P.M. to 1:30 A.M., Thursday through Saturday; phone 923–1419 for reservations.

TOURS TO OTHER AREAS

There are three bus companies in Philadelphia that conduct specialized tours to nearby sites. They are *Gray Line Tours,* 568–6111; *New Jersey Transit,* 567–2947; and *SEPTA Bus Rambles,* 574–7800 or 734–3880. The trips are scattered throughout the year, so call in advance for schedules and rates. For example, at Gettysburg, the site of the Civil War Battlefield and Lincoln's famous address can be visited on an 11-hour-long tour with Gray Line four times each summer. See the chapter on areas outside Philadelphia.

 SPECIAL-INTEREST SIGHTSEEING. Many Philadelphia institutions prefer to have organized groups such as schools or clubs request tours several months in advance. Below are those that welcome visitors anytime.

GUIDED

The Academy of Music, Broad and Locust Sts., offers a one-hour tour one Tuesday per month at 2:00 P.M. during the orchestra's season from October to May. Admission: $1.00; 893–1936.

Black History Strolls and Tours of Philadelphia has, among others, an Art and Music Tour, a Black Business Tour, a Black Women Tour, an Educational Tour, a Haitian Connection Tour, and a Sociological Study Tour with special emphasis on black culture, for $6.50 to $7.00; 923–4136.

The Free Library of Philadelphia, 19th and Vine Sts., has half-hour tours of their rare book department at 11:00 A.M. weekdays. Admission is free; 686–5322.

Masonic Temple, One N. Broad St., is the very ornate, very large headquarters of the Pennsylvania Masons. Each room represents a different architectural style. Tours are weekdays at 10:00, 11:00 A.M., 1:00, 2:00 and 3:00 P.M.; Saturdays, except July and August, at 10:00 and 11:00 A.M. Closed holidays. Admission is free; 988–1917.

Philadelphia Naval Base, South Broad St., is where our mothball fleet docks. Also tour the shipbuilding center and land facilities. By reservation only: Fridays at 10:00 A.M. and Saturdays at 9:00 A.M. and 11:00 A.M. Give as much notice as possible. Admission free; 952–7628.

SELF-GUIDED

City Hall, at Broad and Market sts., is full of interesting places to visit. This is where city and state courts hold their sessions and where the city council meets. There is an elevator and escalator to take you up to Billy Penn's statue; the view of the city is spectacular. Weekdays 9:00 A.M. to 4:30 P.M.; closed holidays. Admission is free; 686–1776.

Pennsylvania Hospital, at 8th and Spruce sts. (The Pine Building), is full of art work, early medical instruments and other items of medical interest. This, the nation's oldest hospital, is open weekdays from 9:00 A.M. to 5:00 P.M. and is closed holidays. Admission free; phone 829–3971.

United States Courthouse, 601 Market St., is the federal court facility for Eastern Pennsylvania. If you report to the Clerk's Office at room 2609, they will direct you to an interesting trial. Open weekdays 10:00 A.M. to 4:30 P.M. Admission free; 597–9368.

United States Mint, 5th and Arch sts., has self-guided tours with audio-visual assistance that explains how coins are made. Open weekdays from 8:30 A.M. to 3:30 P.M. Admission is free; 597-7350.

THEME PARKS. Sesame Place, 100 Sesame Rd., Langhorne (752–4900), about an hour's drive from Center City Philadelphia, is a parent's dream—an amusement park that not only lets children play hard, but educates them, too. Named for the immensely popular public television show, Sesame Place has muppets, animals, a playground, computers, televisions, and food. The park is open daily 10:00 A.M. to 5:00 P.M. from May 4 to September 9. Open til 8 P.M. June 16 to September 16; weekends only from September 10 to October 14. Admission: Adults $7.70; children over 2, $9.90; younger children free. From Philadelphia, take I–95 north to Oxford Valley Mall. The park is right behind the mall. Parking is $2.00.

For information on *Dutch Wonderland,* in Lancaster, and *Hershey Park,* Hershey, see *Practical Information for Lancaster County.*

PARKS. Philadelphia is dotted by five public squares which were planned by William Penn himself. **Franklin Square,** at 7th and Race sts., sits on the Center City's northeast border; in Revolutionary times, it was a burial ground and ammunitions storage location. **Washington Square,** which brightens the southeast section of the city at 6th and Walnut sts., resembles a London square. It is the site of the Tomb of the Unknown Soldier of the American Revolution. **Rittenhouse Square,** by 18th and Walnut sts. in the southwest, has always been a prestigious address. It is the home of many of the city's artistic events. In the northwest section of the city is **Logan Circle,** once Logan Square. The Swann Memorial Fountain by Alexander Stirling Calder sits in its center, surrounded by beautiful flowers, and distinguished museums, public buildings, and hotels. City Hall occupies what was **Centre Square** in Penn's original plan.

Fairmount Park, the largest landscaped city park in the world, has more than 8,500 acres containing historic and cultural treasures, along with woods, meadows, flowers, trees, statues, and five particularly scenic acres along the banks of the Schuylkill River. William Penn dreamed of Philadelphia as a "Greene Countrie Towne," a vision which was realized in 1812 when five acres of land were purchased. Today, the park is a glorious backyard for many city dwellers. Tourists are particularly drawn to the historic houses in the park: *Mount Pleasant,* built by a Scottish sea captain in 1761; *Laurel Hill,* a gracious home dating from 1760; *Woodford,* a Georgian mansion built in 1756; *Strawberry Mansion,* named after the habit of a matron who served visitors strawberries and cream; *Cedar Grove,* a Quaker farmhouse; *Sweetbriar,* an elegant estate built as an escape from the city's yellow fever epidemic; and *Lemon Hill,* originally owned by Robert Morris, a signer of the Declaration of Independence. For more information, see "Historic Sites," below.

Another park attraction is the *Japanese House,* authentically patterned after a 17th-century Japanese residence. Built in Nagoya, Japan, in 1953, it was given to the Museum of Modern Art in New York and later to the City of Philadelphia. The house is open to the public from late April to mid-October, Wednesday to Sunday, 10 A.M. to 5 P.M. Guided tours are available. Admission is $1; children under 12, 50 cents. Phone MU6–1776, ext. 81–220.

One of the few buildings remaining from the Centennial Exposition of 1876 is *Memorial Hall,* which dominates a broad avenue in the center of the park. The park also has two amphitheaters, used for summer concerts: *The Mann*

Music Center in West Fairmount Park is the home of the Philadelphia Orchestra on evenings in June and July. You'll also see performances by popular musicians and ballet companies at the music center. *Robin Hood Dell East,* at Ridge Ave. and Dauphin St., schedules a mix of rhythm and blues and soul sounds in July and August. (See "Music," below.)

At 25th St. and the Benjamin Franklin Pkwy, marking the entrance to the park, is the *Philadelphia Museum of Art.* It has over 1,000,000 dazzling works of art (see "Museums"). Just behind the museum are a series of Greek Revival buildings known as the *Fairmount Water Works* and dating from the early 1800s. The buildings stand over subterranean rooms where machinery pumped water from the Schuylkill River through a series of pipes by steam.

Just beyond, along the East River Drive, are the Victorian houses of *Boathouse Row,* headquarters to the many rowing clubs that make up the "Schuylkill Navy." The *Philadelphia Zoological Gardens,* 34th St. and Girard Ave., is America's first zoo, with 42 acres and 1,800 animals (see "Zoos"). Finally, the park is the site of the *Horticultural Center,* at Belmont Ave. and Horticultural Drive. Here is a display room, greenhouse, and arboretum. For information about the park, phone 686–2176.

Schuylkill Valley Nature Center, 8480 Hagy's Mill Road, Roxborough, has over 500 acres of fields, thickets, ponds, streams, and woodlands, with seven miles of winding trails that lead you through a wildlife haven in the city. Admission $2 for adults, $1.00 for children. Open 8:30 A.M. to 5:00 P.M., Monday through Saturday; phone 482–7300.

Tinicum National Environmental Center is the largest remaining wetland in Pennsylvania and dates back to 1643. These 200 acres, approximately one mile north of Philadelphia International Airport, have more than 280 species of birds, opossums, raccoons, muskrats, and turtles. Visitors can use foot trails, a wildlife observation platform, and a boardwalk. Fishing, bicycling and photography are permitted. Admission is free; hours are 8:00 A.M. to sunset. The Center is at 86th St. and Lindbergh Blvd.; phone 561–0662.

 ZOOS. When the **Philadelphia Zoological Gardens** opened in 1874, people flocked there on foot, by horse and carriage, and even by steamboat. They've been showing up in herds ever since. Today, the country's oldest zoo has over 1,600 animals representing more than 540 species, plus more than 500 species of native and exotic plants, adding all botanical garden to its list of credits. The Victorian entrance pavilions, designed by architects Frank Furness and George W. Hewitt, are noteworthy, but most visitors come to see the animals.

Bear Country is one of the most naturalistic zoo exhibits in the nation. The pools, streams, shade trees, rock formations, and grassy hillsides not only promote the natural behavior of the bears, but give the visitor an unobstructed look at their activities. Polar bears, sloth bears, and spectacled bears all live here. Close by is the five-acre *African Plain* where giraffes, zebras, and other animals roam together.

The *Jungle Bird Walk,* a walk-through aviary with lush tropical foliage, is just as worthwhile. Don't miss the *Wolf Woods* and the zoo's *nursery* where you can watch abandoned babies get special care. A monorail overlooks all this, treating visitors to a bird's-eye view of the zoo. It operates from April to November and is an 18-minute "safari" ride.

The Children's Zoo allows visitors to touch and feed the animals and has an hourly animal show. For an additional fee, children can take pony rides. The

Sea Lion Show is at 11:30 A.M. and 2:30 P.M. year-round. There is even a *cow milking* at 1:30 P.M. daily from April to November.

The zoo sits on 42 acres at 34th St. and Girard Ave. in West Philadelphia (243–1100). By car from Center City, take the Schuylkill Expressway west to the Girard Avenue exit. By public transportation, use SEPTA's Route 38 bus from Broad and Chestnut sts. From the Tourist Center at 16th and John F. Kennedy Blvd., hop on the Fairmount Park Trolley Bus.

The zoo is open daily except Thanksgiving, Christmas, and New Year's Day from 9:30 A.M. to 5 P.M., till 6 P.M. April to October on weekends and holidays. Admission is $4.00 for adults; $3.00 for seniors and children 2 to 11; children under 2 free. Additional fees for Children's Zoo, 50 cents; Jungle Bird Walk, 35 cents; Solitude, 50 cents; and the monorail, adults $2.25, children $1.75 (25 cents more on weekends).

 GARDENS. Philadelphia proudly claims "America's First Botanical Garden" in *Bartram's Garden,* 54th St. and Lindbergh Blvd. Founded in 1728 by the Royal Botanist to King George III, John Bartram, it claimed such visitors as George Washington, Thomas Jefferson, and Benjamin Franklin. The 27-acre garden on the banks of the Schuylkill River hasn't changed much since Bartram's time. It still blooms with exotic flora from all over the "New World." Along with the botanical specimens, the garden offers a tour of Bartram's 17th-century stone farmhouse, picnic grounds, a museum shop, an afternoon tea, and a Greens Sale during Christmas. Gardens are open daily, dawn to dusk. Free admission. Farmhouse open 10:00 A.M. to 4:00 P.M., Tuesday–Sunday, April through October; Tuesday–Friday, November through March. Admission: adults $2.00; students and children, $1.00. Afternoon teas Tuesday to Friday by reservation only, are $4.00 per person. Phone 729–5281.

The *Morris Arboretum of the University of Pennsylvania,* Hillcrest Ave. between Stenton and Germantown aves., Chestnut Hill, features over 3,500 different trees and shrubs from around the world. The 175-acre arboretum is typical of Victorian era design with winding paths, formal parterres, a hidden grotto, and tropical fernery with natural woodlands. The collection comes mainly from the temperate Northern Hemisphere, although the exotic plant collection continues today with flora imported from China and Korea. Open every day except Christmas and New Year's at 10 A.M. Closes 5 P.M. April to October, 4 P.M. November to March. Extended hours to 8 P.M. on Thursday evenings from June to August. Admission: adults $2.00; children and senior citizens $1.00; children under 6 free. Free tours with admission every Saturday and Sunday at 2:00 P.M. starting from the Hillcrest Pavilion. Phone 247–5777.

The *Horticultural Center* in Fairmount Park has a 28-acre arboretum and a wonderful greenhouse with thousands of plants and trees used to beautify the city properties. The center is open to the public Wednesday through Sunday from 9:00 A.M. to 3:00 P.M. A 50 cent donation is asked; phone 561–5100 ext. 1287/88.

About 35 miles south of Philadelphia in the Brandywine Valley lies *Longwood Gardens,* once the country home of Pierre S. Du Pont, of the Du Pont Chemical Co. Of the 1,000-acre estate, 350 acres are open to the public. It is a combination of the Old World pleasure gardens, such as Versailles, and New World vigor. In addition to the outdoor gardens and woodlands, Longwood Gardens has glassed conservatories sheltering 20 indoor gardens, illuminated fountains, a mighty pipe organ, 14,000 types of plants, and the historic Peirce-Du Pont House. During the summer, on Tuesday, Thursday, and Saturday nights, is the Festival of Fountains, with concerts, fireworks displays, and open-air theater performances. In the fall, there is the Chrysanthemum Festival with 15,000 chrysanthemums, family weekends, and craft demonstrations. Open daily. Garden hours are 9:00 A.M. to 6:00 P.M., April to October; 9:00 A.M. to 5:00 P.M. November to March. Conservatories open 10:00 A.M.–5:00 P.M. Admission: adults, $5.00; children 6 to 14, $1.00; children under 6, free. From Philadelphia, follow Route 1 south to Kennett Square.

For additional information and times of festivals, dial 1–388–6741 from Philadelphia.

BABY-SITTING SERVICES. If you'd like to spend a special night out without the children, your first call should be to the hotel's Concierge or Guest Services representative. Most hotels can help you arrange for a baby-sitter—either a member of the hotel staff or one of the carefully screened sitters regularly used by the hotel. They may instead provide you with the name of an outside agency. If your hotel cannot help you, there are two reputable baby-sitting agencies. Prices are steep but you are buying peace of mind. *Rent-A-Granny* (934–3933) mainly hires retired people. Rates are $7.00 an hour for one child; $9.00 an hour for two or more—before midnight. After 12, rates are $8.00 and $10.00, respectively. There is a three-hour minimum. The *University Home Service* (265–6661) uses sitters in their late 20s or early 30s. Their rate is $6.50 an hour, with a four-hour minimum. For the best results, try to give these agencies as much notice as possible.

CHILDREN'S ACTIVITIES. Undoubtedly, the top entertainment for children is the *Please Touch Museum,* 210 N. 21st St. Described as both educational and entertaining, it is specifically for children age 7 and younger. The idea is to teach children by letting them touch the exhibits: Calliope, an exhibit about sound; Cultural Corridor, exhibits from a variety of cultures; Nature Center, with small animals to watch and pet; Tot Spot, an area for crawling, climbing, and exploring; and You Can Be, with puppets, masks, costumes, and uniforms. The museum also has a Little Theater for children, featuring music, mime, storytelling, puppetry, and films. The hours for Please Touch are 10:00 A.M. to 4:30 P.M. Tuesday through Saturday; 12:30 P.M. to 4:30 P.M., Sunday. Admission is $2.50. Phone 963–0666.

Perelman Antique Toy Museum is another stop that is a must for children and adults. The museum has three floors of Early American tin and cast iron toys, the world's largest collection of mechanical and still banks, plus a wide assortment of Automatona toys, animated cap pistols, and Early American toy vehicles. The museum is located at 270 S. Second St. and is open daily from 9:30 A.M. to 5 P.M. Admission is $1.50 for adults and 75 cents for children under 14. Phone 922–1070.

The *Philadelphia Marionette Theater,* 2501 Christian St., gives performances by reservation only, but it's worth the extra effort. There is a small museum in the lobby with replicas of such famous puppets as Howdy Doody and Charlie McCarthy as well as puppets from Bali, Thailand and around the world. Performances on weekdays at 10:30 A.M., Saturdays at 1:00 P.M. Admission is $3.00 per person. Phone 732–6581. The *American Theater Arts for Youth* is also popular. They perform at various locations (563–7460).

The *Franklin Institute Science Museum* and *Fels Planetarium,* 20th St. and Benjamin Franklin Pkwy., are four floors of visitor-activated exhibits, live shows, special lectures about the worlds of aviation, physics, astronomy, light, printing, computers, maritime history, meteorology—and more. Undoubtedly the most famous and long-lasting exhibit is the giant heart—the visitor travels through it as if he or she were a corpuscle. The museum also has an observation deck, from which you can look at sunspots through a telescope. Other exhibits include: Mathematical Puzzles, Weather Station, Fusion, Airplanes and Aerodynamics, Printing and Papermaking, Locomotives, Clocks and Time, Geometric Models, Electricity, Ham Radio, Fire Fighting, Marine and Aviation History, Ben Franklin's World, Illusions, Shipbuilding, Optics, and Earth Sciences. The Museum has a store with science-oriented toys, kits and books, telescopes, globes, and historic reproductions. Open Monday through Saturday, 10:00 A.M. to 5:00 P.M.; Sunday from noon to 5:00 P.M. The Planetarium shows are weekdays at 12:30 and 2:00 P.M.; Saturdays at noon, 1, 2, 3, and 4 P.M.; Sundays at 2, 3, and 4 P.M. The first show on Saturday and Sunday is a Live Constellation Show; the others offer the current feature presentation. Children under 5 are not admitted to Planetarium shows except during the special children's show (for tots 7 and under) Saturdays at 10:30 A.M. Admission: Adults $3.50; children from 4 to 12, $2.75; senior citizens $2.50; children under 4, free. The Planetarium is an additional $1.00 charge; children's show is 75 cents. Phone 448–1200.

The *Academy of Natural Sciences,* 19th St. and the Benjamin Franklin Pkwy., also has a Children's Nature Museum designed for 12 year olds and younger tots. Inside is a fossil cave, dinosaur footprint, green plants, minerals, and live animals. The regular museum is full of dinosaurs, extinct and endangered species exhibits, and has live animal nature programs for all ages. The main museum is open Monday through Friday, 10:00 A.M. to 4:00 P.M.; Saturdays, Sundays, and holidays, 10:00 A.M. to 5:00 P.M. The hours for the children's museum are the same, except it is closed on Mondays. Admission to the museum: adults, $3.00; students 13 to 18, senior citizens, and military personnel $2.75; children 3 to 12, $2.50; and children under 3, free: Phone 299–1000.

The *University Museum of the University of Pennsylvania,* 33rd and Spruce sts., offers a Children's Film Program on Saturdays at 10:30 A.M. from October to March. Last year the museum showed such favorites as *The Black Stallion Returns, Dumbo, Time Bandits,* and *Kim.*

And any child would love the Egyptian and Peruvian mummies and the Crystal Ball of the dowager Empress of China on exhibit in the museum. Hours are Tuesday through Saturday, 10:00 A.M. to 4:30 P.M.; Sunday, 1:00 to 5:00 P.M. The museum is closed Sundays during the summer months. Although admission is free, they do suggest a $2.00 donation. Phone 898–4000; or 222–7777 for a taped message.

The *Annenberg Center Theatre for Children* schedules productions especially for children from time to time. This year they are offering an international children's theater festival in June. In February, Le Théâtre Sans Fil from Quebec will present *The Hobbit* with giant puppets; in March, The Shoestring Players will present *Folktales from around the World.* Tickets are from $4.00 to $5.00; phone 898–6683.

Penn's Landing is full of ships: old ships, tall ships, battleships, and submarines. The *Moshulu* was built in 1904 as a trade vessel between Europe and Chile. Confiscated by the United States during World War I, taken back by the Germans during World War II, she was returned to the United Sates in 1972, and restored as a Maritime Museum and Restaurant. The U.S.S. *Olympia* is the last survivor of the Spanish–American War fleets. As Commodore George Dewey's flagship, she fought in the Battle of Manila Bay and was the flagship of the U.S. Patrol Force during World War I. The U.S.S. *Becuna* is a guppy-class submarine which served in the South Pacific during World War II with Admiral William Halsey's Seventh Fleet; docked nearby is the *Barnegat,* a steam-powered lightship. The *Gazela of Philadelphia* is undoubtedly the pearl of Penn's Landing. Built in 1883, the tall ship sailed to Philadelphia for the Bicentennial celebration and is now a working exhibit and training vessel. For further information about the ships call 923–9030 or 922–1898. The latter four are open to visitors daily for a nominal fee.

 PARTICIPANT SPORTS. Going out to the ball game has taken on new meaning in the "Decade of the Home Athlete," who is just as likely to be playing as observing. And Philadelphia offers a wide variety of arenas for the player to test his skills.

Bicyclists can rent "wheels" for some rides through the park from *Fairmount Park Bike Rental,* 1 Boat House Row (behind the Art Museum), 236–4359. Hours are 10:30 A.M. to 8 P.M. daily during the summer; weekend hours during the fall. Rental rates are $4 an hour with a $10 deposit required on all bikes.

Boating. Those interested in testing the waters of the Schuylkill can head to the Public Canoe House, East River Drive, just south of the Strawberry Mansion Bridge (228–9336). A canoe or rowboat rental goes for $7 an hour with a $10 deposit required; sailboats $10 an hour, $10 deposit.

Fishing: On the opening day of trout season, people are lined up almost shoulder to shoulder at the Wissahickon and Pennypack Creeks, both of which are stocked with trout from mid-April (when the season opens) through mid-May. Fishing licenses are mandatory and can be purchased at many area sporting goods stores. For information, call the Fish Commission at 483–8267.

Golf courses wind their way through Fairmount Park and are open throughout the year. With the exception of *Cobbs Creek,* 7800 Lansdowne Ave. (473–5440), the courses charge $5 per 18 holes Monday to Friday; $6 weekends and holidays. Cobbs Creek charges $6 and $8 for regular and weekend/holiday hours. Locations: J.F. Byrne, 9500 Leon St. (335–8199); Juniata, L and Cayuga sts. (743–4060); Walnut Lane, Walnut Lane and Henry Ave. (686–1776, Extension 81–316); and Franklin D. Roosevelt, 20th St. and Pattison Ave. (467–2418).

Hiking takes on an added exciting dimension for those in the *Wanderlust Hiking Club.* Hikes are scheduled throughout the year on Saturday afternoons. For information, call the Department of Recreation at 686–1776, extension 81–361.

Ice skaters can take to the rink at the *University of Pennsylvania's Class of 1923 Skating Rink,* 3130 Walnut St. (898–1823). The rink is open October through March, Wednesdays, and Friday–Sunday. Call for hours. Admission is $3; rentals are $1. Also, the *Wissahickon Ice Skating Club* at Willow Grove Ave. and Cherokee St. (247–1759) is open weekends, 8:30 P.M. to 10 P.M. Rates are $2.50 an hour; skate rentals are $1.

Joggers can be seen traipsing up and down streets all over the city, but probably no area is favored more than the East and West River Drives, a scenic eight-mile-long route stretching from the Art Museum along the banks of the Schuylkill River. Then, of course, there are the steps of the Art Museum itself, host to Rocky-like runners who raise their arms in salute to an early-morning jaunt.

If the weather is contrary, you can jog indoors—as well as swim, play handball, racquetball and squash, work out, and relax in a whirlpool or sauna—at a few different places. The *Philadelphia Athletic Club,* 314 N. Broad St. (564–2002), welcomes guests for an $8 fee. PAC is open every day but Sunday. The *YMCA,* 1421 Arch St. (241–1225), is open to men and women visitors daily. The fee is $6 and a picture ID is required.

Tennis players have a variety of courts and clubs to choose from. *Fairmount Park,* has some 115 tennis courts available free to the public. However, players must bring their own nets. For information, call the Fairmount Park Department of Recreation: 686–1776, extension 81–221. *Pier 30,* at Delaware Ave. and Bainbridge St. (985–1234), offers courts daily for rental at $12 an hour; from 5 P.M. to 9 P.M., $16; and from 9 to 11, it's $14. These indoor courts are exceptional. The *Robert P. Levy Tennis Pavilion,* on the University of Pennsylvania Campus, 3130 Walnut St. (898–4741), offers eight courts—air conditioned —at $10 an hour. The schedule is Monday to Friday, 7 A.M. to midnight; Saturday and Sunday, 8 A.M. to midnight; and a summer schedule during June to August, 9 A.M. to 9 P.M.

SPECTATOR SPORTS. Philadelphia sports teams no longer have to apologize to their fans for their woeful finishes. Indeed, the city has become known as a "City of Champions," thanks to teams more accustomed to post-season play than not. And they play out their hopes and dreams in a sports complex in South Philadelphia boasting *Veterans Stadium* and the *Spectrum,* both located at Broad St. and Pattison Ave. The Vet and the Spectrum can be reached by subway (end of the line) or by the C bus, which runs south on Broad St. Parking—and there is ample room to accommodate overflow crowds at both facilities—costs $3.

In **baseball,** the National League *Phillies* are perennial favorites, sparked by their win of the World Series in 1980 and their play in the 1983 Series. The Phils play close to 80 home dates, most of which are at night, at the Vet (463–1000). Tickets are available at the ballpark, at Ticketron (John Wanamaker Department Store, 1300 Market St.; 422–2322), and at many area ticket agencies (expect a surcharge of about $2.50). Tickets run from $3 for general admission to $8 for field boxes. General admission for children under 12 is $1.

Since the Phils started playing winning ball in the late '70s, most of the good tickets seem to have been snapped up by season ticket holders, who, even when the team has an off-year, wouldn't think of canceling their orders. Sunday games, which are "give-away" days for youngsters, are usually the most popular, although tight pennant races seldom fail to make the box office cashier happy. Early season games are not that well attended, so there's a shot at getting a good seat—if you can brave the chill. The baseball season runs from early April to early October.

Playoffs are nothing new to the Philadelphia *76ers,* the pro **basketball** team with talent to spare. They can slam-dunk the ball all night and still be ready for a 7 A.M. wake-up call. The Sixers captured the championship in 1983, wiping out memories of past futile seasons. Playing from October to early April, they use the Spectrum as home base (339–7676). The Sixers invariably make the playoffs, but spoiled fans expect nothing but number one from these giants in shorts—which can make for some exasperating talk around the watercooler the day after. The Sixers play some 40 home dates, mostly at night. Tickets are $8 to $20 and are available at the Spectrum, the Vet, or Ticketron in addition to ticket agencies.

The Philadelphia *Eagles,* the city's entry in the National **Football** League, have flown better in the past—namely in 1981 when they rushed all the way to the Super Bowl. But these past few seasons have not been as successful for the Birds, who have had to retrench and try, try again. They also play their games at the Vet (463–5500) and even during unspectacular seasons, tickets are hard to come by. Tickets are $15 and can be purchased at the Vet, Ticketron, or other ticket agencies. Games are usually played Sunday afternoons; the season runs August to December.

In June, the White Manor Country Club, Providence Rd. in Malvern (647–1070), plays host to the *Ronald McDonald LPGA Kid's Golf Classic* featuring the leading names in the golf world.

Sharing the Spectrum—and the same time span—with the Sixers are the *Flyers,* whose championship season of 1974 helped set the pace for the other local teams. The two-time Stanley Cup **hockey** champions have been down on their luck in recent post-season play, but just try to get a seat to a game! These season ticket holders are worse than those clutching ducats for the Phillies. Tickets are $8.50 to $17.50 and are available at the Spectrum, Ticketron, and ticket agencies. Forty home dates are played. There's always hope that the Flyers, now under the watchful eye of former player-turned-GM Bob Clark, will skate off with another title. For information, call 755–9700.

Horse Racing. For those whose idea of track has nothing to do with marathons, there's thoroughbred racing throughout the year at *Keystone Racetrack,* just off of Street Road in Northeast Philadelphia. It is easy to get to Keystone by car; Route I–95, the Pennsylvania Turnpike, and Schuylkill Expressway are readily accessible. Bus service is also available (639–9000); general admission, $3.50; clubhouse, $6. Trotters and pacers line up at Liberty Bell Park, between Roosevelt Blvd. and I–95 on Woodhaven Road at Knights Road. The track is accessible by the Pennsylvania Turnpike, Schuylkill Expressway, and Route I–95. The season runs from February to December. For information, call 637–7100. General admission is $2; clubhouse, $4.

The *U.S. Pro Indoor* **Tennis** *Championships,* set for the Spectrum in January, attracts the top names in the game, including Ivan Lendl, John McEnroe, and Jimmy Connors. For information, call 947–1146.

Other sports on the scene include the *Penn Relays,* a **track** meet featuring the country's best runners, held the last weekend in April at Franklin Field.

COLLEGE TEAMS

The cheers one hears for local sports teams aren't reserved just for the pros. Philadelphia has a longstanding tradition of backing its college teams. Nowhere is that more obvious than with the Big Five of **basketball:** *Temple, La Salle,* the *University of Pennsylvania, St. Joseph's,* and *Villanova.* Games are played at the Palestra (386–0961) from November to March. Tickets are $4 to $10 and are avilable at the colleges or at the Franklin Field ticket office, 33rd and Locust sts.

College **football** also commands attention, although the local teams aren't the national powerhouses they are in basketball. Penn tackles other Ivy Leaguers; Temple's Owls slug it out with such teams as Syracuse and Penn State. Villanova, after years away from competing on the gridiron, is making a comeback.

Philadelphia also is the site of the *Army–Navy Game.* This football classic is played at Veterans Stadium and is scheduled for the weekend following Thanksgiving.

Rowing regattas, in which college teams from around the country compete on the banks of the Schuylkill, take place between March and June. Rowing is a popular attraction in Philadelphia, with teams in practice attracting throngs to watch them from the East and West River Drives.

If you still want more, the best bet is to check the weekend and daily sports sections of the *Philadelphia Inquirer* and *Daily News* which list upcoming events.

HISTORIC SITES. Philadelphia has more historic buildings associated with early American history than any other city in the United States. Many of these buildings are concentrated within an area popularly referred to as "America's most historic square mile." Although some are privately owned and others maintained by private or city organizations, the most important structures have been administered since 1951 by the National Park Service. The removal of several hundred commercial and nonhistoric buildings and the careful research and restoration of many historic ones provides today's visitor with a glorious sight and an excellent lesson in American history. See also "Museums," below.

INDEPENDENCE NATIONAL HISTORICAL PARK

Most of the buildings in *Independence National Historical Park* are open daily from 9 A.M.–5 P.M., although the hours of some buildings are extended in summer to 8 P.M. (Check summer schedule for free walking tours, reenactments of historic events, and the evening "Sound and Light" show in Independence Square.) There is no admission charge to any buildings, but admission to Independence Hall, the Bishop White House, and the Todd House is by tour only. In all other buildings well-trained Park interpreters and volunteer guides are on duty to give talks and answer questions. The sites here are listed in the order a visitor might wish to follow when seeing the park.

Park Visitor Center. 3rd & Chestnut sts.; 597–8974, call 627–1776 for a taped message with current information. If you have more than an hour to spend sightseeing, resist the urge to head for Independence Hall or the Liberty Bell and begin at this modern red brick structure. Most Chestnut Street buses will take you to 3rd St. By car, the nearest large parking lots are at 2nd and Sansom sts. (two blocks away) or 5th St., above Market St. (underground). The Park staff will supply you with a map and outline a personalized tour for you, dependent on your interests and time. Literature is also available in twelve foreign languages. Restroom and souvenir facilities are on the premises as well as exhibits which depict Colonial life. A 28-minute film, *Independence*, dramatizes the events from 1774 to 1800. Don't forget to make reservations before you leave if you wish to take free tours of the two restored Colonial homes (Bishop White & Todd) nearby.

Liberty Bell Pavilion. Market St. between 5th and 6th sts.; 597–8974. The American Bicentennial of 1976 created the need for a permanent home for the Liberty Bell, where it would be secure and yet visible to the greatest number of people 24 hours a day. On January 1, 1976, it was removed from Independence Hall, its home for over two centuries, to its present site. The bell was ordered from England in 1751. To commemorate the 50th anniversary of William Penn's Charter of Privileges, its Biblical inscription was chosen: "Proclaim Liberty throughout all the land, unto all the inhabitants thereof." The State House bell cracked shortly after its arrival in Philadelphia and was repaired by two local men who inscribed their names (Pass and Stowe) on it before it was ever used. The bell rang on July 8, 1776, when the Declaration of Independence was publicly read in Independence Square.

The crack visible today is believed to have occurred on July 8, 1835, while ringing for the funeral of Chief Justice John Marshall. An unsuccessful attempt was made to repair the bell and restore its tone by drilling out the crack and inserting the two bolts which can be seen today. Though the bell is mute, its inscription captured the interest of the abolitionists and their fight against slavery in America. From the original inscription on the State House bell, they gave it not only a new meaning but a new name: it became known as the Liberty Bell. The stories and legends about the bell are endless. Its survival into the 20th century has made it a symbol of freedom throughout the world. Open daily 9 A.M.–5 P.M. The bell is visible and illuminated at night; and by activating a buzzer on the East or West walls of the building, the story of the bell can be heard.

Independence Hall. Chestnut St. between 5th and 6th sts.; 597–8974. This handsome Georgian structure known as America's most historic building was constructed in 1732 as the Pennsylvania State House. What happened here between 1775 and 1787 changed the course of American history—and the name of the building to Independence Hall. In its Assembly Room, the Declaration of Independence and the Constitution of the United States were adopted and signed. The members of the Second Continental Congress met here throughout the Revolutionary period and elected George Washington as Commander-in-Chief of the Continental forces, witnessed Richard Henry Lee's resolution for independence and participated in the debates that ultimately led to the adoption of Thomas Jefferson's Declaration of Independence on July 4, 1776. While fighting raged all around them, the Congress adopted the design of the first American flag, created the first government for the nation, received the first foreign ambassador, and ultimately learned of the final British defeat at Yorktown in 1781.

Six years after the end of the war that established American independence, another group of men returned to the Assembly Room to ensure its survival. The members of the Constitutional Convention, led by George Washington, met secretly for three and a half months in the Assembly Room. The greatest minds of the day wrestled with the weaknesses of the Articles of Confederation and ended by creating a new government in its place. On September 17, 1787, they signed the Constitution of the United States, the oldest written national constitution still in use today.

The Assembly Room is restored with period furnishings to resemble its appearance during these times. The two most treasured items in the room are Washington's chair (the "Rising Sun" chair) and the Syng inkstand used when the Declaration and the Constitution were signed. The tour of the building includes a stop at the Pennsylvania Supreme Court chamber, and on the 2nd floor, the Governor's Council chamber, a committee room, and the long gallery —a 100-foot-long room used for banquets and balls and furnished with a working harpsichord. The room itself has housed American prisoners, a British hospital, and, later, a museum of art and natural history. To see the interior of Independence Hall, you must go with a guide. Tours leave the East Wing every 15–20 minutes. The lines between April and October are very long so plan to arrive early or allow enough time. It takes 15 minutes to see the 1st floor and another 10 minutes if you wish to visit the 2nd floor. Open daily 9 A.M.–5 P.M.

Congress Hall. 6th & Chestnut sts.; 597–8974. Completed in 1789 as a County Court House, this building's most important use was between 1790 and 1800 when Philadelphia was the nation's capital and it was the home of the United States Congress. As you enter the delegates' doorway from Independence Square, you are in the House of Representatives. You may sit in the room and hear the story of the early congressional sessions. Located on the 2nd floor is the smaller but much more elegant Senate Chamber. President Washington was inaugurated for his 2nd term in the Senate in 1793. Four years later John Adams took his oath of office in the House Chamber. Four men who were to become presidents served here—James Madison, James Monroe, Andrew Jackson, and William Henry Harrison. During this decade, the Bill of Rights was added to the Constitution; Alexander Hamilton's proposals for a mint and national bank were enacted; and Vermont, Kentucky, and Tennessee became the first new states. Although few original items are found in Congress Hall today, both the House and the Senate chambers have been authentically restored. Be sure to see the magnificent portraits of Louis XVI and Marie Antoinette (on the 2nd floor); these were a gift from the French government for the American Bicentennial. Open daily, 9 A.M.–5 P.M.

Old City Hall. 5th & Chestnut sts.; 597–8974. This building was constructed to be the first permanent home for Philadelphia's city government. It served that purpose for nearly three-quarters of a century. But it also played a role on the national scene when the United States Supreme Court met in session on the first floor between 1791 and 1800; John Jay presided as the nation's first chief justice over the court sessions here in Philadelphia. Today the courtroom has been re-created, and an 8-minute audio-visual presentation highlights some of the cases and problems that helped define the authority and role of that judicial body before its move to Washington. On the 2nd floor, multi-media exhibits on occupations, education, and entertainment depict the social and cultural life in Philadelphia between 1775 and 1800. Open daily, 9 A.M.–5 P.M.

Philosophical Hall. 104 S. 5th St.; 627–0706. "The American Philosophical Society held at Philadelphia for Promoting Useful Knowledge" sounds as impressive as the organization itself. Founded by Benjamin Franklin in 1743, it is the oldest learned society in America. Membership is limited to 500 Americans and 100 people from other countries chosen for their achievements in the physical and social sciences as well as the humanities. Its membership list reads like an international "Who's Who": Washington, Adams, Jefferson, Tom Paine, Lafayette, von Steuben, Emerson, Darwin, Edison, Pasteur, Churchill, and Einstein—to name just a few. Their headquarters, erected on Independence Square in 1785, is the only private building on the block. Over 200 years later, meetings of the society are still held here twice a year, as distinguished members gather from all over the world. The society offers financial assistance to scholars, publishes books and papers, and maintains a library. Though not open to the public, the building may be visited by special request in writing or by phone.

Library Hall. 105 S. 5th St.; 627–0706. The original building on this site housed another famous Franklin first, the Library Company of Philadelphia. It was founded in 1731 as the first subscription library in North America. In a real sense it was the first public library in the Colonies and a "library of congress" for members of the Continental and Federal congresses that met in Philadelphia. This institution is now located at 1314 Locust St. (see "Libraries," below). The building standing here today was reconstructed in 1959 and houses the library of the American Philosophical Society. The building is open to students and scholars for research, but there are changing exhibits in the lobby that can be seen by entering the door on Library St. Note the statue of Franklin above the 5th St. entrance, which is a copy of the original 1789 structure designed by William Thornton who later contributed his talents to the Capitol in Washington. Open Monday–Friday, 10 A.M.–5 P.M.

Second Bank of the United States. 420 Chestnut St.; 597–8974. Considered one of the finest examples of Greek Revival architecture in the United States, the Second Bank was designed by William Strickland and modeled after the Parthenon in Athens. The bank was chartered in 1816 but did not move into this building until it was completed in 1824. The "bank war" between its president, Nicholas Biddle, and President Andrew Jackson resulted in the demise of the bank as a national institution in 1836. Today the restored interior houses an outstanding collection of portraits (primarily by Charles Willson Peale and family) from the Colonial and Federal periods. Paintings of American statesmen, military leaders, and foreign dignitaries are displayed in a series of rooms. One of the highlights of the museum is the Signers Room with its special exhibits on the signers of the Declaration and the Constitution. The elegantly restored main banking room is devoted to officers of the Revolution and is dominated by the statue of George Washington carved in wood by William Rush. Open daily 9 A.M.–5 P.M.

Carpenters' Hall. 320 Chestnut St.; 925–0167. The Carpenters' Company of Philadelphia, organized in 1724, is the oldest builders organization in the United States. Its members were responsible for the design and construction of most of the important buildings in 18th-century Philadelphia. They constructed this 2-story Georgian meeting hall in 1770. Its original purpose as a meeting place for members has been obscured by its more important role as the gathering place of the First Continental Congress in the fall of 1774. During the Revolution, Carpenters' Hall was a center of military activity and used by both the Americans and the British as a hospital. Many famous tenants occupied the building before the end of the 18th century. In 1798, while the Bank of Pennsylvania was in residence, the first recorded bank robbery in America took place. Now more than 200 years later the Carpenters' Company once again occupies its original home and holds meetings here several times a year. The Carpenters' Company maintains several exhibits inside the building. Open Tuesday–Sunday, 10 A.M. –4 P.M.

New Hall. Chestnut St. between 3rd & 4th sts.; 597–8974. The Marine Corps Memorial Museum is housed in this reconstructed building on Carpenters' Court. On display are early flags, weapons, medals, and uniforms. The exhibits cover the period from 1775 to 1815 and recount the famous battles of the marines from the Revolution (1775–81) through the war with the Barbary States (1801–4) to the victories at Tripoli (1804–5). There is a Memorial Room honoring the marines who have died in battle. Open daily, 9 A.M.–5 P.M.

Pemberton House. Chestnut St. between 3rd & 4th sts.; 597–8974. The Army–Navy Museum is housed in a replica of the 18th-century home of Joseph Pemberton, a Quaker merchant. There are three floors of exhibits that make the history of America's early soldiers and sailors come alive. "Steps to Victory" identifies the location and outcome of important battles of the American Revolution. "Try Your Hand at Maneuvering a Sea Battle" allows the visitor to participate in naval combat. The small museum gives an excellent overview of these two military branches from 1776 to 1805. Open daily, 9 A.M.–5 P.M.

Franklin Court Complex. Market St. between 3rd & 4th sts.; 597–8974. The imagination used in the construction of this area is almost a match for that of its famous owner. In 1763, at the age of 57, Dr. Benjamin Franklin built his first permanent home in Philadelphia, in a courtyard off Market St. Today's visitor returning to Franklin Court will not find his house (which was torn down in 1812) but a unique steel framework which outlines the original house—chimneys and all. Peek through cement portholes and view the original foundations, brick floor, and privy pit unearthed by archaeologists. Pause to read the inscriptions etched in slate from Franklin and his wife describing the house's construction. Then enter the doors that lead you 19 feet underground to a museum that explores the life and accomplishments of this 18th-century genius. The statesman, diplomat, scientist, inventor, printer, and author are all revealed through exhibits, which you can work, watch and listen to. An 18-minute film on Ben and his life in Franklin Court is shown in a modern theater. The houses on Market Street owned by Franklin have been restored and contain a working post office (the only one in the U.S. open 7 days a week and operated by employees in Colonial dress), a print shop and book bindery with ongoing demonstrations, a house left unfinished to show details of construction, and a Benjamin Franklin gift shop where you can buy copies of almost everything he ever said and everything that was ever said about him. Open daily, 9 A.M.–5 P.M.

First Bank of the United States. 116 S. 3rd St.; 597–8974. Completed in 1797, this is considered the oldest bank building in the United States. It was the home of the First Bank of the United States, organized by Alexander Hamilton in 1791 and modeled after the Bank of England. Despite its successful operation, Congress did not renew its charter in 1811. For over 100 years it was operated as a private banking institution. Today the building houses the history and museum branches of the Park Service as well as their library. It is not open to the public except for special events.

Philadelphia Merchants Exchange. 3rd & Walnut sts.; 597–8974. Another structure to be admired from the exterior only—but certainly worth a look—is this building designed by William Strickland. Built between 1832 and 1834, it is a masterpiece of Greek Revival architecture. The building housed the Mercantile and Stock Exchanges, and was a place where merchants would meet to trade and sell their wares. A watchman posted in the tower kept members informed of ship arrivals. For over 50 years it was the commercial center of Philadelphia. The building is used today for the regional offices of the National Park Service. It is not open to the public.

City Tavern. 2nd & Walnut sts.; 923–6059. Reconstructed on its original site is one of the most celebrated and popular meeting places in 18th-century Philadelphia. City Tavern, built in 1773, was called "The Most Genteel Tavern in America" by John Adams. Generals, politicians, merchants, and lawyers all enjoyed the food and hospitality of this famous institution. Banquets and receptions were held here for the Continental and Federal congresses. Today the public is able to dine in the Colonial atmosphere of this present day operating tavern. Open daily 11 A.M.–11 P.M. for lunch and dinner. Call for reservations.

Bishop White House. 309 Walnut St.; 597–8974. William White was first Episcopal Bishop of Pennsylvania, rector of Christ Church for over 64 years and chaplain of the Continental Congress and the United States Senate. Because of his position, many of the nation's great leaders and socially prominent figures visited his home, which he built in 1786 and occupied for almost 50 years. The house has been restored to its former elegance. The living room and dining room are lavishly furnished and decorated. Off the kitchen is an indoor "necessary," uncommon in Philadelphia in the 18th century. The upstairs study is perhaps the most accurately restored room in the house and contains most of the Bishop's original library. Filled with fine period pieces and the contributions of the Bishop's descendants, the house conveys the grandeur and charm of its famous owner. Free tour reservations must be made at the Visitor Center. Open daily, 9:30 A.M.–4:30 P.M.

Todd House. 4th & Walnut sts.; 597–8974. Built in 1775, this house reflects the Quaker simplicity of its early occupants—John Todd, Jr., a Philadelphia lawyer, and his wife, Dolley. The devastating yellow fever epidemic of 1793 left Mrs. Todd a young widow. Shortly thereafter she met a Virginia congressman who changed her name to Dolley Madison. Her lifestyle in the White House as the wife of the 4th president of the United States was quite a contrast to her years in this house. It is modestly furnished with period pieces and reflects the means of a middle class family in 18th-century Philadelphia. Free tour reservations must be made at the Visitor Center. Open daily, 9:30 A.M.–4:30 P.M.

Graff House. 7th & Market sts.; 597–8974. When Jacob Graff, a Philadelphia bricklayer, built this house in 1775 he did not envision having a tenant in it. Working in two rented rooms on the 2nd floor, Thomas Jefferson wrote his rough draft of the Declaration of Independence in June 1776. Jefferson's bedroom and parlor have been re-created and contain copies of many of the items he brought with him from Virginia. A first floor exhibit area is devoted to Jefferson and an interesting display on the Declaration of Independence, including the changes made in the original draft. Jefferson's stay in Philadelphia during the summer of 1776 is depicted in an excellent 12-minute film. Open daily 9 A.M.–5 P.M.

Christ Church. 2nd St. above Market St.; 922–1695. Organized in 1695, Christ Church is the oldest Episcopal Church in America. The present building dating from 1727 is noted for its handsome interior and the grace of its 200-foot tower and steeple. The church is closely associated with America's independence and with the people who helped achieve it. George Washington, John Adams, Benjamin Franklin, Robert Morris, and Betsy Ross all worshipped here. Inside the church is the tomb of Bishop White, its rector for over 60 years. Buried beside the church are James Wilson and Robert Morris, signers of the Declaration of Independence. Open daily, 9 A.M.–5 P.M. Donations welcomed. Guides on duty. Located three blocks east of the church building is **Christ Church Burial Ground,** 5th & Arch sts. Five signers of the Declaration of Independence are buried here. Its most famous "resident" is Benjamin Franklin. It is traditional to throw a penny on his grave for good luck. Open daily (June–October) 9:30 A.M.–4:30 P.M. Guide on duty, weather permitting.

Kosciuszko House. 3rd & Pine sts.; 597–8974. Thaddeus Kosciuszko resided in this 18th-century house during the winter of 1797–98. He was one of the first foreign volunteers to distinguish himself in the American Revolution. This Polish military engineer came to America in 1776 to fight with Washington and his army. His small rented room on the 2nd floor has been restored as a memorial to his efforts. A short film about his activities during the Revolution is shown in English and Polish. Open daily, 9 A.M.–5 P.M.

Edgar Allan Poe House. 532 N. 7th St.; 597–8780. Poe lived in Philadelphia for six years. During his stay he attained his greatest success as editor and critic and published some of his most famous tales. This house is his only residence in the city still standing; he lived here between 1843 and 1844. "The Gold Bug," "The Fall of the House of Usher," "The Tell-Tale Heart," and "Murder in the Rue Morgue" were written at this address. Take the #50 bus north on 5th St. to Spring Garden St. The house is two blocks west at the corner of 7th. An exhibit and audio-visual program on the author, his family, and his literary accomplishments are located in the Poe House visitor center, where guided tours of the house begin. Open daily 9 A.M.–5 P.M.

OUTSIDE INDEPENDENCE NATIONAL HISTORIC PARK

Betsy Ross House. 239 Arch St.; 627–5343. The most popular residence in Philadelphia is easy to find. Just look for the 13-star flag displayed from its 2nd-floor window. Though controversy surrounds Betsy's role in making the first American flag, the popular legend of America's most famous flagmaker will probably last forever. A self-guided tour takes you through the restored 18th-century house, shared by Betsy and her first husband, John Ross, an upholsterer. Its small rooms are furnished with period pieces to reflect the life of this hardworking Quaker lady. Betsy died at the age of 84 (outliving 3 husbands) and is buried in the front garden of the house. Open daily, 9 A.M.–5 P.M. (6 P.M. during Daylight Saving Time).

Elfreth's Alley. 2nd St. between Arch & Race sts.; 574–0560. Dating back to the 1690s, Elfreth's Alley is the oldest residential street in America. Named after an early resident, this 6-foot wide cobblestoned passageway is lined with 30 privately owned homes dating from the early 1700s. It is one of Philadelphia's most charming and photographed sites. Its early residents were the craftsmen and tradesmen of Colonial Philadelphia. It is thought that the ubiquitous Benjamin Franklin resided here briefly. The oldest homes on the street are No. 122

and No. 124; a small museum run by the Elfreth's Alley Association is located in No. 126. The museum is open daily 10 A.M.–4:30 P.M. (Saturday and Sunday only in January and February). Private homes are open only on the first Saturday and Sunday in June (Elfreth's Alley Days).

Fairmount Park Houses. Among the many notable sights in the world's largest city park are several early American mansions which have been restored and in many cases contain their original furnishings. A tour of one or all seven of these houses affords the visitor a unique glimpse into the variety of early American architecture, the superb examples of locally crafted and imported furniture, and the fascinating social history and lore associated with them. You can visit a mid-18th-century Quaker farmhouse with the accumulated furnishings of five generations of original owners (*Cedar Grove);* the Georgian-style home overlooking the Schuylkill River that was once owned by Dr. Philip Syng Physick, "father of American surgery" (*Laurel Hill*); the Federal style house of a wealthy Philadelphia merchant, with its impressive oval drawing rooms (*Lemon Hill*); a beautiful Georgian residence described by John Adams as "the most elegant seat in Pennsylvania" (*Mount Pleasant*); the largest house in Fairmount Park furnished with a fine collection of English Regency and French Empire furniture (*Strawberry Mansion*); the 1797 home of a Philadelphia congressman which was the scene of many lavish parties for both American and French guests (*Sweetbriar*); and the house which was a center for Tory parties during the Revolution and is furnished with an outstanding collection of American-made furniture (*Woodford*). Parking is available at each house. If you drive, be sure to obtain a park map since it is very easy to get lost in the more than 8,500 acres. Call the Park House office (787–5449) to check hours which are subject to change. If you leave the driving to the Fairmount Park trolley driver, he will not only get you there but will narrate your ride enroute. Trolleys leave the Tourist Center at 16th and John F. Kennedy Blvd., Wednesday–Sunday, 10 A.M.–4:20 P.M., about every 30 minutes (April–November). Adults $2; senior citizens $1; children under 12, $.50. You may get on and off to visit as many houses as you wish for one fare. Most houses are open Tuesday–Sunday, 10 A.M.–4:30 P.M. Adults $1; children $.50.

Friends Meeting House. 4th and Arch sts; 241–7199. Open Monday–Saturday, 10 A.M. to 4 P.M. In 1693, William Penn gave the land on which the meeting house sits to the Religious Society of Friends, called Quakers. It was used as a burial place for more than 100 years until the main part of the Meeting House was built in 1804 for the growing number of Friends in the Philadelphia area. This is the oldest Friends meeting house still in use in Philadelphia and the largest in the world. Inside you'll find exhibits depicting the life and contributions of William Penn. Meetings for Worship, to which visitors are always welcome, are held Thursday at 10 A.M., Sunday at 10:30 A.M. Admission is free.

Germantown. For the tourist with some extra time to explore and a spirit of adventure, a visit to Germantown can be a rewarding experience. Located six miles northwest of Center City, Germantown was a thriving community in Colonial times. In 1793–94, it was the capital of the United States as President Washington and most of his cabinet fled the yellow fever epidemic in Philadelphia. The elegant homes, beautiful gardens, Federal charm, and Victorian splendor of this historic area can be experienced by today's visitor. You can tour the stately country house and gardens of a distinguished Pennsylvania chief justice; the scene of the 1777 Battle of Germantown (*Cliveden*, 6401 Germantown Ave.; 848–1777); a quaint Colonial one-room schoolhouse (*Concord School House*, 6309 Germantown Ave.; 438–6328); the residence of President Washington in 1793–94 known as the Germantown "White House" (*Deshler Morris House*, 5442 Germantown Ave.; 596–1748); six 18th-century houses which display period costumes, textiles, and artifacts and serve as the library and headquarters for the local historical society (*Germantown Historical Society Complex,* 5214 Germantown Ave.; 844–0514); the home of the oldest Mennonite congregation in America (*Germantown Mennonite Church,* 6121 Germantown Ave.; 843–0943); the summer residence of a prosperous Philadelphia merchant, used by British officers during the Revolution (*Grumblethorpe,* 5267 Germantown Ave.; 925–2251); an imposing Federal-style house overlooking the city of Philadelphia with original family furnishings (*Loudoun,* 4650 Germantown Ave.; 248–0235); the Victorian mansion of a Philadelphia merchant with its gingerbread architecture, Gothic gables, and leaded glass windows (*Maxwell Mansion,* Green & Tulpehocken Sts.; 438–1861); the Georgian country manor house of James Logan, William Penn's secretary (*Stenton,* 18th & Windrim Sts.; 329–7312); a Federal-style house with original woodwork and fine furniture (*Upsala,* 6430 Germantown Ave.; 247–6113); and the oldest house in Germantown (1690) containing original furnishings and surrounded by two acres of lawns and gardens (*Wyck,* 6026 Germantown Ave.; 848–1690).

Check individual buildings for hours and fees or write the individual houses for an appointment. The Tourist Center at 16th and John F. Kennedy Blvd. has a comprehensive brochure of historic Germantown. The area can be reached by train or trolley from Center City (see "How to Get Around," above). By car, take the Schuylkill Expressway (I–76) or the East River Drive to the Lincoln Drive exit, continue to Rittenhouse St., turn right; make the next right onto Wissahickon Ave., and the next left onto School House Lane to Germantown Ave.

Hill-Physick-Keith House. 321 S. 4th St.; 925–7866. Built in 1786, this handsome residence is the only free standing house in Society Hill. (You should have noticed the famous Philadelphia row houses by now.) It is also one of the most beautiful homes in America. Its most famous owner was Dr. Philip Syng Physick, "father of American surgery" who was on the staff of Pennsylvania Hospital. Chief Justice John Marshall often came to Philadelphia for treatment by the doctor. The elegantly restored interior contains some of the finest Federal and Empire furniture in Philadelphia; many items that belonged to Dr. Physick are on display. Guided tours of house and garden are available. Open Tuesday–Saturday, 10 A.M.–4 P.M.; Sunday, 1–4 P.M. Adults $2; students $1; children $.50.

A Man Full of Trouble Tavern. 127–129 Spruce St.; 743–4225. Built in 1759, this is Philadelphia's only remaining tavern from Colonial times. It contains a barroom with early American and English furniture, the traditional basement kitchen and small low-ceiling lodging rooms on the 2nd floor. This 225-year old tavern has special collections of pewter, English delftware, early wrought iron, and homespun linen sheets and curtains. Its location near the waterfront obviously made it a popular place for sailors and dockers. Open Saturday and Sunday, 1 P.M.–4 P.M. (May–August); other times by appointment. Adults $1; children $.50.

Pennsylvania Hospital. 8th & Pine sts.; 829–3971. Founded in 1751 by Dr. Thomas Bond and Benjamin Franklin, this is the oldest hospital in the United States. The hospital complex has expanded greatly since the 18th century but by entering the 8th St. gate you can view the oldest buildings facing Pine St. The buildings still in use today house America's first medical library, the first medical amphitheater, and the first public dispensary. No less notable is the fact that the hospital was a pioneer in the treatment of the insane. The first scheduled appendectomy and gall bladder operations in America were performed here. One of the hospital's nonmedical treasures is "Christ Healing the Sick in the Temple," a painting by Benjamin West that was given to the hospital by the artist in 1817. Open Monday–Friday, 9 A.M.–4:00 P.M. Tours by appointment.

The Philadelphia Contributionship. 212 S. 4th St.; 627-1752. The offices of the oldest fire insurance company in America are found in this 1836 building designed by Thomas U. Walter (better remembered for the Capitol dome in Washington, DC). In 1752 Benjamin Franklin created this institution in an effort to improve and safeguard Philadelphia and its buildings. The present day offices are open to the public. When you enter you may sign the guest book with a quill pen and receive one as a souvenir. A museum of fire fighting equipment and several rooms tracing the history of this early company can be visited. On many old Philadelphia houses you can still see the fire mark of this company represented by the "hand-in-hand" plaque located on the front of the building. Open Monday–Friday, 9 A.M.–4 P.M.

The Powel House. 244 S. 3rd St.; 627-0364. Built in 1765, this was the home of Samuel Powel, the last mayor of Philadelphia under the British Crown and the first mayor under the new American Republic. Recognized as one of the finest houses in the city, it was the scene of many important social events. John Adams, George Washington, and the Marquis de Lafayette all dined here and were entertained in its 2nd floor ballroom. Period furnishings, including some family possessions, have returned the house to its former elegance. Open Tuesday–Sunday, 10 A.M.–4 P.M. Adults $2; students $1; children $.50.

LIBRARIES. When it comes to Philadelphia libraries, the "oldest," "largest," and "best" are words commonly used to describe their holdings and collections. Many of the city's most important libraries are major centers of research and, in a real sense, are historic museums housing valuable collections of books, paintings, and furnishings. The following list represents those libraries found within walking distance of Center City Philadelphia that contain many of its most outstanding collections. See also "Museums," below.

The Athenaeum. 219 S. 6th St.; 925-2688. The Athenaeum of Philadelphia was founded in 1814 as a private library. It is made up of members who have distinguished themselves in literary, scientific, and artistic fields. Housed in an Italian Renaissance brownstone and surrounded by an important collection of paintings and period furniture is a research library specializing in 19th-century social and cultural history. One of its major collections is on American architecture, numbering over half a million items. It is a storehouse of pre-1900 periodicals in all branches of the humanities and contains other significant holdings in the areas of early American travel and transportation. The Athenaeum is housed in a National Historic Landmark building designed by John Notman, c. 1845, and may be used by the public. Monday–Friday, 9 A.M.–5 P.M. Free admission. Tours by appointment.

Free Library of Philadelphia. 19th & Vine sts.; 686-5322. The main branch of the Philadelphia public library is not just a place for books. It is a concert and lecture hall, a movie theater, and a museum. Exploring all of its sections could keep you busy for days. Besides its permanent collection of over 2 million volumes, the library contains a Map Room with globes, atlases, guide books, and maps from historic to modern times; a Print and Picture collection used in the library's ever-changing exhibits; an outstanding Film Department and collection of theater memorabilia; and a Newspaper Department where a foreign or out-of-town visitor is likely to find a copy of his or her local paper. There is a Children's Library with books and special materials geared for children from pre-school through 8th grade. The Fleisher Collection of Orchestral Music with more than 12,000 completely scored compositions is the largest collection of its kind in the world. The library's most outstanding feature is the Rare Books Department with holdings that span over 5,000 years—from cuneiform tablets and 9th-century European manuscripts through 3 centuries of children's books and 18th-century calligraphic samples of Pennsylvania Fraktur. The Elkins Library which contains many valuable Dickens letters and memorabilia was moved intact from the Philadelphia financier's home and installed in the Philadelphia library. Open Monday–Wednesday, 9 A.M.–9 P.M.; Thursday–Friday, 9 A.M.–6 P.M.; Saturday, 9 A.M.–5 P.M.; Sunday, 1 P.M.–5 P.M. (Closed Sundays, June–August). Tours of Rare Books Department, Monday–Friday, 11 A.M. Free admission.

The Historical Society of Pennsylvania. 1300 Locust St.; 732–6200. With its more than half a million books and 14 million manuscripts, this organization founded in 1824 is one of the most important repositories for the study of American Colonial and Revolutionary history. In its possession are such treasures as the architectural plan of Independence Hall, the printer's proof of the Declaration of Independence, and the first draft of the U.S. Constitution. Its manuscript collection is the largest private collection in the United States and includes the personal papers of William Penn and Pennsylvania's only president, James Buchanan. Its holdings also include one of the most important collections of genealogical records in the nation. In a series of changing exhibits on the first floor are displayed some of the 800 portraits and landscapes and over 5,000 artifacts owned by the Society, including possessions of Franklin, Penn, Washington, Jefferson, and Lincoln. Galleries open Tuesday, Thursday, Friday 9 A.M.–5 P.M., Wednesday 1 P.M.–9 P.M., Saturday 10 A.M.–3 P.M. Free. Library and reading rooms open same times but closed Saturday. Adults $3, students $1.

The Library Company of Philadelphia. 1314 Locust St.; 546–3181. Behind the walls of this modern facade is the oldest subscription library in North America. Like so many other Philadelphia institutions, the Library Company was founded in 1731 by Benjamin Franklin. Its collection, in excess of 400,000 volumes, is particularly rich in the fields of Americana up to 1880, black history to 1915, the history of science, and women's history. It has one of the largest and most valuable collection of rare books in Philadelphia and an outstanding group of Philadelphia prints and photographs numbering over 12,000 items. Special exhibits illustrating the possessions of the library are always on view and include a scene of Philadelphia, dating from 1720, that is the oldest extant picture of a North American city. Open Monday–Friday, 9 A.M.–4:45 P.M. Free.

Library of the American Philosophical Society. 105 S. 5th St.; 627–0706. This prestigious organization's library, located across the street from Independence Square, is one of the principal institutions in the United States today for the study of the history of science. Outstanding volumes in the library's collection are first editions of Newton's *Principia,* Franklin's *Experiments and Observations,* Darwin's *Origin of the Species,* and Priestley's *Experiments and Observations on Air.* American natural history, medical science, and the study of American Indians are subjects represented with outstanding manuscript collections. Included in its holdings are also many of Franklin's original books and papers, the original journals of the Lewis and Clark expedition, and a priceless copy of the Declaration of Independence in Jefferson's own hand. The library is accessible to the public but is used mainly by students and scholars. Open Monday–Friday, 10 A.M.–5 P.M. Free admission.

 MUSEUMS. Philadelphia is clearly one of the great cultural centers of America. It has over 50 museums appealing to a wide range of interests and visitors of every age and taste. Most of the city's major institutions are located on the Benjamin Franklin Parkway and are a short walk from Center City. They can also be reached by car or by the Fairmount Park Trolley Bus which operates from the Tourist Center at 16th and John F. Kennedy Blvd., Wednesday–Sunday, 10 A.M.–4:20 P.M., leaving about every 30 minutes (April–November). Adults $2; senior citizens $1; children under 12, $.50. You may get on and off unlimited times on one fare. See also "Historic Sites," above.

Academy of Natural Sciences. 19th St. & Benjamin Franklin Pkwy.; 299–1000. Founded in 1812, this is America's first natural history museum. It has achieved international fame for its collections of animals, birds, insects, and minerals. A 65-million-year-old dinosaur over two stories high greets you as you enter the museum. The Academy is best known for its large exhibits of mammals from North America, Africa and Asia, realistically displayed in reconstructions of their natural habitats. Dinosaur Hall, Gem Gallery, Mineral Hall, and the Hall of Endangered Species display many of the museum's outstanding collections. A hall devoted only to shells contains one of the largest and most important shell collections in the world. Live animal nature programs and a special children's nature museum *Outside-In* help to make enjoyable learning about nature and our environment. Open Monday–Friday, 10 A.M.–4 P.M.; Saturday and Sunday, 10 A.M.–5 P.M. Adults $3.00; students 13–18 and senior citizens $2.75; children 3–12 $2.50. Children's Nature Museum open Monday–Friday, 1–4 P.M.; Saturday and Sunday, 10 A.M.–5 P.M.

The Afro-American Historical and Cultural Museum. 7th & Arch sts.; 574–0380. Everything in this museum is dedicated to the historic and artistic achievements of black people in America. The building, designed by Theodore V. Cam, a black architect, was opened in 1976 and is the only museum specifically built to house collections of Afro-American culture. Four galleries trace black history and highlight the experiences and achievements of black people from beginnings in Africa and journey to America through the American Revolution and Civil War to the present day. The museum contains a special gallery of paintings, photographs, and sculpture by black artists and features a "Hall of Fame" dedicated to the accomplishments of outstanding Afro-Americans. Open Tuesday–Saturday, 10 A.M.–5 P.M.; Sunday, noon–6 P.M. Adults $1.50; children and senior citizens $75 cents.

The American Swedish Historical Museum. 1900 Pattison Ave.; 389–1776. Modeled after a 17th-century Swedish manor house, this museum is situated on land settled by the Swedes prior to William Penn's arrival. Fourteen galleries contain materials that interpret over 300 years of Swedish influence on American life. Special exhibits on John Ericsson, designer of the Civil War battleship the *Monitor,* and Jenny Lind, the "Swedish Nightingale," are popular attractions. There are many rare examples of early glass, textiles, paintings, and drawings as well as a library of over 12,000 volumes and materials. A museum shop featuring Scandinavian crafts, records, books, and prints offers many interesting items for purchase. Open Tuesday–Friday, 10 A.M.–4 P.M.; Saturday, noon–4 P.M. Adults $1.50; students $1; children under 12 free.

Atwater Kent Museum. 15 S. 7th St.; 922–3031. Housed in an elegant Greek Revival building designed by John Haviland is this museum of nothing but Philadelphia history. The growth of Philadelphia from the 1680s through the 1880s is depicted by the use rare artifacts, paintings, and documents. Included in the museum's collection is a scale model of Philadelphia's most famous street, Elfreth's Alley. Other rooms devoted to Penn and the history of Philadelphia give the visitor a special insight into the growth of the Quaker city. The development of the city's municipal services is traced through prints and vintage equipment. Open Tuesday–Saturday, 9:30 A.M.–4:45 P.M. Free admission.

Balch Institute for Ethnic Studies. 18 S. 7th St.; 925–8090. This museum and library is dedicated to the history of immigration and ethnic cultures in the United States. Open Monday–Saturday, 10 A.M. to 4 P.M. Donations welcomed.

Barnes Foundation. 300 N. Latches Lane, Merion; 667–0290. This treasure house of art is located a short distance from the city but is easily accessible by car or public transportation. Dr. Albert C. Barnes, who invented the patent medicine known as Argyrol, obviously decided to put his money into art instead of the bank. His home contains 23 rooms with paintings and decorative art hung from ceiling to floor and wall to wall. For years his collection was a somewhat well-kept secret except to the students who studied art at his foundation. In 1961, 10 years after Dr. Barnes's death, a court order forced the Barnes Foundation to open the collection to the public. It is now recognized as one of the finest private collections in the world. Degas, Seurat, Picasso, Klee, Utrillo, Rouault, El Greco, Titian, and Corot are just a few of the artists represented. Renoirs, Matisses, and Cezannes seem to be everywhere. The eclectic collection also includes Pennsylvania Dutch bric-a-brac, Mayan ornaments, and 16th-century Chinese Art. Two local artists, Horace Pippin and William Glackens, are also on exhibit.

Since the collection will never leave this house, it is well worth a trip here to see it. Museum is open Friday and Saturday, 9:30 A.M.–4:30 P.M. (100 reserved, 100 unreserved visitors); Sunday 1 P.M.–4:30 P.M. (50 reserved, 50 unreserved visitors). Closed July and August. Call or write in advance for reservations. Directions: From Center City, take SEPTA bus 44 to Latches Lane and Old Lancaster Road and then walk. By car, take the Schuylkill Expressway to the City Line Avenue exit (US Route 1), head south; turn right at Old Lancaster Road; turn left at Latches Lane and follow to museum. Admission: $1; Children under 12 not admitted.

Buten Museum of Wedgwood. 246 N. Bowman Ave., Merion; 664–6601. If you love Wedgwood, this is the place for you; you can even buy some here. Glazed earthenware, porcelain, bone china, unglazed stoneware, vases, and lustreware in all colors, sizes, shapes, and description. More than 10,000 pieces from earliest examples (1759) to some of the most contemporary varieties are exhibited in this home, once the residence of Josef Hofmann, the celebrated pianist and director of the Curtis Institute of Music. Open Tuesday–Friday, 2 P.M.–5 P.M.; Saturday 10 A.M.–1 P.M. Adults $2.50; senior citizens $2. Guided tours of the three galleries take about 1 hour. From Center City, take SEPTA Bus 44 to Bowman Avenue. By car, take the Schuylkill Expressway to the City Line Avenue exit (US Route 1) and head south; turn right on Old Lancaster Road, left on Montgomery Avenue, right to Bowman Avenue.

Firemen's Hall Museum. 149 N. 2nd St.; 923–1438. An authentic firehouse has been converted into a museum detailing the history of American fire fighting from Benjamin Franklin's day to the present. Included are colorful displays of hand- and horse-drawn equipment, old leather buckets, and 18th-century fire marks of the early fire insurance companies. It serves as a reminder that Philadelphia had the first paid fire department in America. Open Tuesday–Saturday, 9 A.M.–5 P.M. Free.

Franklin Institute Science Museum. 20th St. & Benjamin Franklin Pkwy.; 448–1200, 564–3375 for taped message. Founded in 1824 in honor of Benjamin Franklin, the Franklin Institute is a museum-lovers paradise; an adventure in energy, motion, and sound. Four floors of do-it-yourself exhibits explore the science of ship-building, light, mechanics, physics, aviation, and time. Museum demonstrations show how lightning and electricity work, how paper is made, and what combustion is all about. A visitor will find a working weather station, a roof-top observatory, and computers to operate. Proven museum favorites are a giant human heart (15,000 times larger than life) which you can walk through, a telephone exhibit that enables you to listen to your own voice, a ride to nowhere on a 350 ton steam locomotive, a space capsule model for moon landings, and a complete Boeing 707 to explore. Devices that create optical illusions and distortion mirrors are particularly popular with children. Dominating the four floors of the museum is a giant pendulum constantly in motion illustrating the earth's rotation on its axis. Franklin Memorial Hall contains a 20-foot statue of its namesake and an exhibit containing various Franklin memorabilia.

The Franklin Institute includes the country's largest public observatory, the *Fels Planetarium.* Seasonal constellation shows and multi-media programs exploring astronomical phenomena are presented.

Museum is open Monday–Saturday, 10 A.M.–5 P.M.; Sunday, noon–5 P.M. Adults $3.50; children 4 to 12, $2.75; senior citizens $2.50. Admission to the Planetarium is $1 extra. Planetarium shows are scheduled Monday–Friday, 12:30 and 2 P.M.; Saturday, noon, 2, 3, and 4 P.M.; Sunday, 2,3, and 4 P.M. Live Constellation Show, Saturday, Sunday, 1 P.M. Special Children's Show, Saturday 10:30 A.M. 75 cents.

John Wanamaker Memorial Museum. 13th and Market sts., 8th floor; 422–2737. The museum focuses on the life of the store's founder. Open Monday–Saturday, noon–3 P.M. Free admission.

Mutter Museum. College of Physicians, 19 S. 22nd St.; 561–6059. Fascinating collection of medical antiques, memorabilia, and jars of specimens. Open Tuesday–Friday, 10 A.M. to 4 P.M. Free admission.

Mummers Museum. 2nd St. & Washington Ave.; 336–3050. It is difficult, if not impossible, to describe the Mummers to a visitor. These costumed performers dazzle, amuse, entertain. You must experience for yourself the color and pageantry, the sights and sounds of this unique Philadelphia tradition; visiting the Mummers Museum is a good way to do it. The history of the Mummers and their parades is exhibited through several audio-visual devices: the visitor becomes a part of the New Year's Day festivities that have taken place in Philadelphia since the turn of the century. The elaborate and colorful costumes of the Mummers are displayed on mannequins, and a short lesson is offered on the Mummers' "strut" as the distinctive sounds of the Philadelphia string bands are heard in the background. String Band concerts are held outside the museum on Tuesday evenings beginning in early May. Museum open Tuesday–Saturday, 9:30 A.M.–5 P.M.; Sunday, noon–5 P.M. Adults $1.50; children and senior citizens 75 cents.

The National Museum of American Jewish History. 55 N. 5th St.; 923–3811. Erected in 1976, this complex houses the only museum in America devoted to the political, economic, social, and cultural evolution of the Jewish people in America. Its large permanent collection of artifacts and the many rotating exhibits reveal the significant contributions made by Jewish immigrants from the Colonial period to the present day. A permanent exhibit—"The American Jewish Experience from 1654 to the Present"—gives a broad overview of Jewish life and experience in the Americas. Adjoining the museum is a contemporary synagogue of the Mikveh Israel Congregation, the city's oldest and the nation's second oldest Jewish congregation. Museum open Monday–Thursday, 10 A.M. –5 P.M.; Sunday, noon–5 P.M. Adults $1.50; students and senior citizens $1.25; children under 12, $1.

Norman Rockwell Museum. Curtis Building, 6th and Walnut sts.; 922–4345. The work of this American artist, including his *Saturday Evening Post* covers, are displayed here. Open daily 10 A.M. to 4 P.M. Adults, $1.50; senior citizens, $1.25; children under 12 free.

The Pennsylvania Academy of the Fine Arts. Broad & Cherry sts.; 972–7600. This institution houses the oldest art school and museum in the United States. Its present Victorian building, which dates from 1876 and was designed by

Frank Furness, was declared a National Historic Landmark in 1976. The Academy has been collecting and teaching for almost 200 years and has included on its faculty people such as Thomas Sully, Thomas Eakins, Mary Cassatt, and Arthur Carles, all of whom are represented in its holdings. A distinguished permanent collection of more than 4,000 works spanning three centuries of American art—paintings and sculpture by Charles Willson Peale, William Rush, Gilbert Stuart, George Inness, Cecelia Beaux, and John Neagle—are displayed in its galleries. Its collection has grown to include significant works by 20th-century artists such as David Smith, Robert Motherwell, Alexander Calder, Edward Hopper, and Andrew Wyeth. European artists are represented as well, in a small but fine collection. Some of the museum's most popular works are "Penn's Treaty with the Indians" by Benjamin West, "The Cello Player" and "Walt Whitman" by Thomas Eakins, the "Fox Hunt" by Winslow Homer, and the "Lansdowne Portrait" of George Washington by Gilbert Stuart. Open Tuesday–Saturday, 10 A.M.–4 P.M.; Sunday, noon–4 P.M. Adults $2; senior citizens $1.50; students $1. Free on Tuesdays. Museum tours Tuesday–Friday, 11 A.M. & 2 P.M.; Saturday and Sunday, 2 P.M. (No tours in August.)

Penn's Landing. Today's visitor is able to tour several historic vessels docked on the Delaware River waterfront. *Gazela of Philadelphia,* Delaware Ave. & Dock St.; 923–9030. Philadelphia's own tall ship is the world's oldest and largest wooden square-rigged sailing vessel in operable condition. Tours are available of the upper and lower decks of this 100-year-old Portuguese vessel. The *Barnegat,* built across the river in Camden, New Jersey, in 1904, operated as a floating lighthouse and marked the coastal shipping lanes to the Philadelphia port for 63 years. Both vessels are open daily from noon to 5 P.M. Admission $1 (includes both ships). U.S.S. *Olympia,* Delaware Ave. & Spruce St.; 922–1898. Admiral Dewey's flagship was used in the victorious battle of Manila Bay in 1898. Its last mission in 1921 was to return the body of the Unknown Soldier to its final resting place in Arlington Cemetery. The *Becuna* is a World War II submarine resting a few feet from the Olympia. It served as flagship of the Southwest Pacific Fleet under General Douglas MacArthur. The *Becuna* is credited with destroying thousands of tons of Japanese naval and merchant ships and after the war served with the Atlantic Fleet in the Caribbean. Self-guided tours. Open daily 10 A.M.–6 P.M. Adults $2.50; children under 12, $1.25 (includes both ships).

Pennsylvania College of Podiatric Medicine Shoe Museum. 8th and Race sts.; 629–0300, ext. 219. The history of shoes, with samples ranging from Egyptian sandals to modern styles once worn by celebrities. Open Monday–Friday, 10 A.M. to 4 P.M. Call for reservations; tours by appointment only.

The Philadelphia Maritime Museum. 321 Chestnut St.; 925–5439. Since 1961 this museum has been telling the story of Philadelphia's port area. Three floors of exhibits feature outstanding collections of marine art, ship models, early navigational instruments, weapons, and other fascinating and rare items. There is an interesting exhibit where visitors can see how museum pieces are collected and preserved, and a 5,000 volume research library for nautical enthusiasts. The museum maintains a 1935 barge on the Delaware River where classes in all phases of boat building and repair are conducted periodically and open to the public. Museum open Monday–Saturday, 10 A.M.–5 P.M.; Sunday 1 P.M.–5 P.M. Adults $1; children under 12, 50 cents. (Free on Monday, 10 A.M.–noon.)

Philadelphia Museum of Art. 26th & Benjamin Franklin Pkwy.; 763–8100. Call 787–5488 for tape on daily events. One of the greatest treasures of the Philadelphia Museum of Art is the building itself. Constructed in 1928, it sits imposingly on an elevation overlooking the city. The 99-step ascent to the building's entrance was given national recognition by Sylvester Stallone in the film *Rocky* several years ago and offers a magnificent view of the Philadelphia skyline. (You can also enter the building from the back or west entrance where parking is available.) Resembling a Greek temple, the museum occupies 10 acres and contains over 200 galleries and an international collection of over 500,000 works of art. In the Great Stair Hall at the main entrance you can stand under a mobile by Alexander Calder entitled "Ghost," look down the Parkway to Logan Circle and see the Swann fountain designed by his father, or look to the 37-foot statue of William Penn on top of City Hall executed by his grandfather. A statue of Diana at the top of the stairs once served as a weather vane for the first Madison Square Garden in New York. On the surrounding walls are the great Constantine tapestries designed by Rubens.

The museum has several outstanding permanent collections. The John G. Johnson collection of European paintings spans the history of Western art from the Renaissance to the 19th century. Modern and contemporary works are found in the treasures of the A. E. Gallatin and Arensberg collections, represented by such artists as Picasso, Braque, Matisse, Brancusi, and Duchamp. Highlighted in the Near and Far East galleries are some of the museum's popular acquisitions including an Indian Temple, a Chinese Palace Hall, and a Japanese Ceremonial Tea House and Temple. Many Philadelphia artists and craftsmen are on view in the American galleries that survey 300 years of America's artistic development. Through the years, the museum's most popular possessions have been Van Gogh's *Sunflowers,* Picasso's *Three Musicians,* Duchamp's *Nude Descending a Staircase,* an outstanding collection of armor and arms, and the French, English, and American period rooms. Many special exhibits are brought to the museum and have proven to be one of the most popular features for visitors and residents alike. A series of concerts, lectures, and films round out the cultural activities here.

Open Tuesday–Sunday, 10 A.M.–5 P.M. Adults $3; students and senior citizens $1.50. (Free Sunday 10 A.M.–1 P.M.) Museum guides offer tours every hour 11 A.M.–3 P.M., leaving from the West Information Desk. Special tours for the hearing impaired.

Perelman Antique Toy Museum. 270 S. 2nd St.; 922–1070. An 18th-century restored home is a museum devoted entirely to toys. On display are more than 4,000 tin, cast-iron, and wooden toys—locomotives, carousels, wagons, carriages, trains—and the world's largest collection of mechanical banks. Two hundred years of dolls, games, and animated cap pistols from Europe and America will delight both young and old. Open daily 9:30 A.M.–5 P.M. Adults $1.50; children 75 cents.

Port of History Museum. Delaware Ave. & Walnut St.; Penn's Landing; 925–3804. Built by the State of Pennsylvania for America's Bicentennial, this imposing waterfront structure is used to house an ever-changing series of exhibits on national and international fine arts and crafts. Its 500-seat theater has become a popular scene for music, dance, and theater performances. Open Wednesday–Sunday, 10 A.M.–4:30 P.M. Admission $1.

Rodin Museum. 22nd St. & Benjamin Franklin Pkwy.; 787–5476. Considered the jewel of the museums on the Parkway, this 20th-century building houses the largest collection outside Paris of the drawings and sculpture of Auguste Rodin. The museum and its collections were given to the city of Philadelphia in 1926 by Jules Mastbaum, a local theater magnate. An architectural fragment stands at the entrance to the museum and represents a chateau Rodin erected near his studio at Meudon. Before entering the museum itself, you'll see two of Rodin's most famous works on display outdoors—the original cast of "The Thinker" and "The Gates of Hell." The interior of the small museum contains "The Burghers of Calais," "St. John the Baptist Teaching," busts of Balzac, Mahler,

Shaw, and Victor Hugo, as well as personal books, papers, and drawings of the artist. Open Tuesday–Sunday, 10 A.M.–5 P.M. Donations welcomed.

Rosenbach Museum and Library. 2010 Delancey Place; 732–1600. This 19th-century town house consists of three floors furnished with 18th-century English, French and American antiques, including Chippendale, Hepplewhite, and Louis XV furniture; paintings by Canaletto, Sully, and Lawrence, and drawings by Daumier, Fragonard, and Blake. In addition there is a library of over 30,000 rare books and 130,000 manuscripts on English and American literature and American history. If you want to see the first book printed in what is now the United States, the original manuscript of James Joyce's *Ulysses,* the first edition of Ben Franklin's *Poor Richard's Almanack,* or Lewis Carroll's own copy of *Alice in Wonderland,* this is where you will find them. In its outstanding collection of illustrations are over 2,000 drawings by Maurice Sendak. A recent acquisition is the living-room of the American poet Marianne Moore. It was taken intact from her New York apartment when she died and contains her manuscripts and complete library. This jewel of a museum represents the efforts of Philip H. and A. S. W. Rosenbach, Philadelphia collectors for nearly half a century. Open Tuesday–Sunday, 11 A.M.–4 P.M. (closed in August). Adults $2.50; students and senior citizens $1.50.

The University Museum of Archaeology and Anthropology. 33rd & Spruce sts.; 898–4000, 222–7777 for taped exhibit information. Founded in 1887 and located on the campus of the University of Pennsylvania, this museum contains one of the largest U.S. collections of ancient and primitive cultures and is one of the world's leading archaeological museums. The museum has been engaged in more than 300 expeditions and continues to send archaeologists and anthropologists all over the world. Some of their discoveries can be found in the galleries devoted to Southeast Asia, Mesopotamia, China, Africa, and the Americas. The North American collection, with its Indian art and pottery, spears and war bonnets, masks, and kachina dolls, is a favorite of children. There is an American "Gold Room" containing an important collection of gold objects from ancient American civilizations. A highlight of any visit to the museum is the magnificent round Rotunda; its 90-foot high ceiling that covers one of the most important collections of Chinese art in the Western world. From a bronze vessel used in sacrificial ceremonies, c. 1600 B.C., to the late-19th-century crystal ball of the Dowager Empress, the collection represents more than 3,000 years of creative Chinese achievement.

Popular highlights with museum visitors are the Egyptian mummies, the gems of royalty who lived 4,500 years ago, and the 12-ton Sphinx of Rameses II. "The Royal Tombs of Ur," one of the museum's most famous galleries, has recently been redesigned and reopened. A spectacular collection from the Royal Cemetery at Ur (in modern Iraq) includes precious gold artifacts and jewelry from 2650–2550 B.C. with interpretation and the story of their excavation. The Nevil Gallery is a permanent section of the museum for the visually handicapped. Objects of pottery, soapstone, wood, brass, and a variety of musical instruments uncover the magic of archaeology through touch and provide a fascinating experience for the sighted visitor as well. Open Tuesday–Saturday, 10 A.M.–4:30 P.M.; Sunday, 1 P.M.–5 P.M. (Closed Sunday, July and August). Tours Saturday and Sunday, October through May at 1 P.M. $2 donation requested.

Wistar Institute Museum. 36th and Spruce sts.; 898–3708. Anatomical exhibits, skeletons, specimen jars, and more from the realm of development biology, to interest high school level students and above. Open Monday–Friday 10 A.M. to 4 P.M. Free admission.

FILM. Like other major metropolitan cities, Philadelphia offers the latest Spielberg or Lucas flick, not to mention the X-rated films your mother warned you about. Many of the city's first-run movie theaters are located between Broad and 20th on Chestnut St. Both daily papers—the *Inquirer* and *Daily News*—have daily movie listings with special attention given to films in the Friday "Weekend" sections.

Small, independent films and art films have found havens in Philadelphia, where festivals celebrating their existence become more commonplace each year. In Center City, the *Temple Cinematheque,* 1619 Walnut St. (787–1529), has become a password for those film buffs who can't get enough of *The Late, Late Show.* Past offerings have included a tribute to Luis Bunuel and Kubrick's futuristic *A Clockwork Orange.*

In the heart of the South Street area, the *Theater of the Living Arts,* 334 South St. (922–1010), has been in the vanguard of the "small movie" movement for years. Schedules are constantly changing; so if you didn't like the esoteric film playing two days ago, it's possible a Dutch private-eye movie will be playing there today. And let's not forget those midnight screenings of *Pink Flamingoes* and *The Rocky Horror Picture Show,* which have proved a cottage industry for TLA.

Meanwhile, the *Roxy Screening Rooms I* and *II,* 2021–23 Sansom St. (561–0114), is proving to be a legitimate "art" house, showing the intellectual and esoteric. The emphasis is on the hard-hitting or emotionally moving film devoid of glitz and glamour.

Other movie houses off the beaten track: *International House,* 3701 Chestnut St. (387–5125), often celebrating foreign filmmakers; the *University Museum,* 33rd and Spruce sts. (898–4025), with weekend revivals of such films as *King Lear* and *The Weavers: Wasn't That a Time;* and the *Art Museum,* 26th St. and Benjamin Franklin Pkwy., which has been celebrated for its Sunday afternoon film series, featuring films of long ago (763–8100).

Probably, the crown jewel of all the local houses is the *Ritz Three,* 214 Walnut St. (925–7900). It offers the latest in foreign fare as well as an occasional New Wave or small gem. It is also a meticulously cared-for three-screen theater where the patrons actually show respect for the environs.

MUSIC. If there is one art which most effectively shapes the cultural skyline of Philadelphia, it is music. From the world famous Philadelphia Orchestra to chamber music groups, the city offers music for myriad moods and interests.

The *Philadelphia Orchestra,* now under the baton of Riccardo Muti, has for nearly a century held its ranks as one of the country's leading ensembles. In its history, the orchestra (893–1900), which performs its Philadelphia concerts September to May at the *Academy of Music,* Broad and Locust sts., has been dominated by two conductors: Leopold Stokowski and Eugene Ormandy. Stokowski was known for his fiery temper and brilliant work—and was not above telling members of the audience to stop rustling their bags in their seats. Ormandy held a sure hand over the orchestra for some 40 years before retiring a few seasons back. Muti already is establishing an enviable record.

Season tickets to the orchestra are prized items. For years, they were passed down from generation to generation. The Academy of Music January 1986 anniversary concert, celebrating the music hall's 130th year, will most likely be as hard a ticket to come by as it has in years past.

This is not to say it is impossible to gain access to a concert. Single tickets for the classical music concerts occasionally do find their way to the box office, and one hour before each Friday and Saturday performance, tickets for the amphitheater go on sale for $2 each. Get there earlier and be prepared to get in line, which forms to the right.

The orchestra isn't the only work of beauty going on at the Academy of Music (893–1930). The acoustically perfect Academy, which seats close to 3,000, was first opened in 1857; it is filled with ornate splendor. Some sight lines are blocked by columns, but unless you have just bought a ticket behind one of these pillars, it is difficult to quibble about the Academy, billed as the oldest opera house still being used in its original form.

When the orchestra wraps up its season at the Academy, it still has a home to go to. The *Mann Music Center,* in West Fairmount Park, is a remarkable success story, owing a great deal of its success to the time, efforts, and money of its namesake, Fredric R. Mann. This mover-and-shaker gets some of the world's most notable musicians (Zubin Mehta, Isaac Stern) to perform here in the orchestra's open-air season, which runs from mid-June to the end of July. Tickets can be purchased by becoming a Friend of the organization. But the easiest way to see a concert is also the cheapest—free. Coupons appear regularly just prior to and during the season in local newspapers. Just clip a coupon, mail it along with a stamped, self-addressed envelope, and a pair of free tickets will be headed your way. Mail to the Department of Recreation, PO Box 1000, Philadelphia 19105. If you get there early enough, you may also be able to get free tickets on the day of a concert at the Tourist Center, 1525 John F. Kennedy Blvd. For information, call 567–0707. For information about other Mann Music Center concerts, including rock performances and ballet, call 878–7707.

Also making musical news is the new *American Music Theater Festival* (925–0600), with concerts at the *Walnut Street Theatre* and other city sites. The festival specializes in musical theater (a resurrection of Gershwin's "Strike Up the Band!"), opera ("X"), and jazz ("Trio"). The festival is scheduled for June and July. The Walnut Street Theatre is located at 9th and Walnut sts; box office hours are daily, 10 A.M. to 6 P.M.

The *Opera Company of Philadelphia* (732–5811), formed as a merger between the old Lyric and Grand Opera companies, has emerged as one of the nation's most heralded troupes. The company performs at the Academy of Music, Broad and Locust sts., with a season that runs from October to April. OCP attracts the biggest names in the operatic field; indeed, Luciano Pavarotti has made Philadelphia a home away from home, lending his name to a prestigious vocal competition scheduled to conclude in 1985. Winners get to perform with the star in an OCP production. Box office hours are daily, 10 A.M. to 5 P.M.

The *Pennsylvania Opera Theater* (923–8768) performs works with flair, often operas that have not been staged in a while. They also place an emphasis on works done in English. The company performs at the Walnut Street Theatre, April to June.

Leading voices on the choral scene are the *Philadelphia Singers* (732–3370) and *Singing City* (561–3930), performing at varied sites throughout the city and specializing in classical fare.

The *Concerto Soloists of Philadelphia* (735–0202) perform classical music under the baton of Marc Mostovoy. Their Monday concerts are held at the Academy of Music; Sunday concerts at the Church of the Holy Trinity. Their office is at 338 S. 15th St.; season runs from September to June.

Each May, the *Philadelphia College of the Performing Arts* presents its "In Concert" series at the Shubert Theater, 250 S. Broad St. (875–2200). The series showcases the students' many talents. Other events of interest are the *Music from Marlboro* classical music series at the Walnut Street Theatre, held throughout the year (569–4690); the *Kool Jazz Festival,* during June at varied spots (465–3221); and *Mozart on the Square,* a springtime celebration of the composer in the Rittenhouse Square area. Also noteworthy is the schedule of the *Robin Hood Dell East* (477–8810), at Ridge Ave. and Dauphin St., with its July–August mix of rhythm and blues and soul sounds. Moe Septee's *All Star-Forum* season runs from November to May at the Academy of Music, offering such classical artists as Itzhak Perlman and Isaac Stern. For information, call 735–7506. Septee also presents the *Philly Pops,* conducted by Peter Nero, in concerts from October to May at the Academy. The musicians are occasionally aided by some definitely nonmusical personnel, such as Phillies' pitcher Tug McGraw and the Phillie Phanatic, the team's mascot.

Such popular names as John Denver, Ted Nugent, Judas Priest, The Cars, and Moody Blues are in town frequently under the auspices of *Electric Factory Concerts.* For information about who'll be performing where and when, and how to get tickets, call 568–3222 or 976–HITS. The Spectrum Arena (Broad and Pattison, South Philadelphia) is where groups like Yes, Rush, and Van Halen appear on tour. Call 389–5000 for the schedule. Rock, blues and reggae bands appear frequently at *Ripley Music Hall,* 608–610 South, Society Hill. Call 923–1860 to check the schedule.

The city also plays host to free music festivals and concerts during the summer, such as the daily noontime shows at the John F. Kennedy Plaza and weekend performances at Penn's Landing. Big name rock and folk acts appear frequently in the city; they are covered in the Night Life section of this book. And, there's that old favorite, the annual *Philadelphia Folk Festival* (247–1300) each August at the Olde Pool Farm in Schwenksville.

DANCE. The dance scene in Philadelphia has taken a giant step forward in the past few years. Nowhere is that more evident than with the success of the *Pennsylvania Ballet Company,* which performs its repertory at the Academy of Music, Broad and Locust sts. PBC's season runs from September to June and offers an interesting mix of classical and modern. Its "Nutcracker" is a Christmastime favorite for audiences young and old alike. Last year, PBC celebrated its 20th anniversary with a gala that would have seemed unlikely only five years ago. The company is thriving now, showing creativity and flair under the influence of its leaders Robert Weiss and Peter Martins. The company can be reached at 978–1429.

The success has left its imprint on other companies. The *South Street Dance Co.* (925–3619), which specializes in modern, works its magic at sites throughout the city. The *Zero Moving Dance Co.* (843–9974) performs its modern dances at the YM-YWHA, Broad and Pine sts., and at the Conwell Dance Lab on Temple University's Main Campus. The *Philadelphia Dance Co. (Philadanco),* 387–8200, also offers modern dance at the Annenberg Center, 3680 Walnut St., and other theaters. Meanwhile, Annenberg Center plays host to *Dance Celebration '85,* featuring top dance groups from around the world. The celebration runs from November to April (898–6791). Keep your eyes open for the *Waves Dance Company,* (563–1545), who give electrifying contemporary performances at local theaters. They get rave reviews.

THEATER. Philadelphia's reputation as a tryout town has been on the skids for years. While once the favorite of producers, it has been displaced by such sites Washington and Los Angeles.

Touring companies still make the rounds, however. *A Chorus Line* always seems to generate top box office; and a production of "42nd Street" still has them talking at the *Forrest Theatre* (923–1515). The Forrest, 1114 Walnut St., along with the *Shubert Theatre,* 250 S. Broad St. (735–4768), and the *Academy of Music,* Broad and Locust sts. (893–1930) are the prime theaters for musicals in the city, although they are just as liable to host touring dramatic works as well.

Philadelphia is not in such bad shape when one considers the local talent at work. The *Walnut Street Theatre Company,* 9th and Walnut sts. (574–3550), tries to incorporate as many professional local actors as possible into its schedule of musicals, comedy, and drama. Indeed, the theater itself is of prime interest to theater buffs—it is the oldest operating theater in the United States, celebrating its 176th anniversary. The theater company's season runs from November to March.

The *Philadelphia Festival Theatre for New Plays* at Annenberg Center, 3680 Walnut St. (222–5000), is drawing national attention for its TLC of new works and their playwrights. The festival runs from April to June.

The *Philadelphia Drama Guild* also performs at the Annenberg Center (563–7530), with an emphasis on 20th-century works. The season runs from October to May. The Annenberg also plays host to visiting theater companies; the fare is eclectic. The box office number for the Annenberg is 898–6791.

The *Wilma Theater,* 2030 Sansom St. (963–0345), has gained some fine critical notices since its adoption of a policy geared toward hiring Equity actors. Its work is innovative. The season runs October to June.

The *Philadelphia Company of Plays and Players,* 1714 Delancey St. (574–3586), performs plays by contemporary American playwrights, culling from off-Broadway hits. This company has also taken a step to more professional status.

Across the street from the Wilma, at 2031 Sansom St., is *Curtains* (557–7606). *Shear Madness,* a humorous murder mystery that lets the audience play armchair detective, shows year-round here, Thursday through Sunday. The show has been drawing Philadelphia audiences since it opened in 1981.

Also contributing to the Philadelphia theater scene are *Society Hill Playhouse,* 507 S. 8th St. (923–0210), with contemporary works; *Independent City Theater,* at the Walnut Street Theatre (247–2121), offering off-Broadway fare; *Cafe Theatre of Allens Lane,* Allens Lane and McCallum St. (848–9384), eclectic fare.

For **children,** *American Theater Arts for Youth* has found considerable success performing at Theater of the Living Arts, 334 South St., and at Penn's Landing (563–7460). (See also "Children's Activities.")

Dinner theaters in the area specialize in Broadway musicals such as "Mame" and "Fiddler on the Roof": the *Riverfront Dinner Theatre* is located at Poplar St. and Delaware Ave. (925–7000); *City Line Dinner Theatre,* 4200 City Line (879–4000); and the *Huntingdon Valley Dinner Theatre,* 2633 Philmont Ave., Huntingdon Valley (947–6000).

Tickets are generally accessible in Philadelphia. But don't expect to get two on the aisle Saturday morning for that night's performance of "42nd Street." Call in advance. Also, ticket agencies usually can come up with the tickets you need—at a premium of course. For half-price tickets on the day of the performance, look to the discount ticket booth at the northwest corner of 15th and Market sts. (Full-price advance tickets can also be purchased here.)

For information about what is happening on the local theater scene, read the weekend listings section in either the *Philadelphia Inquirer* or *Daily News*.

SHOPPING. No need to travel to New York for a shopping spree; the shopping in Philadelphia is world class. Fashions range from conservative to avant-garde. You'll find branches of some high-fashion shops that are at home in Beverly Hills and Paris, as well as boutiques exclusive to the city. There are luxury goods in every category and good bargains to be found. Stores are within easy walking distance of the historic area; many are indoor complexes which make them suitable for rainy day shopping excursions.

Radiating off Rittenhouse Square is a fashionable residential area with shops to match, boutiques that could just as well flank New York's Fifth Avenue. Along Walnut St. and on intersecting 17th and 18th streets are fine men's and women's clothing stores, beauty salons, art galleries, gourmet shops, and toy stores.

The city's main shopping street is Chestnut, which from 18th to 6th sts. is a pedestrian mall, closed to all traffic except public transporation. *John Wanamaker* is the main attraction here; it's been a grand department store since President Taft dedicated it in 1911. The huge store and it's Eagle statue is as familiar to Philadelphians as is the Liberty Bell.

The *Gallery at Market East* was the country's first enclosed inner-city shopping mall. In the glass-roofed shopping center, spanning Market St. from 8th to 11th, are three leading department stores—*Strawbridge & Clothier, Gimbels,* and *J.C. Penney*—and more than 250 shops (many are moderately priced chain stores) and restaurants. In the basement is *Market Fair,* with more than 25 international eateries. The Gallery keeps later hours than most stores; it is open until 8 P.M. daily (Wednesdays until 9). Sunday hours are from noon to 5 P.M.

The *Bourse,* on Independence Mall just opposite the Liberty Bell Pavilion, houses up-to-the-minute designer fashions from Cacharel and Saint Laurent and others in an elegant, restored Victorian commodities exchange. Even if the specialty shops are beyond your budget, be sure to get a look at the Bourse. You can lunch on ethnic goodies along the third floor cafe.

NewMarket in Society Hill is a surprising mixture of quaint Colonial storefronts and ultramodern multileveled glass boxes. The indoor/outdoor complex, between Pine and South sts., overlooks the Delaware River. You'll find native American crafts, toys, fashions, and goodies, as well as some popular dining and drinking spots.

South Street, from Front to about 8th, is the place to find funky fashions, vintage clothing, antiques, hard-to-find books, natural foods, and endless oddities. South Street merchants keeps a different schedule than most Center City shopkeepers; many stores don't open until noon; they keep their doors open until the wee hours, which means until midnight on Friday and Saturday. The restaurant scene is booming here; you can get a munch at almost any hour.

Though antique shops are scattered throughout the city, dozens of antique dealers and collectors are clustered along Pine Street's *Antique Row,* especially between 9th to 12th sts. A comparatively long history has endowed the city with a fair share of vintage 19th- and early 20th-century furnishings and Colonial heirlooms.

The windows sparkle with diamonds, gold, and precious stones on *Jewelers Row,* in the vicinity of 8th and Sansom sts. Shoppers will find a wide selection and good, competitive prices in these jewelry stores.

Chestnut Hill, on the outskirts of the city, is another fashionable shopping and dining area. You'll find quality goods—classic but conservative clothing, luxuries like linens, stationery and gourmet cheese, and antiques—in the quaint shops between 8000 and 8700 Germantown Ave. The Chestnut Hill West commuter train, which leaves from Suburban Station (across from the Tourist Center at 16th and John F. Kennedy Blvd.) ends at the Chestnut Hill shopping district.

There are more fine shops in Philadelphia, and more categories of merchandise, than can be listed here. We've included a sampling of interesting and reputable establishments.

SPECIAL SHOPPING NOTES

Sales are held throughout the year, so if you are looking for a special item, check the daily newspapers first. Although hours vary, stores generally open Monday through Saturday at either 9:30 or 10 A.M. and close at 6 P.M. Many shops extend their hours on Wednesday evenings. On Sundays, some major department stores and malls are open. It's best to phone for current hours.

Almost all stores accept major credit cards (Visa, MasterCard, American Express). Diners Club and Carte Blanche are not as widely used. Because of the large number of bad checks that shopkeepers receive, they may or may not accept a personal check with identification. It's safer and easier to use traveler's checks. Be sure you have an I.D. with you. Cash is always welcome, but as in any big city, it is not wise to carry much money on you.

A 6 percent state sales tax will be added to the price tag of all items except clothing, which is exempt. Although restaurant meals are taxed, gourmet chocolates and other take-home foods are not.

DEPARTMENT STORES

As Bloomingdale's is to New York, *John Wanamaker* is to Philadelphia. The world-famous landmark at 13th and Market sts. occupies a city block and was one of the first of the great department stores in the country. Even if you don't want to buy, come hear the pipe organ concerts at 11:15 A.M. and 5:15 P.M. each day, in the marble, pillared Grand Court. From the bargain basement to the 9th floor gift department, Wanamaker's is exciting. The listing of their departments occupies three columns in the phone book. A fashion boutique features the best collections from Paris; for men, there is an international designer shop and the classic London Shop. Furniture is another specialty; visit the Williamsburg and Baker galleries.

High-tech electronics, a grandfather clock hall, and extensive houseware departments are other drawing cards. A full-service store, Wanamaker's also has a travel agency, ticket office, watch repair desk, and beauty salon. You can dine in the elegant Crystal Room, the Terrace on the Court, or in any number of less formal restaurants. The Center City store is open 10 A.M. to 7 P.M. Monday through Saturday (til 9 P.M. on Wednesdays) and Sunday, from 11 A.M. to 6 P.M. In addition to their own charge card, they accept American Express, Visa and MasterCard.

Strawbridge & Clothier is another Philadelphia favorite. The main store is in The Gallery at Market East at 8th and Market sts. A family-owned and run business since 1868, Strawbridge's strong points include their traditional and updated fashions for the whole family, an outstanding decorative home furnishing department, a large collection of Oriental rugs, and a business and personal computer department. Their Food Hall (see Gourmet Foods below) is a culinary paradise.

Strawbridge & Clothier has monthly Clover Day sales which offer great values. Check the local papers for the exact dates. You'll find the store's sales associates particularly helpful, and the folks at the Information Desk maintain a list of employees who speak foreign languages. The store is open Monday to Saturday, 10 A.M. to 6 P.M. (Wednesday night til 9 P.M.) and Sunday from noon to 5 P.M. MasterCard and Visa are accepted in addition to the store's own plate.

WOMEN'S CLOTHING

The well-known department stores offer a wide variety of fashions to tempt women of all ages. Another is *Bonwit Teller,* an upscale woman's specialty department store at 1700 Chestnut St., which is small enough to provide personalized service. Bonwit's has classic fashions for the career woman, moderately priced sportswear for juniors, and the latest from the hot designers. On the ground floor are fine accessories, cosmetics, and a men's department.

The sportswear at *Paraphernalia,* 1717 Chestnut, has a European look and is moderately priced. *Pegasus,* in an eclectic setting at 18th and Walnut sts., offers progressive ready-to-wear fashions exclusive to the boutique. They'll help you coordinate an outfit or a wardrobe; their accessories are art pieces that can make even a plain dress sensational.

At *Jaeger International Sportswear,* 1719 Walnut, the tailored English look has been adapted into stunning sportswear for the executive and society woman. *Toby Lerner,* 117 S. 17th St., offers European high-fashion apparel with strong classic lines. *Knit Wit,* 208 S. 17th, features fun, trendy sportswear and unique cocktail clothes. Both stores have a full line of shoes. At 128 S. 17th is *Plage Tahiti,* showcasing its own collection of avant-garde original fashions that are sold nationally. You'll find whatever is most current here, in addition to swimwear, year-round. The raiment at *Philip Mendelsohn,* on Rittenhouse Square, is more classic and sophisticated. The petite and small-framed woman can find fashionable clothing in sizes 0 to 6 at *Piaffe,* 1708 Sansom St.

For lingerie, try *Body & Sole Fashions* or *Intima.* Both boutiques, on the 1700 block of Sansom St., have a good selection of silks and satins, laces and cottons.

In the Bourse is *Cacharel,* selling classics in linen and raw silk from the French designer, and *Cazou,* which features all-cotton Le Sport Sac sportswear and Panache dresses.

The young-at-heart will find avant-garde sportswear, shoes, and jewelry to their liking at *Neo Deco* on South Street at 414.

MEN'S AND WOMEN'S CLOTHING

The finest in European and American designer apparel for men and women can be found at *Nan Duskin,* an exciting, elegant fashion store at 1729 Walnut St. A marble pillared entranceway leads you to a treasure-trove of furs, fine jewelry, Bottega Veneta leather goods, fragrances, millinery, lingerie, and edible delicacies.

The prestigious British firm of *Burberry's,* named for the gentleman who first designed the trenchcoat, has a store at 1705 Walnut St. In addition to their line of raincoats, overcoats, and sportcoats, they carry cashmere sweaters. *Ultimo,* 1425 Walnut, features men's and women's sportswear imported from Milan.

In The Bourse: *Howard Heartsfield* sells gorgeous handmade clothes woven, knit, or crocheted by fiber artists. The one-of-a-kind apparel—sweaters, bikinis, camisoles, and more—are nothing less than works of art. The handwoven and handknitted clothing sold at *Celtic Weavers* is imported from the United Kingdom. The yarn is for sale, as is the Irish crystal and china. The world's largest

Saint Laurent boutique calls the Bourse home. The designer's high-fashion day and evening wear and accessories are for sale.

Aero offers innovative fashions from Japan, Britain, and Italy—from swimsuits to tuxedos—in their store at 325 South St.

MEN'S CLOTHING

Like women's, men's clothing runs the gamut from American conservative to urban funk. *Allure,* 1509 Walnut, features handsome Italian imported dress and sportswear and a collection of lizard wallets and belts. *Wayne Edwards Men's Loft,* 1517 Walnut, sells exclusive lines of classic but contemporary European fashions. Both stores are known for fine quality, good service, and impeccable tailoring.

Dimensions, 1627 Chestnut St., is one of the city's finest men's stores. The store offers contemporary European elegance as well as the classic preppy look of Ralph Lauren in their Polo Shop. French, Italian, and West German furnishings of highest quality, with prices to match, are found at the elegant *Cote d'Azur,* 212 S. 17th St. Their Italian handmade shoes are noteworthy.

Boyd's, at 1217 Market St., is more of an Everyman's store. The largest men's store in the city and the second largest in the country, Boyd's has been a Philadelphia tradition since 1937. The five shops cater to those after a traditional English look, chic Italian imports, or other more contemporary styles. The extra-big, extra-short, and extra-tall man can find clothing to suit here. Fine tailoring, attentive service, and valet parking make shopping at Boyd's very pleasant.

Brooks Brothers, 1500 Chestnut St., the oldest men's clothing store in America, is a bastion of dignified, conservative wares for those who feel most comfortable in button-down shirts and striped ties. *M.L. Lawrence,* at 121 S. Broad St., has updated the conservative Brooks Brothers' look with British-styled business clothing in natural fabrics. For garb to wear on your day off, try *Urban Guerilla,* 1630 Sansom, 132 N. 3rd, and in the Bourse, for the latest in urban funk and military chic.

CHILDREN'S CLOTHING

The major department stores have fine children's clothing departments. For more unusual tiny-tot wear and toys, try the delightful *Born Yesterday* at 1901 Walnut. The handmade goods (they have t-shirts for adults, too) and imported fashions are styles you won't see elsewhere. There's a more conservative look to the infant-to-preteen garb at the *Children's Boutique,* 126 S. 18th St, which offers complete wardrobes, specialty gifts, and handmade items.

SHOES AND ACCESSORIES

Many of the men's and women's clothing stores mentioned above carry a full line of shoes. Other stores sell shoes only. *Strega,* 1505 Walnut, has a wide range of looks for men and women, representing the best in exclusive, superb quality footwear made primarily in Italy.

The latest designs from Paris, manufactured in Florence, are at *Roland Pierre,* a shoe salon for women in the Bourse. Here you'll find unique shoes and unusual color combinations. At *Beige,* 1715 Walnut, Italian imported women's footwear is more moderately priced. For men's fine brand-name shoes at discount prices, try *Sherman Bros. Shoes,* 1520 Sansom St. The shop specializes in hard-to-fit and difficult sizes.

BEAUTY SALONS

Nan Duskin and *Bonwit Teller* have full-service beauty salons, as does the Bellevue Stratford Hotel, home of the *Pierre & Carlo Salon.* All cater to both men and women. *Zagobi Beauty Center,* 1722 Walnut, offers many services including hair styling, ear piercing, massage, and makeup application. (Under the same roof, at *La Belle Amis,* are the latest women's fashions.)

Cezanne, 1735 Walnut, specializes in emergency services, including makeup, sculptured nails, and hair styling. *Christine Valmy,* on Locust east of 18th, is known for luxurious European facials and skin care.

When you've had enough sightseeing, take a total body break at *Toppers on the Bourse Mezzanine,* a salon (hair, nail, and skin care) and health spa (massage, sauna, nautilus gym) open until 9 each night.

JEWELRY

J.E. Caldwell, at Juniper and Chestnut, has been a local landmark since 1839. The store, with chandeliers by Baccarat, is as elegant as the jewels therein. In addition to the traditional and more modern jewelry, Caldwell's boasts one of the city's largest crystal selections, giftware, stationery, and a bridal registry. The world-reknowned *Bailey Banks & Biddle,* at 16th and Chestnut, is known for diamond and gold jewelry, fine china and crystal and silverware and stationery. *Pearson Campbell,* in the Bellevue Stratford, has gold jewelry ranging from $70 gold stud earrings to $250,000 treasures.

The shops on Jewelers Row are well-stocked and reputable. In *Jack Kellmer's* beautiful showroom at 717 Chestnut are diamonds, gold jewelry, and gift items at a discount. *Robbins,* 801 Walnut, is a diamond specialist; *Harry Sable,* 8th and Sansom, is the "king of wedding bands." Also of note, on the 700 block of Sansom, are *Safian & Rudolph, Sydney Rosen,* and *Perlstein.*

My Jewel Shop, Inc., 202 S. 17th St., has precious stones and custom-made handcrafted jewelry in gold. Across the street, *Richard Kenneth* specializes in jewelry from the late Georgian, Victorian, art nouveau and deco periods. At *Wesley Emmons,* 257 S. 16th St., you'll find custom-designed jewelry and estate and antique pieces in prime condition.

For fabulous fakes, try *Replique Fashion Jewelry* in the Warwick Hotel, 17th and Locust. The shop specializes in reproductions of fine gems and unique designs by local artisans.

LUGGAGE AND LEATHER GOODS

Robinson Luggage Company, Broad and Walnut sts., offers better name brands of luggage, leather, and travel accessories marked down at least 20 percent. Their selection of briefcases is the largest on the East Coast. *Pacific Briefcase & Luggage Co.,* 1626 Chestnut, also discounts their quality top-of-the-line luggage, handbags, and accessories. For wearable leathers, try *Patricia's Leather Lines,* whose skin, leather, and suede clothes, belts, bags, and shoes are made in their own factories in India and sold exclusively at their store on 1724 Walnut St.

COSMETICS, PERFUMES, AND TOILETRIES

Sample the white rose toilet water that Dolley Madison favored at *Caswell-Massey,* the oldest perfumer in America. The store, at 1630 Sansom St., has a great selection of fragrances, soaps, and toiletries. Pick up a copy of their famous catalog. You can also pamper yourself with British toiletries and comestibles at *Crabtree & Evelyn,* 1701A Chesnut St. and in NewMarket. A basket filled with jams and honey, or tea and biscuits, makes a terrific gift.

VERY SPECIAL SHOPS FOR GIFTS AND LUXURIES

There are a few special shops in the city that don't quite fit neatly into any category. They are great stores for unusual presents for friends, hosts, and hostesses—or for yourself. *Touches,* 1500 Locust St., is a tiny shop filled with wall-to-wall pleasures: handmade shawls, stunning handbags and belts, and unusual jewelry. It's a store where you can always find a gift in your price range. Almost everything is handmade at *Dandelion 2,* at 17th and Locust sts.: the unusual jewelry, original handcrafted ceramics, porcelains, and glass, and the clothing—some imported from India and Indonesia, as well as American hand-woven and batiked craft pieces.

The fabrics, clothing, and home accessories are all in sweet English floral prints at *Laura Ashley,* 1721 Walnut. You can buy wallpaper, picture frames, and a dress to match. Linens and domestics from the popular French Primrose Bordier collection can be found at *Descamps,* 1733 Walnut. Romantic is the word at *The Parlour,* a clothing boutique store with accessories at 131 S. 18th St. Year-round, you'll find white clothing, from Edwardian to new-wave. Jewelry representative of the French deco era and American heirloom furnishings, like handworked table linens and silk flowers, are specialties here.

For items made by hand with tender loving care, visit the *Elder Craftsmen,* 1628 Walnut St. All the charming gifts and children's clothes at this non-profit shop are made by senior citizens.

Your teenagers will enjoy the *Philadelphia T-Shirt Museum,* at 118 S. 18th St., with its large selection of unique silk-screened t-shirts and sweatshirts.

The art of topiary began in the Roman Empire and continues today at *Exotic Blossoms,* 510 S. 5th St. The arbor artist who decorated the Epcot Center sculpts plants into hundreds of decorative shapes, such as swans, dancing bears, and airplanes. The store will ship a plant anywhere in the United States.

The nationally reknowned *Holt's Tobacconist,* at 16th and Sansom, is the city's oldest and largest purveyor of pipes and tobacco, cigars and lighters. *Paper Moon,* 329 South St., may be the city's best stocked newsstand with more than 800 titles, cards, and candy.

GAMES AND TOYS—FOR CHILDREN AND ADULTS

The creative *Past Present Future,* 24 S. 18th St., features fantasy crafts and handmade toys, wooden or soft sculptured, for all ages. The world's largest exhibit of toy ray guns is on display at *Rocketships and Accessories,* an emporium of sci-fi and high-tech toys and collectibles at 625 S. 4th St. Enter the military and fantasy worlds at *The Compleat Strategist,* 2011 Walnut St. Strategy games like the Battle of Waterloo and Dungeons and Dragons, military posters and prints, war-related history books, and miniatures are available.

SPORTING GOODS AND CLOTHING

Eddie Bauer, 1425 Chestnut, is geared to the well-dressed active set with its outdoor casual clothing for men and women, camping gear and walking and hiking shoes. For the less adventurous, there's an indoor comfort area with goodies like warm slippers and flannel sheets.

Not as stylish, but just as practical, are the items at *I. Goldberg*, an army-navy —and everything store—at 902 Chestnut. The shop is crammed with government surplus and military style clothing, jeans and work clothes, footwear, camping gear, and lots to keep you warm in the winter. Rummaging here is an not-to-be-missed experience.

Runners get special attention at the *Philadelphia Running Center*, 1915 Walnut St., where knowledgeable salespeople can help you select appropriate gear. For a large selection of sports equipment, head to *Pearson Sporting Goods* at 1128 Chestnut.

BARGAIN SHOPPING

For the thrill of bargain shopping, we suggest the *Fashion Direct Outlet* at 2313 Chestnut St. You'll find first-quality over-runs, cancellations, and new test styles from high-fashion designers at discount prices; notable are the Fenn Wright & Manson knits and linens and the Calvin Klein accessories. At *Post Horn*, a division of J. G. Hook at 2130 Arch, traditional, nautically inspired women's sportswear is available at low outlet prices. For men's suits and sportswear, try *Today's Man*, at 1528 Chestnut St. They offer 30-to-40 percent off retail prices on brand names like Cardin, Adolfo, and Nino Ceruti. You'll fine similar discounts on men's clothing at *Max Golden & Son*, 1520 Sansom St. They'll make immediate alterations for out-of-town buyers. Women's designer leather shoes, boots, and handbags can be had at bargain prices at *The Warehouse Bootery*, 1835 Chestnut. *Bernie Robbins*, 1625 Sansom St, is a high-class catalog showroom with good values on jewelry, luggage, small appliances, etc.

FINE FOODS AND GOURMET SHOPS

Bon Appetit, 213 S. 17th, has fine gourmet cookware, cutlery, specialty foods, and a complete selection of gourmet cooking utensils, from a whisk to a duck press. You'll find lots of French copper and porcelain here. *The Cook Nook*, 257 S. 20th St., imports classic cookware for the gourmet and professional directly from France. They have an extensive collection of cookbooks in both English and French, and a large assortment of ingredients like oils, vinegars, and mustards. Both stores have a well-informed sales staff. *Pottery Barn*, 1610 Chestnut St., offers functional cookware at moderate prices.

For gourmet food, much of it ready-to-eat, head to *The Market at the Commissary*, 1710 Sansom St., or to *Viking Pastries* and *The Fruit Lady Charcuterie*, both at 1717 Walnut. They offer salads and other prepared goodies, cheeses, coffees, and fresh pasta. *The Food Hall*, at Strawbridge and Clothier's 8th and Market St. store, is an emporium in the European tradition. Eat-in at the cafe or take out breads, cheeses, salads, and Bassetts ice cream. Daily cooking demos with samples and the Delaware Valley's largest candy department attract shoppers. Sweet tooths can be satisfied at *Confiserie Suisse*, 225 S. 17th St., a chocolate boutique with handmade confections flown in weekly from Switzerland.

BOOKS

The largest bookstore in the city is *B. Dalton Bookseller*, at 1431 Chestnut St. The three floors hold a broad selection; the store is especially strong in cookbooks, sports, and fiction. You'll find a good selection of Philadelphia titles, tour books, and maps. *Encore Books* is a discount chain with thousands of titles. Their three locations—1413 Walnut St., 609 Chestnut, and 34 S. 17th—give up to 35 percent off on *New York Times* bestsellers and as much as 80 percent off on closeouts and remainders.

Sessler's, 1308 Walnut St., is loaded with personality and may be Philadelphia's favorite bookstore. It is best for rare and special-order books and art and travel volumes. They've added a collection of current fiction. Visit their antique map and print gallery. For old-fashioned, caring service, your best bet is the *Joseph Fox Bookshop,* 1724 Sansom St., which carries a small, choice collection of fiction and nonfiction, gift books, and volumes on the arts. The *Architecture Book Information Center,* at 17th and Sansom sts., is a treasure-trove for books on architectural theory, building construction, interior design, and furnishings. But there are also travel and children's books, blueprint posters, and international magazines.

The *How-To-Do-It Book Shop,* 1608 Sansom, offers self-instruction guides for doing practically anything, including woodworking, gardening, boating, and raising a pet. *Whodunit,* 1931 Chestnut, has one of the world's largest selections of mysteries, spy stories, and adventure books. You'll find many out-of-print books in stock here.

Until 2 A.M. Friday and Saturday nights, you can browse through an eclectic collection of used books and records at the *Book Trader* at 501 South St.

RECORDS AND MUSIC

The largest volume of classical and popular records and tapes can be found at *Sam Goody's,* 1125 Chestnut St. For harder-to-find jazz and soul records at good prices, check *3rd Street Jazz and Rock,* at 10 N. 3rd. If you are looking for unusual records—bird calls, sound effects, exercise, or language instruction—*Royer Smith,* 2019 Walnut, will special order them for you if he doesn't already have them in his unique collection. The store carries a large sampling of classical records. For sheet music, head to the back room at *Jacob's,* 1718 Chestnut St.

ANTIQUES

There are many reputable dealers on Pine St. If you are looking for antique quilts and 18th- and 19th-century country antiques, visit *M. Finkel & Daughter,* 936 Pine. At 1004, *Gary A. Friedman* has oversized Victorian and period-style furniture. Look for collectibles at *Schaffer Antiques,* 1014 Pine, and at *Joseph Davidson,* 924 Pine.

Edward G. Wilson, 1802 Chestnut St., has an amazing collection of smaller items like antique coins, lamps, and jewelry. If you love a good auction, you'll find it at *Samuel Freeman's,* 1808 Chestnut. On Tuesdays and Wednesdays at 10 A.M., they auction off furniture, china, and more. Freeman got the highest price ever for a printed document—$404,000 for one of the original flyers on which the Declaration of Independence was printed and posted throughout the city.

Euro-Pine, 309 Arch St., specializes in country pine furniture crafted during the 19th and early 20th centuries by artisans from Northern Europe. For art and accessories from the '30s, try *Ogetti di Bella,* 522 S. 4th St. The *Calderwood Gallery* at 746 South St. has art nouveau and art deco furniture and glass.

Gargoyles, 512 S. 3rd., features antique and reproduction architectural pieces like archways, mantles, and entranceways. Victorian embellishments from saloons and apothecaries are among the goods available at the *Architectural Antiques Exchange,* 715 N. 2nd St.

Whether you collect Teddy Roosevelt campaign buttons or baseball cards, you'll find it at *Love of Past,* 205 S. 17th. There's a wealth of Americana collectibles and memorabilia, particularly ads, magazines, and postcards from the 1850s to 1950s. Collectors and musicians favor *Vintage Instruments,* 1529 Pine St., known for its antique strings and woodwinds and for making fine instruments as well. Bibliophiles prefer *Bauman Rare Books,* at 1807 Chestnut St. There is a fine collection of volumes from the 19th century and earlier, especially books on English lit, law, black history, and travel and exploration. Also noteworthy are the prints and map collection.

 ART GALLERIES. Philadelphia has many more art galleries than can be included in any one listing. For current shows, it's best to check the monthly guide in *Philadelphia Magazine* or in the Weekend Section of Friday's *Inquirer.* Many galleries are in the vicinity of Rittenhouse Square; a few dot South Street; others are scattered about. Here are a few notables:

Peale House Galleries of the Pennsylvania Academy of the Fine Arts, 1820 Chestnut St., 972–7600, have rotating exhibits of works by alumni, faculty, and students. *Philadelphia Art Alliance,* 251 S. 18th St., 545–4302, displays changing mixed-media exhibits in an elegant Rittenhouse Square mansion. *Philadelphia College of Art,* Broad and Spruce Sts., 893–3100, features works of students, faculty, and local artists.

Suzanne Gross, 1726 Sansom, features painting, sculpture, and original works on paper by area and internationally recognized artists; *Marian Locks,* 1524 Walnut, exhibits primarily Philadelphia and regional contemporary artists. *David David Gallery,* 260 S. 18th, is noted for American and European paintings, drawings, sculpture, and prints from the 16th-to-20th centuries. Japanese antique and contemporary prints can be found at the *Gilbert Luber Gallery,* 1220 Walnut St.

The city's oldest and largest fine arts gallery is the *Newman Gallery* at 1625 Walnut. The showings range from 19th-century American and European paintings to contemporary graphics. *Frank S. Schwarz and Son,* 1806 Chestnut St., has stunning examples of 19th- and 20th-century American and European paintings. *Gross-McCleaf Gallery,* 1713 Walnut St., displays major works by prominent and emerging artists with an emphasis on outstanding Philadelphia painters. *Muse,* 1915 Walnut, is a woman's cooperative gallery which strives to improve the visibility of women artists. *I. Brewster,* 1742 Sansom, favors art nouveau and deco, and posters and paintings by Louis Icart and Erte.

At her gallery on 1721 Walnut St., *Helen Drutt* showcases American and European artists of the late 20th century, focusing on ceramics, textiles, wood and contemporary jewelry. Contemporary fine art pieces—wood, glass, furniture, and sculpture—adorn the *Snyderman Gallery* at 317 South St.

The craft galleries are as diverse. *Janet Fleisher,* 211 S. 17th, displays pre-Columbian, American Indian, and 20th-century American folk art, often in the form of pottery and jewelry. The sculptures, textiles, and jewelry of Africa, Indonesia, and the South Pacific are highlighted at *Jane Steinsnyder,* 1608 Pine St. Here you'll find costumes and contemporary clothing fashioned from ethnic textiles. *Swan Galleries,* 132 S. 18th, displays works—clay vessels, wall hangings, art wear—by the country's most recognized and collected craft artists. *The Works,* at 319 South St., is a contemporary gallery specializing in hand-blown glass, wood, jewelry, ceramics, and fiber.

At NewMarket, the *Artisans Cooperative* shows off an interesting collection of authentic native crafts from Appalachia, the South, New England, and the Midwest.

DINING OUT. Fifteen years ago, a guide to fine dining in Philadelphia would have been one of the shortest—and saddest—books in the world. With very few exceptions, the local restaurant scene was a woeful collection of chop houses and pretentious "Continental" establishments that were expensive (at least for those days) and uniformly mediocre. They had a certain captive audience in out-of-town visitors on expense accounts, but for the most part Philadelphians preferred to eat at home or in their clubs, figuring rightly that they didn't need to pay restaurant prices to get overcooked lamb and tough veal cutlets.

All that started to change in the late '60s. Small "boutique" restaurants began opening, particularly in the Society Hill section of town where gentrification was well underway, bringing young enthusiastic entrepreneurs and a new generation of sophisticated diners into the area. As more people traveled abroad and discovered good food, they became the core of demanding restaurant-goers and responsive restaurateurs which was the nucleus of Philadelphia's widely heralded "restaurant renaissance." Pretention went out the door. It was the age of the storefront restaurant—usually a long, narrow room with a shop window in front—offering an eclectic chalkboard menu in an atmosphere of mismatched china and flatware, hand-me-down furniture, poster art, and jungles of hanging plants. The food—characteristically an artful blend of American, French, and Oriental—was likely to be as highly personal as the decor. When one of the experimental dishes obviously wasn't working, another would replace it, the chalkboard would change slightly and the experience would help the kitchen learn and grow.

These days Philadelphia is enjoying the second generation of the restaurant renaissance, sort of "Son of Storefront." The "Early Attic" decor has been replaced with a sleek, frequently contemporary setting. Service is somewhat more mature. And the food continues to be a creative blend of the familiar and exotic.

Obviously not all the restaurants in town are practitioners of "Philadelphia cuisine." The steakhouses and various ethnic restaurants do their own thing. But most of the American and International places have been influenced by the trend, and some restaurants—*Frog, The Commissary, 20th Street Cafe,* and *Lickety Split*—epitomize it.

There is another Philadelphia cuisine that doesn't get much attention from *Bon Appetit* or *Gourmet* magazines. That's Philadelphia junk food. Hoagies, cheesesteaks, and soft pretzels are unique to this area, and few Philadelphians aren't addicted to at least one of them. Soft pretzels are available from street-corner vendors all over town. They're large and doughy and definitely an acquired taste. The natives eat them with mustard. You can get them fresh and hot out of the oven from *Fisher's Ice Cream* in Reading Terminal Market Thursday through Saturday. A hoagie is the Philadelphia version of the typical Italian submarine sandwich made of lunch meats, cheese, lettuce, tomato, and onion. They're traditionally ordered with oil (rather than mayonnaise) and hot peppers, but it's an individual choice. To sample state-of-the-art hoagies, visit *Charlie's Water Wheel,* 1526 Sansom, Center City, or *Grand Old Steak and Sub* in The Bourse, 5th at Independence Mall. Cheesesteaks are sandwiches of thinly-sliced steak, fried and served on an Italian roll. Fried onions and ketchup are the traditional accompaniments, and the traditional source of cheesesteaks in Philadelphia is *Pat's,* 9th and Passyunk in South Philadelphia, where you order a "cheese with" to get cheesesteak with fried onions, and then stand to eat under an outside awning trying to keep from dripping everything all over your feet. *Jim's* at 400 South Street in Society Hill also has exemplary cheese-steaks.

Ethnic cuisines are fairly well represented here, particularly French, Italian, and Chinese. Philadelphia has a handful of remarkably good French restaurants. Unfortunately none of them is inexpensive. The Italian restaurants, on the other hand, range from inexpensive to deluxe with a wide variety to choose from. Chinese restaurants used to be hard to find outside of Chinatown, but these days some of the best of them are located in other parts of the city. Many of the Chinatown restaurants tend to be touristy chop suey parlors or the sort of place that offers one menu of "safe" dishes for Occidentals and another for the Chinese themselves. The better restaurants make use of fresh, seasonal ingredients and are aware of the prevalent concern about MSG. While most Philadelphia Chinese restaurants don't yet rival the best of New York and San Francisco, they generally offer a range of cuisine choices from Szechuan to Cantonese.

Philadelphia's better restaurants are concentrated in the downtown area defined by the Schuylkill and Delaware Rivers, Vine St. to the north, and Federal St. south. To help you get around the restaurants, we've sub-divided parts of that area into the following geographical categories: **Center City, Old City, Society Hill, South Philadelphia,** and **Chinatown.** Center City is roughly bounded by the Schuylkill River to the west, 6th St. to the east, Lombard St. to the south and Race St. to the north. Old City is encompassed by 6th, the Delaware River, Race and Sansom; Society Hill by 6th, the Delaware, Bainbridge and Walnut. South Philadelphia is the area south of Bainbridge. The area between 9th and 11th, Vine and Arch sts. is Chinatown.

Two areas outside that broad reach are also defined here: **West Philadelphia,** the part of the city west of the Schuylkill, and the **Art Museum area,** a triangle north of the Benjamin Franklin Pkwy. with Broad St. and Poplar forming its other two borders.

A listing of restaurants in **Chestnut Hill** can be found at the end of this restaurant section.

Price Classifications and Abbreviations. The price classifications of the following restaurants, from inexpensive to deluxe, are based on the cost of an average three-course dinner for one person for food alone; beverages, tax (6 percent), and tip would be extra. *Inexpensive* means less than $8; *Moderate,* $8 to $15; *Expensive* $15 to $25; and *Deluxe,* over $25. One restaurant, *Le Bec-Fin,* has been designated Super Deluxe. This is the finest French restaurant in Philadelphia, and the prix fixe dinner here is $62 per person.

Abbreviations for credit cards are AE, American Express; CB, Carte Blanche; DC, Diners Club; MC, MasterCard; V, Visa. Most restaurants that do not accept credit cards will take travelers' checks. Many of the larger ones will accept a personal check if you have a major credit card.

Abbreviations for meal codes are B, breakfast; L, lunch; D, dinner; SB, Sunday brunch. Restaurant hours and days change frequently. Particularly in the summer, it's a good idea to check on lunch hours. It's wise to call for hours in any case, and it never hurts to make reservations. Philadelphia hosts frequent conventions, and restaurants can be fully booked at almost any time. A good source for up-to-the-minute restaurant information is *Philadelphia Magazine,* a monthly publication with extensive restaurant listings. The February issue of the magazine always features a major section on dining out and listings for hundreds of local restaurants.

AMERICAN-INTERNATIONAL

Deluxe

The Fountain. Four Seasons Hotel, 18th and the Parkway, Center City; 963–1500. This is one of the best restaurants in Philadelphia, offering exceptional food in an opulent setting overlooking the Swann Fountain in Logan Circle. The menu is in English, the waiters sound like Americans, but the kitchen is in the deft hands of French chefs who use classic techniques to create deceptively simple magic. Ordering a la carte can run up the bill, but they offer a daily four-course prix fixe menu for under $30. B, L, D daily. SB. All major cards.

Expensive

Adrian. 747 N. 25th, Art Museum area; 978–9190. A cozy neighborhood place with an interesting blackboard menu that changes frequently, and live music. L, D Monday–Friday; D only Saturday. AE, DC, MC, V.

Apropos. 211 S. Broad, Center City; 546–4424. The decor is high-tech modern with a California-style menu that includes entrees like grilled pork paillard, pizza with goat cheese and pancetta, and smoked duck lasagna with green noodles. B, L, D Monday–Saturday. AE, DC, MC, V.

Bridget Foy's. 200 South, Society Hill; 922–1813. Steaks, chops and seafood in two dining rooms. Downstairs it's woody and cozy; upstairs it's chandeliers and candlelight. L and D Monday–Saturday. SB. All major cards.

Cafe Nola. 328 South, Society Hill; 627–2590. A little bit of New Orleans with an oyster bar and Creole specialties in a rather noisy setting that's vaguely reminiscent of the French Quarter. D daily. SB. All major cards.

Friday, Saturday, Sunday. 216 S. 21st, Center City; 546–4232. A blackboard menu and a casually romantic atmosphere make this a particularly popular dining spot, but they don't take reservations for dinner. L, D Monday–Friday; D only Saturday and Sunday. AE, DC, MC, V.

Frog. 1524 Locust, Center City; 735–8882. This restaurant is the quintessential Philadelphia restaurant. Upgraded into an attractive townhouse from its humble storefront beginnings, Frog offers a constantly changing menu of seasonal delicacies like pasta with oysters and fresh asparagus, creative desserts, and an excellent American wine list—all in an informal, contemporary setting. L, Monday–Friday; D, daily; SB. All major cards.

The Garden. 1617 Spruce, Center City; 546–4455. A lovely townhouse has been turned into an attractive restaurant with multiple dining rooms and a cheerful patio and covered porch for outdoor dining. The food tends toward French country cooking with seasonal specialties. L Monday–Friday; D only, Saturday. AE, DC, MC, V.

Hoffman House. 1214 Sansom, Center City; 925–2772. Walking into this restaurant is like stepping into a cottage in the Black Forest. The decor—ornate wood paneling, stuffed boars' heads, colorful steins, and stained glass—is enough to tell you this is basically a German restaurant. The menu has expanded to include other cuisines, but the game dishes and wurst are still excellent. Try the steak tartare with a mug of Dortmunder dark. L, D Tuesday–Friday; D only Saturday. All major cards.

Knave of Hearts. 230 South, Society Hill; 922–3956. A variety of Continental dishes imaginatively prepared and served in cozy candlelight characterizes this restaurant. They don't take reservations and it's a popular spot, particularly with young urban dwellers—expect to wait unless you're early. L, Saturday only; D daily; SB. AE, CB, DC.

Lautrec. 408 S. 2nd, Society Hill; 923–6600. The walls of this tiny restaurant are decorated with—what else—classic Toulouse-Lautrec art work, but the kitchen produces its own unique cuisine: light French created with American ingredients. If you eat dinner here, you can listen to jazz downstairs at the *Borgia Cafe* for free—otherwise there's a cover charge. D, Monday–Saturday. SB. All major cards.

Lickety Split. 4th and South, Society Hill; 922–6660. One of the charter members of the restaurant renaissance, this little storefront hideaway boasts a waterfall, a forest of plants, and an inventive Continental menu. D daily. All major cards.

MARS. 714 South, Society Hill; 627–7333. The food is a combination of French and Italian, but the decor is other-worldly: the mirrored ceiling of the bar is illuminated to look like the star-studded heavens, and the atmosphere of the small, dimly-lit dining room is of the Restaurant at the End of the Universe. D daily. All major cards.

Monte Carlo Living Room. 2nd and South, Society Hill; 925–2220. Imported furniture, crystal chandeliers, and impeccable Continental service are the elegant background for French and Italian dishes featuring fresh fish, good veal, and homemade pasta. Dinner guests can continue the evening upstairs at the private club, dancing and enjoying live entertainment every night but Sunday. D, Monday–Saturday. AE, MC, V.

Morgan's. 24th and Sansom, Center City; 567–6066. The food at this charming little restaurant is inspired by France and Northern Italy, but the interpretation is unique. Game dishes are a specialty. L, Monday–Friday; D only, Saturday. All major cards.

October. 26 S. Front, Old City; 925–4447. Regional American dishes like buffalo, pheasant, and Philadelphia pepperpot soup in a serene environment. L, Monday–Friday. D daily. All major cards.

Raymond Haldeman. 110–112 S. Front, Old City; 925–9888. This restaurant features several beautifully decorated dining rooms and an eclectic cuisine that includes a variety of intriguing dishes like cappellini primavera, chicken and almond strudel, and stuffed red snapper in puff pastry. There is also a selection of gourmet dishes prepared for special diets. L, D Monday–Friday; D only, Saturday. All major cards.

La Terrasse. 3432 Sansom, West Philadelphia; 387–3778. This is Penn's unofficial faculty club. The bar is particularly popular, and the food—mainly a mix of French classic and nouvelle—is generally excellent. The atmosphere is sort of grown-up 60s, with hanging plants and classical music, pleasant if not fancy. L, Monday–Friday; D only, Saturday; SB. AE, MC, V.

Tripp's. 1425 Locust, Center City; 735–1129. You get a spectacular view of the city from this attractive penthouse restaurant. The menu features an interesting mix of light dishes and Roumanian specialties. At night the candlelight and twinkling cityscape make this a particularly romantic setting. L, D Monday–Friday; D only, Saturday. All major cards.

20th Street Cafe. 261 S. 20th, Center City; 546–6867. Stark white walls provide a backdrop for an imaginative, eclectic menu ranging from chili and pasta primavera to sauteed duck. L, D Monday–Saturday; D only, Sunday. SB. All major cards.

Two Quails. 1312 Spruce, Center City; 546–8777. American regional cooking is the current trend and it's done particularly well here. The menu changes frequently, but there are generally dishes like blackened redfish or fresh Oregon salmon with sorrel. The emphasis is on seasonal ingredients, there's a good American wine list, and the tiny dining room is casually sophisticated. L,D Tuesday–Friday; D only, Saturday. AE, DC, MC, V.

USA Cafe. 1710 Sansom, Center City; 569–2240. This casual restaurant, located upstairs at *The Commissary* (see below), is All-American from the Harley-Davidson motorcycle and baseball paraphernalia hanging on the walls to its Tex-Mex-and-Cajun menu. Try pasta in green chili sauce or beef filet with a cumin-jalapeno glaze. L, D Monday–Friday; D only, Saturday. All major cards.

Versailles Restaurant. Bellevue Stratford Hotel, Broad and Walnut, Center City; 893–1776. There's some hotel restaurant gimmickry here—wine is stored on racks that run all the way up to the ceiling along one wall, and the steward has to use a library ladder to retrieve the bottles—but it's a serenely elegant room, a womb of taupe with high-backed upholstered chairs that shield you from the outside world. And the kitchen does an admirable job with French and Continental specialties. L, Monday–Friday; D only, Saturday. All major cards.

Moderate

City Bites. 212 Walnut, Society Hill; 238–1300. "Eclectic" barely describes this restaurant, with a decor ranging from Doric temple to high punk. It's a fun place and has the best piped-in music in the city—a wonderful mix of tunes from commercials, TV themes, and 50s hits. The menu is as diverse as the decor; pizza, hamburgers, pasta, and fresh charcoal-grilled fish are available. L, D daily; SB. All major cards.

The Commissary. 1710 Sansom, Center City; 569–2240. Upstairs is *USA Cafe*, see above. Downstairs is a gourmet cafeteria with soups, salads, omelets, patés, desserts, and daily entree specials. Browse through the cookbook library while you sample wine by the glass and watch your omelet cook. B, L, D, daily. All major cards.

Downey's. Front and South, Society Hill; 629–0525. This is ostensibly an Irish pub, with traditional decor and fare—corned beef and cabbage, Irish stew—but the menu is mainly steaks, chops, and seafood. The bread pudding is exceptional, and they have a good selection of imported beers and ales. L, D Monday–Friday; D only, Saturday and Sunday. Brunch Saturday and Sunday. Upstairs is a fancy dining room with live music and a Continental menu, open for dinner only Wednesday–Saturday. All major cards.

Head House Inn. 400–402 S. 2nd, Society Hill; 925–6718. Early American simplicity in this restaurant/tavern. The traditional menu offers lamb, veal, and steak specialties. L, D daily. All major cards.

The Restaurant. 2129 Walnut, Center City; 561–3649. Potluck is the order of the day in this restaurant run by students and staff of the nationally known Restaurant School. It's on-the-job training for chefs and waiters, and if you're willing to be a guinea pig, you can frequently get a very good meal in the attractive Victorian brownstone that houses the school as well. D, Tuesday–Saturday. All major cards.

Rib-It. 1709 Walnut, Center City; 568–1555. 52 S. 2nd, Old City; 923–5511. Barbecue is the specialty here, with ribs, chicken, and steak available. Try the "funion loaf," a block of fried onion rings. L, D daily. AE, MC, V.

CAFES AND DELIS

When you want a quick, light, inexpensive meal, the place to head is a cafe or a deli. Philadelphia is loaded with them. Many of these places are open late, most have liquor licenses (exceptions are noted), and all have an interesting variety of dishes, from entrees to snacks.

The Brasserie. The Warwick Hotel, 17th and Locust, Center City; 545–4655. This chic little cafe is open 24 hours and offers omelets, burgers, and salads. Late night revelers at *élan,* the cocktail lounge down the hall, stop in here for eggs Benedict. Open daily. AE, DC, MC, V.

Corned Beef Academy. 121 S. 16th, Center City; 665–0460. 18th and J.F. Kennedy Blvd., Center City; 568–9696. 400 Market, Old City; 922–2111. Thoroughly modern delis with traditional fare and excellent french fries. B,L Monday–Saturday. Beer available at 18th St. location. No cards.

Eden. 1527 Chestnut, Center City; 972–0400. A stylish cafeteria that features gourmet stir fry dishes, salads, quiche, delicious homemade soups and desserts, and burgers. B, Monday–Friday; L,D Monday–Saturday. No liquor. No cards.

Eden. 3701 Chestnut, West Philadelphia; 387–2471. This Eden is just like the one described above only it's open from lunch til midnight daily and has a bar. No cards.

The Famous Delicatessen. 4th and Bainbridge, Society Hill; 922–3274. This 50-year-old deli is a Philadelphia landmark. The food is better-than-average deli favorites, and the milk shakes and chocolate chip cookies are world-class. B,L daily. SB. No liquor. No cards.

Houlihan's Old Place. 18th across from Rittenhouse Square, Center City; 546–5940. An instant-nostalgia atmosphere of posters, antiques, and plants is the casual setting for a menu that ranges from steaks and burgers to quiche and nachos. L,D daily, til midnight Friday and Saturday. All major cards.

H.T. McDoogal's. NewMarket, 407 S. 2nd, Society Hill; 592–7460. Described as a "fun 'n' foodrinkery," this restaurant offers a wide selection of choices from chicken and seafood to salads and burgers in a casual setting. L, D daily. SB. AE, MC, V.

The Irish Pub. 2007 Walnut, Center City; 568–5603. A popular bar and cozy dining rooms add to the pub atmosphere of this restaurant. A few Irish specialties are available along with a variety of burgers, chili, and sandwiches. L,D daily. AE.

McGillan's Old Ale House. 1310 Drury, Center City; 735–5562. A very casual dining spot featuring a lunch-time buffet sandwich counter (the roast beef is a favorite with local attorneys) and beer by the pitcher or mug. There's table service upstairs and a combo plays on weekends. L,D Monday–Saturday. AE, DC, MC, V.

Pizzeria Uno. 511 S. 2nd St., Society Hill; 592–0400. Chicago-style deep-dish pizza is the specialty in this zippy spot that's decorated like a wholesome saloon. Sandwiches, salads and soups are also available. L, D daily. AE.

Saladalley. The Bourse (upper level), Independence Mall East, Old City; 627–2406. 1720 Sansom, Center City; 564–0767. The draw here is the salad bar, a good selection of greens and goodies, along with soups and a limited selection of entrees and desserts. There's also a seafood bar Friday–Sunday evenings. L, D daily. SB. No cards.

Sassafras Cafe. 48 S. 2nd, Old City; 925–2317. A cozy little place with a Victorian bar and a fireplace, this cafe is known for its hamburgers (and the fact that they don't serve ketchup with them). L, D Monday–Saturday. No cards.

Silveri's. 315 S. 13th, Center City; 545–5115. This is a friendly neighborhood bar that serves food; famous for Buffalo chicken wings. Other menu items include salads and homemade pasta. L, D Monday–Friday; D only Saturday and Sunday. MC, V.

16th Street Bar and Grill. 264 S. 16th, Center City; 735–3316. A chic rendition of a classic bar and grill, this restaurant serves grilled fish, pasta, hamburgers, and pizza, along with a good selection of beers and American wines. A well-stocked jukebox. L, D Monday–Friday; D only, Saturday and Sunday. All major cards.

Tavern on Green. 21st and Green, Art Museum area; 235–6767. Salads and sandwiches, ribs and pasta in a sleek, contemporary atmosphere. L, D Monday–Saturday; D only, Sunday. SB. AE, DC, MC, V.

What's Cooking. 263 S. 15th, Center City; 735–0400. A small but tasty selection of salads, soups, and quiches with daily entree specials in an attractive, two-level, modern setting. L, D Monday–Friday. AE, MC, V.

H. A. Winston & Co. 15th and Locust, Center City; 546–7232. The setting is vaguely Victorian and the specialty is burgers with other dishes available. L, D daily. AE, DC, MC, V.

CHINESE

A variety of Chinese cuisines is available in Philadelphia, from the subtle Cantonese fare to the fiery delights of Szechuan and Hunan Provinces, with many restaurants offering dishes from several different areas. If you like your spicy food on the mild side, just ask. Most of the menus are fairly clear about what's hot and what's not, and many are specific about exactly what ingredients are in everything. Except where noted, the following restaurants all have liquor licenses. Many of the smaller places don't, so be sure to check before you go.

Moderate

Diamond Palace Seafood Restaurant. 1002 Arch, Chinatown; 238–1225. It calls itself a seafood restaurant, but you can get virtually anything you want here. Lobster is a specialty as well as beef sate and Mongolian lamb. L, Monday–Saturday; D, daily. AE, MC, V.

Empress. 1711 Walnut, Center City; 665–0390. This is a comfortable mid-town place with good Szechuan specialties. Peking duck, Mongolian lamb, and seafood preparations are featured. L, Monday–Saturday; D daily. AE, MC, V.

Golden Inn. 134 N. 10th, Chinatown; 627–4158. This is a very popular restaurant, attractively decorated with a lot of gold leaf and mirrors. The Chinese patrons frequently outnumber the others, especially at lunch when dim sum is available. L, D Monday–Saturday; D only Sunday. AE, MC, V.

Ho Sai Gai. 1000 Race, Chinatown; 922–5883. 10th and Cherry, Chinatown; 925–9384. 17th and Snyder, South Philadelphia; 389–0300. Although these aren't among the best of the local Chinese restaurants, they have an extensive menu and are open late—until 3 A.M. every day—a real advantage if you get a craving for lo mein at midnight. L, D daily. AE, DC, MC, V.

Hu-Nan. 1721 Chestnut, Center City; 567–5757. Exquisite Chinese cuisine that features fresh seasonal ingredients imaginatively prepared. The atmosphere is more Western than Oriental, a serene gold-and-blue dining room that used to be a private club. Among the most loyal patrons are chefs of Philadelphia's best French restaurants. L, Monday–Friday; D daily. All major cards.

Imperial Inn. 941 Race, Chinatown; 925–2485. 142–46 N. 10th, Chinatown; 627–2299. A variety of Szechuan, Mandarin, and Cantonese dishes served in well-appointed surroundings. Dim sum served daily. L, D daily. All major cards.

Joy Tsin Lau. 1026 Race, Chinatown; 592–7227. A large, fancy restaurant specializing in Szechuan, Mandarin, and Cantonese cooking, with dim sum available at lunch. L, D daily. All major cards.

Szechuan Garden. 1322 Walnut, Center City; 735–1833. Szechuan special-ties, obviously, with a good selection of other dishes. L, Monday–Friday; D daily. All major cards.

Tang's. 429 South, Society Hill; 928–0188. A small, very pleasant restaurant with seasonal specialties. D daily. All major cards.

EASTERN EUROPEAN

Expensive

Magyar Hungarian Restaurant/Bakery. 2048 Sansom, Center City; 564–2492. Traditional Hungarian fare with game dishes featured on weekends. Pastries are a specialty. No liquor. AE, MC, V.

Warsaw Cafe. 306 S. 16th, Center City; 546–0204. Borscht, beef Stroganoff, and other dishes from Poland, Russia, and Hungary are the specialties at this pleasant little cafe. L, D Monday–Saturday. AE, CB, DC.

FRENCH

Philadelphia is fortunate in having a handful of exceptional French restaurants. Most of them are in the Deluxe category, but if you're willing to spend the money, you'll get a first-rate French meal. There are also a few good Expensive French restaurants, less ambitious but quite adept at what they do. Almost all of the places are very popular, so plan to make reservations well in advance. *Le Bec-Fin* is liable to be booked as much as a month in advance for Saturday night—it's a small restaurant and they have only two seatings a night.

Super Deluxe

Le Bec-Fin. 1523 Walnut, Center City; 567–1000. Philadelphia's premier French restaurant and one of the best French restaurants on the East Coast, Le Bec-Fin offers classic French cuisine in a setting Louis XVI would feel right at home in: apricot silk walls, crystal chandeliers, and gilt-framed mirrors. Service is invisible, and the seasonal menu features the best of ingredients imaginatively prepared and beautifully presented. Master Chef and proprietor Georges Perrier learned his skills in the kitchens of France's legendary Pyramide and Baumaniere. Lunch is a la carte; dinner is prix fixe at $62 a person. Reservations are essential. L, D Monday–Thursday; D only, Friday and Saturday. AE, DC.

Deluxe

Cafe Royal. The Palace Hotel, 18th and the Parkway, Center City; 963–2244. This small dining room is filled with flowers and overlooks the panorama of the Parkway at Logan Circle. The excellent French cuisine is inventive and fairly light with liberal use of fresh seasonal ingredients and gossamer sauces. Dinner music is provided by a classical pianist in the adjacent lounge. L, D Monday–Friday; D only, Saturday. Brunch Saturday and Sunday. All major cards.

Deja-Vu. 1609 Pine, Center City; 546–1190. The decor of this tiny jewel-box of a restaurant is reminiscent of a belle epoque boudoir, all pink brocade and trompe l'oeil, glitter and gilt. The food is essentially French as interpreted by chef and owner Salomon Montezinos in his own unique style. His herb sorbets, offered as palate cleansers, have to be tasted to be believed. D, Tuesday–Saturday. All major cards.

Deux Cheminees. 251 S. Camac, Center City; 985–0367. This lovely 19th-century townhouse, filled with antiques and Oriental rugs, is a French restaurant for aristocrats. The cuisine is classic, beautifully prepared and presented; a specialty is crab marguerite, an ambrosial creamy crab soup. Private rooms are available. D daily. AE, MC, V.

La Truffe. 10 S. Front, Old City; 925–5062. Step through the door here and you'll think you're in a fine French provencial inn. But while the cozy dining room is traditional, the menu reflects the nouvelle trend of lighter dishes and exquisite presentation. L, Tuesday–Friday; D only, Monday and Saturday. All major cards.

Expensive

Alouette. 528 S. 5th, Society Hill; 629–1126. French cuisine with a slight Oriental accent is served here in a charmingly romantic atmosphere of exposed brick walls and candlelight. The chef-owner is Thai, and his interpretation of classic French cooking includes a sprinkling of dishes like chicken with Thai curry. This small restaurant is one of the most popular in the city, and deservedly so. Make weekend reservations well in advance. D daily, except Tuesday. MC, V.

La Camargue. 1119 Walnut, Center City; 922–3148. The Camargue is cowboy country in southern France. This restaurant serves provincial specialties in an atmosphere of white-washed walls, French country furniture and classical guitar music in the evenings. L, Monday–Friday; D only, Saturday. All major cards.

INDIAN

Expensive

Siva's. 34 S. Front, Old City; 925–2700. The food is quite good: North Indian cuisine with tandoori specialties (the clay tandoor oven is in the glass-enclosed kitchen), breads, and freshly made chutneys served in attractive surroundings. L,D. Monday–Friday; D only, Saturday and Sunday. All major cards.

ITALIAN

Philadelphia has always had good Italian restaurants thanks to the Italian immigrants who gravitated to South Philly. Originally "Italian" cooking inevitably meant "Sicilian"; dishes like spaghetti with red gravy ("gravy" being the local designation for tomato sauce), ravioli and veal parmigiana were the standard fare. But in the past five years, other Italian cuisines have become widely available as well, with Florentine, Roman, and Northern Italian restaurants enjoying particular popularity.

Deluxe

Ristorante DiLullo. 7955 Oxford, Northeast Philadelphia; 725–6000. Unquestionably the best Northern Italian restaurant in the city, DiLullo's menu was developed by Italian food authority Marcella Hazen and features seasonal specialties like mushroom pasta with wild mushroom sauce. Their out-of-the-way location has been a drawback, but at presstime, DiLullo's was just about to open in Center City (1405 Locust, 546–2000), in a smashing bilevel renovation of an old theater. It should be worth checking out. L, D Monday–Friday; D only, Saturday. All major cards.

Expensive

Alfredo the Original of Rome. The Bourse, 4th between Market and Chestnut, Old City; 627–4600. Bringing this fancy Italian restaurant to Philadelphia was a classic coals-to-Newcastle move, but it's attractively contemporary, the food's not bad, and there aren't many other Italian places in the neighborhood. Local cabbies were given a complementary meal here when the restaurant first opened, a point to keep in mind if you've had it recommended on the way from the airport. L, D daily. All major cards.

La Famiglia. 8 S. Front, Old City; 922–2803. This elegant family-run restaurant, one of the best in the city, offers a range of Northern and Southern Italian specialties, including ricotta gnocchi and superb veal dishes. L, D Tuesday–Sunday. AE, MC, V.

Gaetano's. 705 Walnut, Center City; 627–7575. Dining here is like eating at the home of upscale Italian friends. If you're early, you wait downstairs in the sitting room of this traditionally decorated townhouse. The dining rooms are up a curving flight of stairs. There are no menus—the prix fixe selections for the five-course meal are recited. The fare is typically Italian, heavy on veal, with an outstanding fisherman's soup. L, D Tuesday–Friday; D only, Saturday. AE, MC, V.

Il Gallo Nero. 245 S. 15th, Center City; 546–8065. Here the accent is Florentine and the ambience cooly elegant. Service has a tendency to be slow, but the food can be worth the wait; fresh white truffles in season, homemade pasta and gelati, and game dishes are specialties. L, D Monday–Friday; D only, Saturday. All major cards.

La Grolla. 782 S. 2nd, South Philadelphia; 627–7701. The cuisine in this small restaurant is mainly Italian with a few French dishes. The small dining room is attractively cozy, and there are also tables in the bar if you want a more casual atmosphere. D daily. All major cards.

Osteria Romana. 935 Ellsworth, South Philadelphia; 271–9191. This friendly, informal restaurant features Roman specialties as well as a roast suckling pig feast (available with 72 hours' notice). Particularly recommended are the gnocchi gorgonzola and the Italian bouillabaisse. Don't fill up on the bread, a crusty loaf you could make a meal of. D, Tuesday–Sunday. All major cards.

Ristorante La Buca. 711 Locust, Center City; 928–0556. This traditional, fancy Italian restaurant features Tuscan specialties. The day's catch is presented at tableside, so you can pick your own fish. L, D Monday–Friday; D only, Saturday. All major cards.

SPQR. 2029 Walnut, Center City; 496–0177. A charming little dining room in a townhouse is the setting for central Italian cooking that can be very good. It's a friendly, family-run place. L, D Monday–Friday; D only, Saturday. AE.

Moderate

Dante's and Luigi's. 762 S. 10th, South Philadelphia; 922–9501. An old-fashioned, simple neighborhood place, the specialties of this kitchen are steamed mussels, manicotti, and calamari. L,D daily. No cards.

Fratelli. 1701–03 Spruce, Center City; 546–0513. The atmosphere is contemporary, but the food here is traditional, with Mama in the kitchen. Homemade pasta, chicken, and veal dishes, and a chocolate cake that defies description. The shameless order it a la mode with white chocolate gelato. L, D Monday–Saturday; D only, Sunday. AE, DC, MC, V.

Phillips. 1145 S. Broad, South Philadelphia; 334–0882. A long-time Philadelphia favorite, this restaurant offers Italian classics like saltimbocca as well as more unusual dishes. L, D Tuesday–Sunday. AE, DC.

Villa Di Roma. 932–36 S. 9th, South Philadelphia; 627–9543. An old favorite in the Italian Market. Special pasta dishes like ziti with asparagus are featured here. Make reservations if you go for lunch. D Tuesday–Sunday; L Friday and Saturday. No cards.

Inexpensive

Triangle Tavern. 10th and Reed, South Philadelphia; 467–8683. This casual neighborhood spot is as popular with suburbanites as it is with the folks on the block. Old-style Italian cooking—ravioli, manicotti, mussels in white or red sauce—just like Mama used to make. D daily. No cards.

JAPANESE

Expensive

Kanpai. NewMarket, 2nd and Pine, Society Hill; 925–1532. Dramatic knife-flashing *teppanyaki* (table cooking) is the attraction at this slick restaurant. Or you can opt for sushi at the upstairs sushi bar. L, D Tuesday–Friday; D only, Saturday–Monday. All major cards.

Moderate

Hikaru. 607 South, Society Hill; 627–7110. Remove your shoes and sit on the floor Japanese-style in the tatami room of this small, attractive restaurant. Specialties include sushi and sukiyaki. L, Monday–Friday; D only, Saturday and Sunday. No liquor. AE, DC, MC, V.

MEXICAN

Moderate

El Metate. 1511 Locust, Center City; 546–0181. The best of the downtown Mexican restaurants, this casa offers the standard tortilla dishes as well as a range of Mexican-inspired seafood dishes. It's a particularly attractive, contemporary restaurant with a popular bar. L, D Monday–Friday; D only, Saturday and Sunday. All major cards.

MIDDLE EASTERN

Expensive

Marrakesh. 517 S. Leithgow (between Lombard and South, 4th and 5th), Society Hill; 925–5929. As if you were on the road to Morocco. The decor is hammered brass and Moroccan rugs, and you sit on low, cushioned benches and eat with your hands. The set meal includes salads, bastilla, chicken, couscous, and dessert. Lots of good, clean fun. Reservations are essential. D daily. No cards.

The Middle East. 126 Chestnut, Old City; 922–1003. It's not terribly authentic, but it appeals to everyone who likes shish kebab and belly dancers. It's customary to stick dollar bills in the dancing girls' costumes as a token of art appreciation. An American menu is available along with Lebanese specialties. D daily. All major cards.

Moderate

Salloum's. 1029 S. 10th, South Philadelphia; 922–2445. There's nothing fancy about this tiny family-run Lebanese restaurant located upstairs over a luncheonette, but the food is authentic and good. The cheerful decor is enhanced by colored lights, and Middle Eastern music and belly dancers on weekends. Reservations are necessary for Friday and Saturday and useful other times. No liquor. D Monday–Saturday. No cards.

SEAFOOD

Philadelphia has a handful of good seafood restaurants, as well as having good seafood dishes—like good steaks—available in most of the better restaurants.

Deluxe

Bookbinder's Seafood House. 215 S. 15th, Center City; 545–1137. Best known of the seafood houses—in fact, best known of all of Philadelphia's restaurants—is Bookbinder's. What isn't as well known to out-of-towners is that there are two very distinct and very dissimilar Bookbinder's located in different parts of the downtown area. Depending on which cabbie you ask or where you are when you're looking for their sign, you could end up at Old Original Bookbinder's in Society Hill (see below), or Bookbinder's Seafood House in Center City. Bookbinder's Seafood House is owned by scions of the family that founded the original. While it's not in the same league with Old Original—the food isn't as good and it isn't as impressive a place—it's still popular, particularly with the local business community. The atmosphere is traditional seafood house, with stuffed marlin cavorting on the walls and captain's chairs surrounding the tables. The prices are somewhat lower than the other and the atmosphere is pleasantly woody and traditional. L, Sunday–Friday; D daily. All major cards.
  Old Original Bookbinder's. 125 Walnut, Society Hill; 925–7027. "Old Original" is in the same location as the original restaurant which was established in 1865 by the Bookbinder family. It is now owned by restaurateur John Taxin. This is probably the restaurant that has made Bookbinder's such a tourist attraction. But because of its touristy reputation (they even have a souvenir shop on the premises) and astronomic prices, many locals avoid it, in spite of the fact that it's the best seafood restaurant in the city. It's also the place you're most likely to see a celebrity since they cater shamelessly to the famous and merely infamous. L, D daily. All major cards.

Expensive

Dockside Fish Company. 815 Locust, Center City; 925–6175. Grilled fish, shellfish, and chowders in a contemporary atmosphere. L, Monday–Saturday; D, daily. All major cards.
  The Fish Market. 124 S. 18th, Center City; 567–3559. Fresh fish and shellfish in attractive, multilevel dining rooms. L, Monday–Saturday; D, daily. All major cards.
  Sanna's. 239 Chestnut, Old City; 925–4240. Unusual preparations of fresh seafood, with dishes like steamed fish and white bouillabaisse. The atmosphere is young, chic, and romantic. L,D Monday–Friday; D only Saturday. AE, MC, V.

Moderate

Philadelphia Fish & Company. 207 Chestnut, Old City; 625–8605. Mesquite grilled fish and shellfish is the specialty here. L, Monday–Friday; D, daily. AE, MC, V.
  Sansom Street Oyster House. 1516 Sansom, Center City; 567–7683. The best raw oysters in town are found in this small, informal fish house. L and D, Monday–Saturday. All major cards.

DiNardo's Famous Crabs. 312 Race, Old City; 925–5115. Roll up your sleeves and dig into hardshell crabs and a variety of other seafood. Very casual. L, D Monday–Saturday; D, Sunday. All major cards.

Inexpensive

Walt's King of Crabs. 804–6 S. 2nd, South Philadelphia; 339–9124. Good fresh seafood in a casual atmosphere. L, D daily. No cards.

STEAKHOUSES

Philadelphia has surprisingly few steakhouses for a city of its size. That may be partly due to the fact that excellent steaks can be had at most of the better restaurants. The quality of the beef is high, the preparation generally careful—order it medium rare and you get it medium rare. (Or try that Philadelphia favorite, "Pittsburgh rare"—juicy red on the inside and charred black on the outside.)

The following restaurants are basically steakhouses although *Saloon* has an extensive Italian menu as well.

Deluxe

Harry's Bar and Grill. 22 S. 18th, Center City; 561–5757. Hunting prints and dark wood set the tone for this exceptionally handsome restaurant. They specialize in steaks although fresh fish and pasta dishes are offered as well. L, D Monday–Friday. All major cards.

Expensive

Arthur's Steak House. 1512 Walnut, Center City; 735–2590. This restaurant has been Philadelphia's premier steakhouse for 50 years specializing in filet mignon, prime rib, and Chateaubriand. The steak displayed in the refrigerated front window is real, and it's replaced every day; it has even been specifically ordered from time to time by adventurous diners. Well-lit and traditionally decorated, this is a no-nonsense place popular with businessmen. L,D Monday–Friday, D only Saturday. All major cards.

Saloon. 750 S. 7th, South Philadelphia; 627–1811. In the heart of the city's Italian district, Saloon offers a staggering selection of Italian specialties and some of the best steaks in town. It's a particularly attractive restaurant with old wood paneling, Victorian antiques, and lots of brass accents. There are no written menus, but the waitresses are patient about repeating the extensive list of possibilities. Two warnings: they don't take reservations on Saturday night, and it's a cash-only operation—and an expensive one at that. L,D Monday–Friday; D only Saturday.

THAI

Moderate

Bangkok House. 117 South, Society Hill; 925–0655. Authentic Thai dishes ranging from subtle to fiery, with asterisks on the menu to warn the unwary, served in an attractive storefront restaurant. D daily. All major cards.

Siam Cuisine. 925 Arch, Chinatown; 922–7135. A particularly pretty setting of pastel walls, floral tablecloths, and greenery is the background for good Thai food. Pork with mint leaves and chili is a specialty. No liquor. L, D Tuesday–Sunday. MC, V.

Thai Royal Barge. 23rd and Sansom, Center City; 567–2542. The atmosphere is luncheonette but the food is authentic and good, with unusual dishes like soft-shelled crab with spicy cucumber-peanut salad. L, Tuesday–Friday; D daily. All major cards.

VIETNAMESE

Moderate

Saigon. 935 Washington, South Philadelphia; 925–9656. It looks like all the family works in this unpretentious, small restaurant. Steamed fish is a specialty and the spring rolls with fish sauce and beef in vine leaves are popular. No liquor. L, D weekdays, except Tuesday. No cards.

Vinh Hoa. 746 Christian, South Philadelphia; 925–0307. This roomy restaurant is another family affair with an Oriental-Formica decor and a large ornamental fish tank. The food is basically Vietnamese with some Chinese dishes. Happy pancakes and deep-fried fish are the specialties. No liquor. L, D daily. All major cards.

 DINING OUT IN CHESTNUT HILL. This section of Philadelphia, across the Schuylkill River and a considerable distance from Center City, has several noteworthy restaurants. Don't make a trip just for the food; while these restaurants are good, you can eat as well in town—but if you're in the area, here are some suggestions.

Expensive

Chautauqua. 8229 Germantown; 242–9221. Classic and nouvelle cuisines meet nicely in this attractive, very contemporary dining room upstairs at the old Chestnut Hill Hotel. There's lighter fare in the oyster bar where a pianist entertains nightly from Wednesday to Saturday. L, D Tuesday–Saturday, D only, Sunday–Monday. SB. All major cards.

21 West. 21 W. Highland; 242–8005. The atmosphere here is country inn, the food, classics like rack of lamb, and the diners have been coming here for years. Before or after dinner, you can sing along at the piano bar. L, D Monday–Saturday. All major cards.

Under the Blue Moon. 8042 Germantown; 247–1100. An unusual decor of batik linen, Mexican tile, and polished blond wood is the background for good, creative cooking. D, Tuesday–Saturday. No cards.

Moderate

Rollers. 8705 Germantown; 242–1771. This light, noisy, chic little cafe, located at the top of the hill where the trolley turns around, has a constantly changing menu of international, eclectic dishes. There's a tiny wine bar and a take-out section, and you can watch your food being cooked. L, D Tuesday–Saturday; D only, Sunday. SB. No cards.

 BRUNCH. Sunday brunch is particularly popular with late-rising city dwellers. The Sunday *New York Times* seems to be an integral part of the brunch ceremony, and the food can vary from deli bagels and whitefish to elegant multiple-course service in white-tablecloth surroundings.

The most lavish brunch in town is the buffet at *élan* in the Warwick Hotel, 17th and Locust, 546–8800. The fancy, dark cocktail-lounge atmosphere is a little strange for a morning meal, but the food makes up for it. There's a large table of cold dishes including bagels and lox and a variety of fruits and salads, and a hot table that offers, among many other dishes, Chateaubriand, breakfast meats, eggs, and pancakes. Muffins and Danish abound and there's even a make-your-own-sundae bar and other desserts if you can face the prospect. A complimentary Bloody Mary or glass of champagne comes with your meal; for an additional $3 you can get unlimited amounts. Hours are 10:30 A.M.–2:30 P.M. No reservations, so come early or expect to wait in line. All major cards.

Many of the better restaurants serve Sunday brunch. Descriptions, addresses, and phone numbers for the eateries recommended here can be found under their appropriate headings in the "Dining Out" section, above. Prices for brunch are generally much lower than dinner prices. Except where noted, brunch is available only on Sunday.

American-International: *The Commissary, The Fountain, Frog, 20th Street Cafe, Cafe Nola, Downey's, Knave of Hearts, Lautrec, La Terrasse.*

Cafes and Delis: *Famous Deli, Houlihan's* (Saturday brunch available), *Tavern on Green.*

Others: *Le Beau Lieu.* The Barclay Hotel, 18th and Rittenhouse Square, Center City; 545–0300. Buffet brunch with a harpist, white tablecloths, and chandeliers. All major cards.

Le Bistro. 757 S. Front, Society Hill; 389–3855. International specialties with a view of Penn's Landing and the Delaware. All major cards.

Miss Headly's Wine Bar. Upstairs at 54 S. 2nd, Old City; 627–6482. Complimentary champagne and the Sunday paper included with brunch at this small cafe. All major cards.

Once Upon a Porch. 414 S. 2nd, Society Hill; 923–3525. This gingerbready, Victorian ice cream parlor offers brunch in a year-round sky-lit "garden." No liquor. No cards.

Society Hill Hotel. 3rd and Chestnut, Old City; 925–1919. A small bed-and-breakfast hotel with a pleasant, casual brunch. All major cards.

TEATIME. Nothing is as restorative as a soothing cup of tea in the middle of a hectic day. These places offer a traditional afternoon tea.

Bellevue Stratford Hotel. Broad and Walnut, Center City; 893–1776. Tea is served in Stratford Court, the main lobby of this plush hotel, from 3:30 til 5 P.M. Monday–Saturday, with a selection of tea sandwiches, pastries, and ice cream concoctions available as well as cocktails. All major cards.

Crystal Room at John Wanamaker. 13th and Market, Center City; 422–2809. Tea at the Crystal Room has sustained many a Philadelphia matron through countless shopping expeditions. The room is impressive, with fluted columns and crystal chandeliers, and the fare is an Americanized version of what you'd expect to find in a modern London tearoom: small sandwiches, pastries, and (more's the pity) tea bags. Served from 2:30–3:30 P.M. Monday–Saturday, til 4:30 P.M. Wednesday. AE, MC, V.

Dickens Inn. NewMarket, 2nd between Pine and Lombard, Society Hill; 928–9307. This aggressively English restaurant is an ideal setting for a cuppa. Originally an 18th-century coaching inn, the building is now cheerfully decorated with all matter of Dickensiana. Tea is a fairly proper affair with good scones, though service is somewhat casual. Monday–Friday from 3 to 5 P.M. All major cards.

Four Seasons Hotel. 18th and the Parkway, Center City; 963–1500. A very proper tea is available in the plush Swann Lounge with a restrained piano tinkling in the background. Scones, tea sandwiches, and pastries are served every afternoon from 3:15 until 4:45 P.M. All major cards.

Palace Hotel. 18th and the Parkway, Center City; 963–2222. Another elegant spot for an afternoon's pause. Tea sandwiches and pastries are available daily from 3 until 5 P.M. All major credit cards.

NIGHT LIFE. Reports that Philadelphia has no nightlife are greatly exaggerated—you just have to know where to look. And what you're looking for. If your idea of late-evening entertainment is a nightcap to the tune of mellow piano music, many of the hotel cocktail lounges will be ideal. If you want the light shows or pick-up scenes, they're available, too.

Certain clubs are members-only, after-hours places that can stay open after the 2 A.M. legal closing time because they're "private." The reality is that anyone can join them on the spot by paying the yearly dues, usually a nominal amount, or by paying a guest fee. Most of these clubs close by 4 A.M., with no one allowed in after 3.

Clubs open and close and change personalities almost overnight. A hot spot this season could be out of favor in six months. Or a gay-couples-only club could evolve into a popular singles gathering place as quickly. Hours and prices change as well. Don't count on using credit cards. Most night spots are cash-only operations. Another caveat: many of these places have strict ideas about proper dress. Some frown on jeans, others expect men to wear jackets. The best plan is to call ahead to find out about dress and hours and who the night's bands and performers might be.

MUSIC AND DANCING

Black Banana. 247 Race, Old City; 925–8677. This used to be one of the city's more interesting boutique restaurants. It's been turned into a private club and is one of the more popular dancing spots with the young crowd. It's still trying to shake its gay-club image, and these days the dance floor is filled with an attractive, diverse mix of people, including some real Beautiful People. The membership fee of $38 entitles you to bring as many guests (for $6 cover each) as you'd like, and your membership is good for a year. Open Wednesday–Sunday, 10 P.M.–3 A.M.

Chestnut Cabaret. 3801 Chestnut, West Philadelphia; 382–1201. Located by the Penn campus, this concert hall/dance club features live music of the "old wave" variety—Jerry Jeff Walker, Levon Helm, and similar rock and rhythm & blues musicians—as well as "new" music programmed by local disc jockeys. The cover is minimal and varies depending on the time, day, and whether the music's live or not. Popular, as you might expect, with college students and other university folks. Casual, but men's shirts should have collars. Open Thursday–Saturday.

The Down Under. 5 Penn Center Plaza, Center City; 567–3553. This place is hard to find—look for a flight of outdoor stairs leading down from the area of the northwest corner of 16th Street and Market. In the summer there's a lot of activity on the patio, particularly during happy hour from 4 to 7:30 P.M., when a hot and cold buffet attracts a crowd of young professionals. There's a DJ and dancing from 4 P.M. til 2 A.M. Closed Saturday and Sunday.

élan. Warwick Hotel, 17th and Locust, Center City; 735–6000. Philadelphia's magnet for mature business people and professionals who stop by for the great happy hour buffet or show up at 9 P.M. for dancing. It's a sophisticated place with sleek decor and backgammon tables, but the dance floor is fairly small, and it's hard to escape the meat-market atmosphere. A DJ programs the music from 9 till 3. Members only, but you can get a one-day $15 membership starting at 4:30. Dinner by reservation at 7 and 9. Closed Sunday.

East Side Club. 1229 Chestnut, Center City; 564–3342. For a while this was the city's most popular hot spot, with live local bands most weeknights and DJ dance nights Sunday and Wednesday. The crowd is mostly young, with blacks favoring the Friday night dance party sponsored by a local radio station, and the Saturday night dance party hopping with predominately white rock and rollers. Admission varies from $6 to free, depending on whether the music's live or recorded. Open daily.

Equus. 254 S. 12th, Center City; 545–8088. This is one of Philadelphia's best gay bars. But it's also popular as a disco with straights who come to dance in couples and groups. The bar is open from early afternoon til 2 A.M. daily. Disco opens weeknights at 10, weekends at 9, with a $4 cover charge that includes one drink.

Glitters. 427 South, Society Hill; 592–4512. This handsome hot spot is up a flight of stairs, all a-glitter in deep blue reflected in chrome, glass, and mirrors. You can snack in the dining area, spend happy hours at the long bar, or kick up your heels in the glass-enclosed dance area to DJ-programed music from 9:30 P.M. Tuesday through Saturday. No jeans after 9 P.M.

Horizon's. Franklin Plaza Hotel, 16th and Race, Center City; 448–2901. Shades of Fred and Ginger, this rooftop restaurant and lounge with its black and silver decor will take you back to the days when hotel dining rooms were the chi-chi places to be. The view, 27 stories above the street, is lovely, and there's a dance floor for cheek-to-cheeking it to a combo from 9 til 1. Closed Sunday.

Kennel Club. 1215 Walnut, Center City; 592–7650. We have seen the future, and this must be it—lots of video screens and computer graphics programmed by a VJ to complement the prerecorded new wave, synth-pop, and reggae music. Weird and wonderful and popular with a wide range of young rockers—preppies, stylish blacks, and gays. Open Wednesday–Sunday from 9 P.M. til 3 A.M. It's a private club with a $10 membership fee. Cover is $1.

Key West. 207 S. Juniper, Center City; 545–1578. This is another popular gay bar, but straights aren't unwelcome. The dance floor is good, and there's a large, comfortable bar area. Open daily from midafternoon til 2 A.M. with free disco admission til 10 Friday and Saturday; after 10, it's $3, but that includes a drink ticket.

Khyber Pass Pub. 56 S. 2nd St., Old City; 627–6482. Live music is featured at this popular bar nightly. It's one of the remaining showcases for local groups, with rock, blues, and country music attracting a young crowd. The bar also attracts foreign sailors in port who come in to quaff beer and ale imported from all over the world. Open daily except Sunday til 2 A.M. Cover charge of $2 Friday and Saturday nights.

MARS. 714 South, Society Hill; 627–7333. Wednesday, Friday, and Saturday starting at 10 there's a disco upstairs above this funky restaurant. The crowd is young, and there's no cover.

Monte Carlo Living Room. 2nd and South, Society Hill; 925–2220. If you eat dinner in the restaurant, you have guest privileges upstairs in the ultra-plush lounge. Non-diners pay a $10 cover. It's a sophisticated little watering-hole, with a pianist singing and playing chansons for touch-dancing and a DJ spinning Top 40s hits between sets. Jackets are required. Open Monday–Saturday from 9 P.M. till 2 A.M.

PT's. 6 S. Front, Old City; 922–5676. Although this nightspot is owned by the same people who own *élan,* the atmosphere is different. A younger crowd, not so seriously into the singles scene, come here to mingle. There are all sorts of attractions—from backgammon tables to all-male revues, live orchestras to Sunday afternoon T-dances. The cover changes nightly depending on the evening's attraction, but it's seldom over $2.

Ripley's. 608 South, Society Hill; 923–2370. This large nightclub features special computerized lighting and an "urban environment." Tuesday, Wednesday, and Thursday nights (and occasionally Monday), live local and international bands and theme parties provide entertainment. A DJ programs dance music and videos on Friday, Saturday, and Sunday. Dress is fashionable. The club swings from 9 till 2. There's a $5 cover on weekends; the cover varies for live entertainment.

Second Story. 1127 Walnut, Center City; 925–1127. Among the best nightspots in town, particularly if you're under 30. An interesting mix of people, great light show, and good dancing. There's even space for talking and drinking, though things tend to get a little claustrophobic when it's crowded. It's a private club with a $10 nonmember cover charge Friday and Saturday, reduced cover for members. Open Friday–Sunday.

Scruples. 119 South, Society Hill; 627–8531. This private club ($10/year membership) is beginning to catch on with an older college crowd, having been a hangout for mid-twenties kids from South Philly. It also attracts young locals from Society Hill and South Street—a mixed crowd who come for the two large dance floors and pleasant bar. A DJ programs the music. Open daily till 3 A.M.

BARS WITH MUSIC

The Bar. Hershey Hotel, Broad and Locust, Center City; 893–1600. A handsome lounge with a combo from 9 til 1 nightly except Sunday. You can even foxtrot to the contemporary and '40s music.

Brasserie Cafe & Bar. Warwick Hotel, 17th and Locust, Center City; 545–4655. There is live music in this 24-hour cafe during happy hour from 5 till 8 weekdays. On weekend nights watch major sports events on the large-screen TV.

Bridget Foy's. 2nd and South, Society Hill; 922–1814. Local musicians play light jazz and pop piano from Wednesday through Sunday in this attractive restaurant. Come for dinner or just stop by for cocktails and music.

Cafe Borgia. 406 S. 2nd, Society Hill; 574–0414. Jazz is the drawing card at this tiny room downstairs at Lautrec restaurant. The music plays nightly except Monday, and if you are a dinner guest, there's no cover charge. If you didn't eat dinner, you ante up for each set.

Cafe Royal. Palace Hotel, 18th and the Parkway, Center City; 963–2244. The cocktail lounge adjoins an elegant, intimate French restaurant, and the atmosphere is sophisticated, particularly with the pianist delivering classics from Chopin to Gershwin. Only "grownups" in jackets and ties will be happy here. The lounge is open seven nights a week with music Wednesday–Saturday.

Fairmount Firehouse. 2130 Fairmount, Art Museum area; 236–3440. This bar used to be an old firehouse. A friendly, casual, young professional crowd meets around the huge, oval bar, and from Wednesday through Saturday music is provided by a singer, bass, and piano.

Joe's Speakeasy and Piano Bar. 114 S. 12th, Center City; 922–5875. Upstairs at New London Restaurant you'll find good local jazz and swing combos every Friday and Saturday from 9 till 1 P.M.

Not Quite Crickett. 17th and Walnut, Center City; 563–9444. A dark, pleasant lounge with a big sound: Gershwin and big band music Monday through Thursday, jazz Friday–Sunday with a weekend jam session featured.

Piano Bar at the Commissary. 1710 Sansom, Center City; 569–2240. Sometimes it's piano music, other times jazz musicians are featured at this attractive little lounge where you can also get light sandwich-salad-nachos fare. Live music Tuesday–Saturday evenings, but the bar is open Monday–Saturday starting at 11:30 A.M.

Society Hill Hotel. 301 Chestnut, Old City; 925–1919. Piano renditions of Gershwin and pop favorites Tuesday–Saturday at this casual, friendly watering hole.

Top of Centre Square. 15th and Market, Center City; 563–9494. The view from the bar here is spectacular, 41 stories above the city. There is live music Wednesday through Saturday. This is a particularly popular spot with young single professionals who flock here for happy hours.

Versailles Lounge. Bellevue Stratford Hotel, Broad and Walnut, Center City; 893–1776. This plush, beautiful lounge is a relaxing place to stop for a nightcap and enjoy the pianist/singer on Friday and Saturday nights til midnight. During the week, the music moves into the Lobby Court from 5 till 8 for cocktail time.

GOOD BARS

While these bars are popular spots with singles, they aren't quite the meet-markets PT's and élan are. They're restaurant bars, pleasant places to stop by for an early drink before the dancing starts elsewhere. Descriptions can be found in the "Dining Out" section, under the headings indicated below.

American-International: *City Bites,* 212 Walnut, Society Hill; 238–1300.

Cafes and Delis: *Brasserie.* The Warwick Hotel, Center City; 925–2317.

Houlihan's Old Place. 225 S. 18th, Center City; 546–5940.

H.T. McDoogal's. 407 S. 2nd, Society Hill; 592–7460.

Sassafras. 48 S. 2nd, Old City; 925–2317.

O'Brien's. Bellevue Stratford Hotel, Walnut and Broad, Center City; 893–1852. This is a meeting place for older singles who don't want to dress up for *élan.* The atmosphere is Tiffany-lamp Nostalgic, with a wide-screen TV for sports events. Open Monday–Saturday.

AN OLD-FASHIONED SUPPER CLUB

Palumbo's. 824 Catharine, South Philadelphia; 627–7272. This is a huge, noisy Philadelphia institution that features family-style entertainment like Patti Page and James Darren. Shows change frequently and are included with the price of dinner (entrees start at $14). No cards.

COMEDY TONIGHT

Comedy Connection. 2031 Sansom St., Center City; 557–9041. Nationally acclaimed comedy talent at this new comedy cabaret. Performances Thursday–Saturday nights, with late-night shows on the weekends.

Comedy Factory Outlet. 31 Bank (between Market and Chestnut, 2nd and 3rd), Old City; 386–6911. Funny stuff ranging from local comics (open-stage night is Thursday) to the young pros Thursday–Saturday nights.

Comedy Works. 126 Chestnut, Old City; 922–5997. Philadelphia's original full-time comedy club is located upstairs over The Middle East restaurant. Top young comics from both coasts perform nightly Wednesday–Sunday. Wednesday is open-stage night when anyone who thinks they're funny can sign up at 8 and prove it at 9.

Going Bananas. 613 S. 2nd, Society Hill; 226–2621. No open stage night at this comedy nightclub, just professional comics with performances at 9 and 11:30 on Friday night, 8:30 and 11 Saturday night. Admission $6.

OUTSIDE PHILADELPHIA

Beyond Philadelphia's city limits lie farms and small cities, green rolling hills and wooded countryside. Here is a land rich in the memories of the American Revolution: battles were won and lost, men suffered through brutal winters, Washington and his troops made the historic crossing of the Delaware River. The area became home for many Colonists. German and Swiss immigrants, later called "Pennsylvania Dutch," settled here, including the Amish who can still be seen on the highways in their horse-drawn buggies.

First this chapter will explore the area south of Philadelphia—Brandywine Valley, home of the wealthy Du Ponts. North of Philadelphia, Bucks County offers historic sites, as well as the popular town of New Hope with its many shops and galleries. West of Philadelphia is Valley Forge, a turnpike-ride from Reading, the "Factory Outlet Capital of the World." Farther west is the Pennsylvania Dutch Country of Lancaster County.

EXPLORING THE BRANDYWINE VALLEY

The rustically beautiful Brandywine Valley is an area rich with history, the site of one of the more dramatic turns in the American Revolutionary War. This is Wyeth Country, where three generations of the famous artistic family have found suitably handsome landscapes to test their talents. However, Brandywine Valley is perhaps best known as the "kingdom" of the wealthy Du Ponts, the French bureaucratic family (originally named Du Pont de Nemours) who fled post-Revolutionary France and settled in upper Delaware. The family's fortune was first made here in gunpowder and iron, later in chemicals and textiles. Many of the Du Ponts' spectacular estates and gardens are now open to the public.

Brandywine Valley, about 35 miles south of Philadelphia, actually incorporates parts of three counties in two states: Chester and Delaware counties in Pennsylvania, New Castle County in Delaware. Chester, first settled in 1655, was the first colony in the state of Pennsylvania. Seventeen years later, William Penn arrived in the area and set up what later would serve as a governmental structure; Chester was to become Pennsylvania's first capital. Brandywine Valley is dotted with museums, antique shops, high-quality restaurants, cozy country inns, and reliable bed and breakfasts.

Longwood Gardens

Longwood Gardens (Route 1, Chadds Ford), with its 350 acres of meticulously landscaped gardens, is arguably the Valley's leading attraction. The home of Pierre Samuel Du Pont (1870–1954), the more than 1,000 acres of gardens originally were used as a summer estate in which Du Pont would play host to his many friends and relatives. His frequent trips abroad explain the use of styles simulating the French, Italian, and English. Du Pont developed a horticulturist's flair, with a keen understanding of wide varieties of flowers.

Longwood Gardens attracts hundreds of thousands of visitors each year—necessitating 190 full-time employees and numerous part-time help to maintain it. The feel here is of eternal summertime; the conservatories are always in bloom. Longwood Gardens also presents concerts and festivals throughout the year, replete with summer "dancing waters" displays. It is clearly one of the world's foremost public gardens.

Brandywine Battlefield Park, also in Chadds Ford, is a popular site for history buffs. The Battle of Brandywine took place nearby on September 11, 1777, a major defeat for General George Washington and his troops. The army then fled to Lancaster, leaving Philadelphia

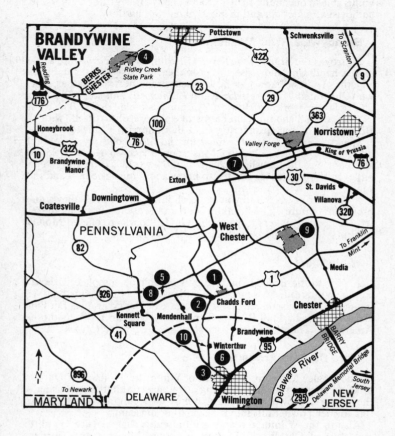

Points of Interest

1) Brandywine Battlefield Museum
2) Brandywine River Museum
3) Hagley Museum
4) Hopewell Village National Historic Site
5) Longwood Gardens
6) Nemours Mansion & Gardens
7) People's Light & Theater Co.
8) Phillips Mushroom Place
9) Tyler Arboretum
10) Winterthur Museum & Gardens

vulnerable to oncoming British troops. The park's Visitor Center offers audiovisual materials and displays about the battle.

Brandywine River Museum

Nearby is the Brandywine River Museum, a former grist mill turned into a handsome showcase for prominent artists—most notably the Wyeths: Andrew, known for his landscapes and portraits; father, N. C., who illustrated *Treasure Island* and *Kidnapped;* and son Jamie. Also on display are works by Howard Pyle and Maxfield Parrish. The woodsy area around the museum seems like a work of art itself, with the Brandywine River meandering right by unhurried picnickers.

Spend several hours at the museum and then move onto an entirely different experience—Phillip's Mushroom Place, in Kennett Square, also known as the "mushroom capital of the world." Here you can find out everything you ever wanted to know about mushrooms—and then some!

A short drive away and you can cash in on one of the Valley's most profitable ventures: The Franklin Mint and Museum, in Franklin Center. (Keep your fingers to yourself!) Guided tours are offered Monday to Friday at this, the largest mint in the world.

Winterthur

A visit to the Brandywine Valley wouldn't be complete without a stop at Winterthur Museum and Gardens, just six miles north of Wilmington. The museum, actually the estate of Henry Francis Du Pont, displays silver by Paul Revere, furniture by Duncan Phyfe, and other Americana. There are 196 room settings made prior to 1850.

More Du Pont Properties

The Hagley Museum, just south of Winterthur, is another Du Pont property turned into an intriguing attraction. Exhibitions focusing on the industrial growth of the country since its beginnings help transform this former powdermill into a fascinating museum.

Also in the Wilmington area are museums that capture the glitter and style of Old World Europe. Nemours Mansion and Gardens, owned by Alfred I. Du Pont, offers 300 acres of French gardens. Antiques abound, with the mansion done in the style of Louis XVI. Some of the paintings here date back five centuries. (It should be noted that children under the age of 16 are not allowed entry.)

Rockwood, the Shipley-Bringhurst-Hargraves Museum built in 1851 by Joseph Shipley, is English in nature, with 400 years' worth of decorative art on display.

The Historical Society of Delaware in Wilmington displays a wide spectrum of material that helped shape the area's history. The Delaware Art Museum, meanwhile, offers a permanent display of art by

Howard Pyle, the "father of American illustration." In addition to displays of several schools of American art there is a collection of works from Victorian England.

In a day trip out of Philadelphia, pack a picnic lunch and head first to Longwood Gardens, then the Brandywine River Museum, then Winterthur. If you have more time, an overnight stay at a country inn and a leisurely exploration of more of this beautiful area makes a great getaway after city sightseeing.

PRACTICAL INFORMATION FOR THE

BRANDYWINE VALLEY

HOW TO GET THERE. Philadelphia will be your gateway. See "How to Get There" in *Practical Information for Philadelphia*. **From Philadelphia by car:** head south on Route 1. Brandywine Valley is about 35 miles from Philadelphia. **By bus:** Both *Greyhound* (215–568–4800) and *Trailways* (215–569 –3100) have bus service from Philadelphia to Wilmington, Del.

TELEPHONES. The area code for the Pennsylvania section of the Brandywine Valley is 215 (from Philadelphia, dial "1" before the number); for the Wilmington, DE, section it is 302. Directory assistance is available by dialing 1–555–1212. Operator assistance is available by first dialing "0" before your number. For directory information from outside the area, dial "1," the area code and then 555–1212. To find out if establishments have toll-free numbers, dial 1–800–555–1212.

HOTELS AND MOTELS. Lodging is plentiful in the Brandywine Valley—from country inns to luxurious resorts; it is relatively easy to find a hotel/inn to your liking. Hotel rates listed below are based on double occupancy, European Plan, unless otherwise noted. Accommodations are grouped by location and price: *Super Deluxe,* $100 and up; *Deluxe,* $80 and up; *Expensive,* $70 to $79; *Moderate,* $60 to $69; and *Inexpensive,* $50 to $59. See *Facts at Your Fingertips* at the beginning of this book for more information on our accommodation categories.

DOWNINGTOWN

Ramada Downingtown Inn. *Super Deluxe.* Route 30; (215) 269–2000. A truly luxurious 469-room resort with pools, sauna, miniature golf, indoor rifle range. Dining room, dinner theater, and nightclub. Modified American Plan.

Tabas Hotel. *Super Deluxe.* Route 30; (215) 269–6000. With some 300 rooms and varied sports facilities, this resort offers something for everyone. Dining room, dinner theater, and night club. Modified American Plan.

EXTON

Duling-Kurtz House and Country Inn. *Deluxe.* 146 S. Whitford Rd.; (215) 524–1830. One of the finest inns in the state. Lovingly, meticulously restored with a homey, yet sophisticated touch. 18 guest rooms named after prominent Americans—and Winston Churchill. Continental breakfast included in rate.

HONEY BROOK

Waynebrook Inn. *Deluxe.* Route 322 and 10; 273–2444. An elegant inn in Pennsylvania Dutch Country. Redesigned, the 17 guest rooms are roomy yet cozy. A special package includes such items as Continental breakfast, dinner, champagne, and a welcome fruit and cheese tray.

KENNETT SQUARE

Longwood Inn. *Inexpensive.* 815 E. Baltimore Pike; (215) 444–3515. A family-owned operation with 28 rooms. Convenient to Longwood Gardens.

LIONVILLE

Holiday Inn of Lionville. *Moderate.* Route 100; (215) 363–1100. 213 rooms. Two pools.

MENDENHALL

Mendenhall Inn. *Inexpensive.* Route 52; (215) 388–1181. A lovely 15-room inn ideally situated for many of the area's attractions.

POTTSTOWN

Coventry Forge Inn. *Inexpensive.* RD 2, off Route 23, 1½ miles west of intersection of Routes 23 and 100; (215) 469–6222. A nice country inn with five rooms. Continental breakfast included.

ST. DAVIDS

St. Davids Inn. *Expensive.* 591 East Lancaster Ave.; (215) 688–5800. With 174 rooms, this nicely situated hotel offers many amenities.

WILMINGTON (DE)

Hotel Du Pont. *Super Deluxe.* 11th and Market sts.; (302) 656–8121. An elegantly styled 280-room hotel with an Old World feel.

BED-AND-BREAKFASTS. See under *Practical Information for Philadelphia.*

TOURIST INFORMATION. For information, you can call or write to the following organizations: *Chester County Tourist Bureau,* 33 W. Market St., West Chester, PA 19380 (215–431–6365). *Delaware County Tourist Bureau,* 602 E. Baltimore Pike, Media, PA 19063 (215–565–3679 or 353–8108). *Greater Wilmington Convention and Visitors Bureau,* Box 111, Wilmington, DE 19899 (302–652–4088).

SEASONAL EVENTS. Each month seems to bring a different highlight to the Brandywine Valley. **January:** *"Welcome Spring" at Longwood Gardens* (continuing to April 30). **February:** *Tyler Arboretum Maple Sugar Festival,* last Sunday of the month. **April:** *Longwood Gardens Easter Conservatory Display; Pennsylvania Crafts Fair* at Brandywine River Museum. **May:** *Winterthur Point-to-Point Races; Devon Horse Show and Country Fair,* country's oldest horse show featuring world-championship horses competing in 34 divisions at Devon Fairgrounds, Rt. 30; 964–0550; *Brandywine River Museum Annual Antique Show and Sale.* **June:** *Longwood Gardens Illuminated Fountain Displays* (through Labor Day). **July:** *Hopewell Village 4th of July Celebration.* **August:** *Nottingham County Fair.* **September.** *Battle of Brandywine Reenactment; Chadds Ford Days and Country Fair.* **October:** *Yellow Springs Antique Show.* **November:** *Hagley Museum Crafts Fair; Longwood Gardens Chrysanthemum Festival.* **December:** *Yuletide at Winterthur; Longwood Gardens* (month-long) *Christmas Display.*

TOURS. *Gray Line Tours,* (215) 568–6111, *New Jersey Transit,* (215) 567–2947, and *SEPTA Bus Rambles,* (215) 574–7800, all offer tours to Longwood Gardens and Winterthur throughout the year. Call for more information.

GARDENS. While many museums and historical sites in the area are beautifully landscaped, none can touch the grandeur of *Longwood Gardens,* Route 1, Kennett Square (388–6741). The gardens are in bloom year round. Open every day of the year and many evenings. Adults $5; children 6–14, $1; children under 5 free.

HISTORIC SITES. (See also "Museums," below.) The *Brandywine Battlefield Park,* Route 1, Chadds Ford (459–3342), is a prime attraction for thousands of visitors. Nearby, Washington and his men fought in the Battle of Brandywine, a major loss for the Colonials during the American Revolution. On the site is a renovated farmhouse which once served Washington and Lafayette. Open April–October, noon to 5 P.M. Adults $2; seniors citizens and children; $1; under 6 free.

The *Historical Society of Delaware.* 505 Market St., Wilmington; 655–7161. Walk back through the early days of Wilmington's history in the society's handsomely renovated Old Town Hall Museum at 512 Market St. Mall, with its nine-foot wooden statue of George Washington. Open Tuesday to Friday, noon to 4 P.M.; Saturday, 10 A.M. to 4 P.M. Free.

MUSEUMS. If it appears that the Brandywine Valley has a museum on each peak—well, it just seems that way. In reality, the region affords a large number of first-quality museums, covering varied aspects of culture and history. (See also "Historic Sites.")

The Brandywine River Museum. At Routes 1 and 100, Chadds Ford; 388–7601. This is Wyeth country and the three generations are well-represented here in a beautiful country setting. Open daily 9:30 A.M. to 4:30 P.M. Adults $2, seniors, students and children, $1; under 6 free.

Delaware Art Museum. 2301 Kentmere Parkway, Wilmington; 571–9590. Specializing in collections from the "Brandywine School" of painting, it also houses the largest collection of English Pre-Raphaelite paintings in the country. Admission free. Open Monday–Saturday, 10 A.M. to 5 P.M.; Sunday, 1 P.M. to 5 P.M.

Franklin Mint and Museum. Route 1, Franklin Center; 459–6168. The largest private mint in the world. Guided tours. Open Monday–Friday, 9 A.M. to 3 P.M. Museum features exhibits of collectibles, jewelry, and art and the documentary film *Of Art and Minting.* Open Tuesday–Saturday, 9:30 A.M. to 4:30 P.M.; Sunday, 1 P.M. to 4:30 P.M. Admission to both is free.

The Hagley Museum. Wilmington; 658–2400. Another Du Pont site, once a powdermill, Hagley is now a restored mill community and powder yard featuring equipment demonstrations. Tuesday–Saturday, 9:30 A.M. to 4:30 P.M.; Sunday, 1 P.M. to 5 P.M. Adults $4; seniors $3.50; children $1; under 6 free.

Mushroom Museum. Route 1, Kennett Square, one-half mile south of Longwood Gardens; 388–6082. Exhibits relate everything you ever wanted to know about mushrooms. Open daily 10 A.M. to 6 P.M. Free admission.

Nemours Mansion and Gardens. Rockland Rd., Wilmington; 651–6912. A 300-acre estate comparable to France's Versailles Palace. Open Tuesday–Sunday, May through November. Call for tour reservations and fees.

Rockwood, the Shipley-Bringhurst-Hargraves Museum. 610 Shipley Rd., Wilmington; 571–7776. Four hundred years of arts and archives from here and abroad. Open Tuesday–Saturday, 11 A.M. to 4 P.M. Adults $2; seniors and children, 75 cents.

Winterthur Museum and Gardens. Route 52, Winterthur; 654–1548. The world's greatest collection of decorative arts made or used between 1640 and 1840—furniture, silver, paintings, textiles—displayed in appropriate room settings. Tuesday–Saturday, 10 A.M. to 4 P.M.; Sunday, noon to 4 P.M. Just show up for unreserved tour ($7) or call ahead for special tours of various sections of the museum ($10).

 THEATER. The *People's Light and Theater Company,* 38 Conestoga Rd., Malvern (644–3500), offers a varied schedule during their April to January season, including a summer New Play Festival.

 DINING OUT. Fine dining is available throughout the Brandywine Valley. The following restaurants are grouped according to location and divided into price categories determined by the cost of an average meal for one person, not including drinks, tax, or tip: *Deluxe:* $20 and up; *Expensive,* $15 to $20; *Moderate,* $8 to $15; and *Inexpensive,* under $8. For credit card and meal abbreviations used below see "Dining Out" in *Practical Information for Philadelphia.*

EXTON

Duling-Kurtz House and Country Inn. *Deluxe.* 146 S. Whitford Rd.; 524–1830. Fine dining in a romantic atmosphere. This restaurant even offers a secluded table for two with personally engraved napkin holders. L, D Monday–Friday; D only, Saturday; SB. All major cards.

HONEY BROOK

Waynebrook Inn. *Deluxe.* Routes 322 and 10; 273–2444. Gourmet dining in a spirited atmosphere. B, L, D Tuesday–Saturday. All major cards.

LIONVILLE

Vickers Tavern. *Deluxe.* Welsh Pool Rd. and Gordon Drive; 363–6336. A lovely, intimate restaurant with separate rooms holding a surprisingly large number of diners. Food is creatively gourmet; service impeccable. Tavern was once used as a station for the underground railroad. Pottery dinnerware is made on the premises. L, D Monday–Friday; D only, Saturday. AE, MC, V.

POTTSTOWN

Coventry Forge Inn. *Expensive.* 1½ miles west of intersection of Routes 100 and 23, just off 23; 469–6222. Nice atmosphere for some delightful French cuisine. The duck is a specialty and one can easily see why. D Tuesday–Saturday; D Monday, May to October only. AE, MC, V.

CHADDS FORD

Chadds Ford Inn. *Moderate.* Route 100; 388–7361. A beautiful inn with good, hearty food expertly served. Right in the heart of the Valley. L, D Monday–Saturday; D only, Sunday. All major cards.

EXPLORING BUCKS COUNTY

Bucks County could have remained 625 square miles of sleepy countryside full of old stone farmhouses, lush rolling hills, and quaint covered bridges if it hadn't been discovered by New York's Beautiful Brainy People in the '30s. Luminaries like writers Dorothy Parker and S.J. Perelman and composer Oscar Hammerstein bought country homes here, an easy commute from Manhattan. Pulitzer Prize and Nobel winning-author Pearl S. Buck lived here, choosing the area because it was "a region where the landscapes were varied, where farm and industry lived side by side, where the sea was near at hand, mountains not far away, and city and countryside were not enemies." Over the years, Bucks County has become known for its arts colonies and antiques, pre-theater tryouts and country inns. And while parts of the county have fallen prey to urban sprawl and the developers' bulldozers, there are places in Upper Bucks County that remain as bucolic as they were 50 years ago.

Pennsbury Manor

The county is a treasure trove for history buffs. Among the most interesting sites to visit is Pennsbury Manor, a careful reconstruction of the brick Georgian-style mansion William Penn built for himself in the late 1600s. Situated on a gentle rise 150 yards from the Delaware River, the manor house was the scene of lavish entertainments put on by Penn in his role as governor of the colony. Penn actually lived in Pennsbury Manor for only eighteen months, starting in 1700. His daughter and second wife didn't care for country life, so he was compelled to move back to the city. History portrays the man as a dour, drably dressed Quaker, but he enjoyed the good life, importing the finest of provisions and keeping a vast retinue of servants and slaves. All his extravagances led to increasing financial difficulties that resulted in the 9 months Penn spent in debtor's prison in 1708.

The manor house, the work buildings, and 40 of the original 8,400 acres of the estate have been reconstructed to provide a microcosm of seventeenth-century life in America. Among the antique furnishings in the house are some fine William and Mary and Jacobean pieces as well as some of Penn's own furniture. Formal gardens, vineyards and orchards, an ice house, smokehouse, bake and brew house, and collections of tools attest to the orderly, self-sufficient nature of Penn's early community.

Fallsington, the Colonial village six miles away where Penn went to church, mirrors three centuries of American architecture, from a seventeenth-century log cabin to Victorian excesses of the late 1800s. Four historic buildings, including the log cabin, have been restored and furnished and are open to the public for guided tours. Two dozen eighteenth-century houses are still standing, occupied by descendants of the original settlers or by owners who enjoy being a living part of history.

Washington Crossing Historic Park

North of Fallsington on Route 32 is Washington Crossing Historic Park. This 500-acre park on the banks of the Delaware marks the site where George Washington and 2,400 troops crossed the icy river on Christmas night 1776 to successfully surprise the Hessian mercenaries at Trenton. In the Lower Park, at the fieldstone Memorial Building, you will find a reproduction of Emanuel Leutze's famous painting of the crossing (the original is in the Metropolitan Museum of Art in New York) and hear a ten-minute narration of the events leading up to the attack. (Even more realistic is the annual Christmas Day reenactment of the crossing, when local businessmen dress in Colonial uniforms and

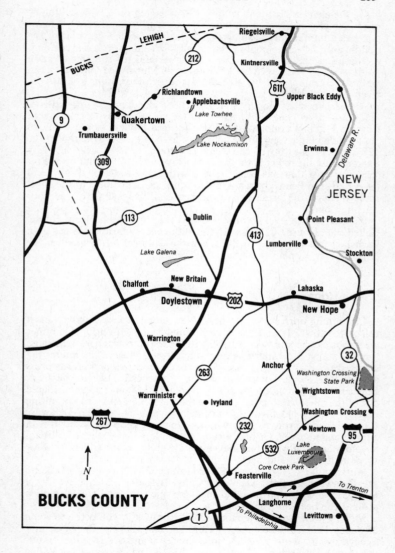

BUCKS COUNTY

brave the elements in small boats.) The Washington Crossing Library of the American Revolution, in the west wing of the Memorial Building, has a number of Washington's letters on display. In front of the building is a reflecting pool with a statue of Washington at one end and, at the other, stairs leading down the riverbank to the embarkation point. A short walk away is the restored and furnished Old Ferry Inn where the general and his staff ate dinner while waiting to cross the river.

About five miles north on Route 32 is the Upper Park with its landmark, Bowman's Hill, named after a surgeon who sailed with Captain Kidd. Washington used the hill as a lookout point. You can get a much better view of the countryside than he did by climbing the 121 steps to the top of the memorial tower erected here in 1930. Surrounding the tower is the 100-acre Bowman's Hill Wildflower Preserve, an area that has been planted with flowers, trees, shrubs, and ferns native to Pennsylvania. Guided tours are available, but the short trails through the preserve are marked and bring you back to your starting point.

Farther up the river to New Hope is the Thompson-Neely House. Called the "House of Decision," the 18th-century farmhouse has been furnished to look just as it did when the Colonial leaders met in the large kitchen to plan the attack on Trenton.

New Hope

Continuing upriver, you come to New Hope, Bucks County's most celebrated town. It's a village, really, and best seen on foot. Summer weekends can be mob scenes here, with pedestrians wandering through the tiny shops and galleries along Main Street. Most of the interesting sights are clustered along four blocks of Main Street and on the cross streets—Mechanic, Ferry, and Bridge—that head down to the river. Bucks County Playhouse is on the river side of Main. Long considered one of the finest summer theaters on the East Coast, it is still mounting productions of old favorites and soon-to-be classics. The Delaware Canal threads through the town, and you can glide lazily down it in a mule-pulled barge. Or take a ride on the New Hope Steam Railroad, an old steam railway that makes an 8½-mile round trip from New Hope to Lahaska and back.

North of New Hope, River Road (Route 32) winds scenically along the Delaware, and the Delaware Canal is frequently in view. It's a lovely drive with charming old inns and ancient stone houses hidden around the bends in the road.

Moving west from New Hope along Route 202, you come to some of Pennsylvania's wine country. Here you can visit the Bucks County Vineyards and Winery, see the small museum and taste the local product. South off Route 202 on Route 413 is the Buckingham Valley Vineyard and Winery, open for tours and tastings.

Not far from here is the town of Lahaska, the center of antique shopping in Bucks County. The bargain-priced American treasures that gave the area its early reputation as an antique-hunter's paradise are few and far between these days, but there are a number of excellent shops with good reputations for quality. In addition to antiques (there is good prowling all the way from New Hope to Doylestown on Route 202), Lahaska has three popular shopping areas. Peddler's Village is a colony of 45 quaint shoppes and restaurants where you'll find clothing, Colonial crafts, and antiques. The Yard and Penn's Market are two other complexes.

Home of Henry Mercer

Continuing west on Route 202 you'll reach Doylestown, the county seat. An important coach stop in the eighteenth century, the town is best known as the home of Henry Chapman Mercer. Bucks County has seen its share of eccentrics, but even in such august company Henry Mercer stands out. The curator of American and Prehistoric Archaeology at the University of Pennsylvania Museum, master potter, self-taught architect, and writer of gothic tales, Dr. Mercer left a legacy of artistic creativity when he died in 1930 at the age of seventy-four. He also left a house, a museum and a pottery and tile works that's still functioning today. These three monuments make up what's known as Mercer Mile in Doylestown. The buildings (all of which are open to the public from March through December) are distinguished by being built entirely of reinforced concrete—even built-in cabinets and shelves are concrete. His mansion, Fonthill, took twenty-eight years to complete, and every room is decorated with the Moravian tiles Dr. Mercer became famous for designing. It's an enormous, bizarre house with rooms of varying shapes and sizes and multiple levels connected by narrow winding stairs. The Moravian Pottery and Tile works are on the grounds of the estate. Here "Mercer" tiles, the unique picture tiles that he created, are made. They can be found in houses all around Eastern Pennsylvania, decorating fireplaces or inset into exterior masonry.

Perhaps the most unusual of his legacies is the Mercer Museum. Dr. Mercer was an inveterate collector, and as early as 1897 he was gathering implements, tools, and crafts from all over Bucks County that were to form the basis for a collection that ultimately included over 40,000 objects. These are attractively and cleverly displayed in the museum which he designed himself—an arrangement of galleries around a central courtyard. Items from the collection are wired to ceilings and walls, or grouped together by trade behind windows in the rooms facing the galleries. The collection includes such unrelated things as a log-sled, cheese press, fire engine, and bean huller.

North of Doylestown are some of Bucks County's famous covered bridges. Thirteen of the original thirty-six bridges are still standing. They're delightful to stumble upon, but if you're serious about seeing them, you can get a brochure with the history and precise location of each from the Bucks County Tourist Commission.

Also in the northern part of the county are some fine parks—many with canoes for rent—well-marked trails for biking and hiking, and camping facilities. Among the best are Lake Nockamixon, a 1,450-acre lake surrounded by a state park near Quakertown; Tohickon Valley Park and Ralph Stover Park, county and state parks respectively, joined along Tohickon Creek near Point Pleasant; and Lake Towhee east of Applebachsville. In the south are Core Creek Park, 1,200 acres with fishing and boating on Lake Luxembourg; and Neshaminy State Park near Croydon.

PRACTICAL INFORMATION FOR BUCKS

COUNTY

HOW TO GET THERE. For information on getting to Philadelphia, the gateway to Bucks County, see "How to Get There" in *Practical Information for Philadelphia*. Bucks County is a large area—40 miles long and 16 miles across at its widest—and it's almost impossible to tour it without a car. The easiest way to get there by car from Philadelphia is via I–95. *SEPTA* has limited bus service from Philadelphia to some areas of Bucks County. For information, call (215) 574–7800 or 734–3880. *Greyhound Bus Lines* (215–568–4800) offers service to Quakertown and Doylestown from Philadelphia. From Doylestown, it's possible to get to New Hope and Lahaska via the *West Hunterdon bus line* (215–345–0468). *New Jersey Transit* (215–567–2947) travels between Philadelphia and New Hope. (See also "Tours," below.)

TELEPHONES. The Bucks County area code is the same as Philadelphia's—215. From Philadelphia, dial "1" before dialing the local Bucks County number. For toll-free directory assistance outside the area, call 1–215–555–1212. To determine whether a business you want to reach has a toll-free 800 number, call 1–800–555–1212 for information.

HOTELS, MOTELS, AND INNS. Bucks County has lodging that ranges from the most modern of the motel chains to quaint bed-and-breakfast spots where you have to share the bathroom. The smaller inns frequently require two-nights' minimum stay on weekends. Price categories are *Inexpensive,* under $55 for double occupancy; *Moderate,* $55–75; *Expensive,* $75–95; *Deluxe,* $95–125. Credit cards accepted unless noted.

DOYLESTOWN

Doylestown Inn. *Inexpensive to moderate.* 18 W. State; (215) 345–6610. A historic Victorian inn with 21 rooms. Private baths, air conditioning, Continental breakfast, and tax included in room rates. All meals available, evening entertainment.

ERWINNA

Golden Pheasant Inn. *Inexpensive.* River Road north of Pt. Pleasant; (215) 294–9595. Victorian antiques furnish the 14 rooms of this inn. Shared baths, Continental breakfast, and tax included in room rates. No dinner service Monday.

LUMBERVILLE

Black Bass Hotel. *Moderate to deluxe.* River Road north of New Hope; (215) 297–5770. Built in 1745, this small hotel offers rooms with shared baths and deluxe suites with private baths. Continental breakfast included. No dinner service Sunday. Evening entertainment weekends.

1740 House. *Moderate.* River Road north of New Hope; (215) 297–5661. Balconies, terraces, and private bathrooms are among the amenities offered in this inn located on the banks of the Delaware. Swimming, boating available. Breakfast included. Dinner available. No cards.

POINT PLEASANT

Innisfree Inn. *Moderate.* Cafferty Rd.; (215) 297–8329. An old fieldstone mill has been converted to a romantic inn with 10 rooms, most with private baths. Breakfast, tea included. No cards.

NEW HOPE

Holiday Inn. *Moderate.* Route 202; (215)862–5221. All the comforts of modern motel living, including a restaurant and cocktail lounge, and entertainment nightly.

Hotel du Village. *Inexpensive to moderate.* N. River Rd. and Phillips Mill Rd.; (215)862–9911 and 862–5164. Hidden around a bend on River Road, this hotel has an excellent restaurant and rooms, located in a separate building, that are pleasant and modern rather than charming and romantic. Private baths. Continental breakfast included. AE only.

New Hope Motel in the Woods. *Inexpensive.* Rt. 179; (215) 862–2800. This modern AAA-member offers color TV, swimming pool, and, of course, private baths. Two night minimum on weekends, three night minimum on holiday weekends.

QUAKERTOWN

Best Western. *Inexpensive.* 1446 W. Broad St. off Rt. 309; (215)536–2500. Modern accommodations near shopping and restaurants.

WARRINGTON

Warrington Motor Lodge. *Inexpensive.* Rts. 611 and 132; (215)343–0373. Swimming pool, restaurant, and lounge.

BED AND BREAKFASTS. See reservation services under *Practical Information for Philadelphia.*

 SEASONAL EVENTS. January: *Yardley Antique Show.* **February:** *Gingerbread at the Thompson-Neely House,* Washington Crossing Historic Park. **March:** *Charter Day at Pennsbury Manor.* **May:** *Strawberry Festival,* Peddler's Village; *Kite Flying Day,* Core Creek Park; *Folk Fest,* Mercer Museum grounds, Doylestown; *Green Hills Farm Country Fair,* Dublin. **June:** *Craft Fair,* Wrightstown; *Buckingham Antiques Show,* Tyro Hall; *Village Fair,* Doylestown; *Flower Show,* New Hope. **July:** *Heart of Bucks Antique Auto Show,* Doylestown; *Tinicum Art Festival,* Erwinna; *Warrington Lions Horse Show,* Warrington. **August:** *New Hope Auto Show; Middletown Grange Fair,* Wrightstown; *Market Day and Festival,* Quakertown; *Antique Show,* Doylestown. **September:** *Polish Festival,* New Britain Township; *Market Day,* Newtown; *Scottish Country Fair,* Pipersville; *Open Gate Farm Tour,* Bucks County Farms; *Harvest Day,* Canal Street, Yardley. **October:** *Phillips Mill Art Exhibit,* New Hope. *Historic Fallsington Day,* Fallsington; *Historic Bristol Day,* Bristol. **November:** *Apple Festival,* Peddler's Village; *Antique Show,* New Hope; *Antique Show,* Newtown. **December:** *Buckingham Antiques Show,* Tyro Hall; *Open House Tour,* Newtown; *Christmas Festival,* Peddler's Village; *Holly Night,* Pennsbury Manor; *Reenactment of Washington crossing the Delaware,* Christmas Day, Washington Crossing Historic Park.

 TOURIST INFORMATION. Brochures, maps, and information about Bucks County are available from the *Bucks County Tourist Commission,* 152 Swamp Rd., Doylestown, PA 18901; (215) 345–4552. Phone, write or drop in weekdays from 8:15 A.M. til 4:15 P.M. Specific information about the area around *New Hope* is available from that town's information center at the corner of S. Main and Mechanic sts., open daily; (215) 862–5880.

 TOURS. During the spring there are *SEPTA* "Rambles"—bus trips several times a month from Philadelphia to attractions like New Hope, Peddler's Village in Lahaska, and the farmers' market in Quakertown. Call (215) 734–3880 for schedules and rates.

 **SPECIAL INTEREST TOURS.** *Mule Barge,* New and S. Main sts., 862–2842. One-hour narrated excursions rides up the Delaware Canal in a mule-drawn barge. Season: April 1–November 15. April 1–April 20: Wednesday, Saturday, Sunday, 1, 2, 3, and 4:30 P.M. May 1–October 15: daily at 11:30 A.M., 1, 2, 3, 4:30, and 6 P.M. October 16–November 15: Wednesday, Saturday, Sunday, 11:30 A.M., 1, 2, 3, and 4:30 P.M. (other days as well, weather permitting). Adults $4.95, senior citizens $4.50, students (with I.D.) $4.25, children under 12 $2.75.

New Hope Steam Railway, station near canal off W. Bridge St., 752–1942. Ride through scenic Bucks County in an old steam train, over the curved trestle made famous in the rescue scenes from the *Perils of Pauline* movies. May–October, Saturday 1:30 and 3:30 P.M.; Sunday 1:15, 2:45, 4:15 P.M.; November, Sunday 1:30 and 3:15. Adults $5, senior citizens $4.75, children $3. For more information write to P.O. Box 352, Penndel, Pa. 19047.

PARKS. For brochures and additional information about Bucks County Parks, write to the *Bucks County Tourist Commission,* 152 Swamp Rd., Doylestown, Pa. 18901; 345–4552.

Core Creek Park, Bridgetown Pike, Langhorne. Fishing and boating, boat rental in summer, bike path, horse trails, tennis, baseball fields, pavilions, picnic areas.

Lake Nockamixon State Park, Route 563, Quakertown. Boating and boat rental, swimming pool, bike path and bike rental, hiking trails, ice skating and sledding in winter, trap shooting, picnic areas.

Lake Towhee Park, Old Bethlehem Pike, Applebachsville. 17 campsites (call 757–0571 for application form), baths and showers, fishing, boating, pavilions, and picnic areas.

Neshaminy State Park, State Rd., Bensalem. Boating, hiking trails, swimming pool, picnic areas, food concession.

Tohickon Valley Park, Cafferty Rd., Point Pleasant. 28 campsites, 3 cabins and a lodge available for rental (for camping application form, call 757–0571), swimming pool, pavilion, ballfield, creek fishing.

Ralph Stover State Park, State Park Rd., Pipersville. Cabin camping (call 982–5560 for application form), pavilions, playground, rock climbing, and scenic view of neighboring Tohickon Valley Park from "High Rocks" overlook.

CHILDREN'S ACTIVITIES. *Sesame Place* (I-95 at Levittown-Oxford Valley exit, Langhorne; 757–1100) is a recreation park designed for kids from 3 to 13 (but older children—and adults—enjoy it just as much as the youngsters do). Featured are water slides (bring bathing suits), a computer gallery, the Count's Gallery (a room filled with 180,000 balls to climb through), and a variety of other activities named after Bert and Ernie and Big Bird and all the Sesame Street favorites. Open daily 10 A.M. to 8 P.M. from mid-April to mid-October. Children's admission $8.80; adults $6.60; children under 6 free.

HISTORIC SITES AND MUSEUMS. *Fallsington,* south off Rt. 1 at Tyburn Rd.; 295–6567. The pre-Revolutionary village where William Penn worshipped. Four buildings have been restored and furnished. Open March 15 to November 15, Wednesday–Sunday, 11 A.M. to 4 P.M. Adults, $2; students $1, children between 6 and 12, 50 cents.

Fonthill. Rt. 313 and E. Court St., Doylestown; 348–9461. Henry Chapman Mercer's bizarre concrete castle and home. Guided tours. Reservations suggested. Open March to December, Tuesday–Sunday, 10 A.M. to 3:30 P.M. Adults $3; senior citizens $2.50; students $1.50.

Mercer Museum. Pine St., Doylestown; 345–0210. Over 40,000 tools and household items collected by Henry Chapman Mercer during his lifetime and artfully arranged. Self-guided tours. Open March to December, Monday–Saturday, 10 A.M. to 4:30 P.M.; Sunday, 1 P.M. to 4:30 P.M. Adults $3; senior citizens $2.50; students $1.50.

Moravian Pottery and Tile Works. Rt. 313 and E. Court St., Doylestown; 345–6722. Mercer tiles are still made here. Open March to December, Wednesday–Sunday, 10 A.M. to 4 P.M. Adults $1.75; senior citizens and students $1; family $3.50.

Pennsbury Manor. Rt. 13 off Tyburn Rd., Morrisville; 946–0400. A reconstruction of William Penn's country plantation. Open Tuesday–Saturday, 9 A.M.

to 5 P.M.; Sunday, noon to 5 P.M. Frequent tours. Adults $2.50; senior citizens $1.75; children ages 6 to 17, $1.

Washington Crossing Historic Park. Upper Park, Rt. 32, 3 miles south of New Hope. Lower Park, Rt. 32, 8 miles south of New Hope. 493–4076. The site of George Washington's historic crossing of the Delaware. The embarkation point is delineated. In addition to the historic buildings there are picnic pavilions and restrooms. Upper Park contains Bowman Hill Tower, a wildflower preserve, and the Thompson-Neely House. Lower Park is home of Memorial Building (inside is a replica of the famous painting commemorating the crossing) and the Visitor Center, the McConkey Ferry Inn and the Mahlon K. Taylor House. Open year-round. Buildings closed Monday during the winter. Free admission to grounds; fee charged for admission to historic houses.

 THEATER. *Bucks County Playhouse,* S. Main, New Hope. 1985 will mark this popular theater's 46th season. While it's long been known as a "summer theater," the Playhouse season runs from May through the first week of December, with nine scheduled performances each week. 1985 productions include hits like *Dracula, Mr. Roberts, Oklahoma, Evita,* and *Sweeney Todd.* For tickets and information, call 862–2041.

 SHOPPING. **New Hope** has long been known for its **antique** shops featuring collectibles that range from extremely fine examples of Early American craftsmanship to fun kitsch. The shops are generally open on weekends with weekday hours by appointment. It's safest to call first. Among the better establishments are *H & R Sandor, Inc.,* Rt. 202 and Reeder Mill Road, 862–9181; *Joseph Stanley Antiques, Ltd.,* Rt. 202, 862–9300; *Sterling,* 1 N. Main St., 862–3444; *Hobensack & Keller, Inc.,* W. Bridge St., 862–2406; and *Olde Hope Antiques,* Rt. 202, 862–5055.

Peddler's Village, The Yard, and **Penn's Market** are three clusters of shops that are located adjacent to each other on Route 202 between Lahaska and New Hope. Peddler's Village consists of over 45 restaurants and shops in an attractive Colonial-style setting. Here you can buy books, cookware, leather goods, dried wreaths, posters, candles, and a host of other decorative items. The Yard, while somewhat smaller, has a similar selection of attractive shops, and Penn's Market boasts a couple of antique shops in addition to more contemporary boutiques. Hours are 10–5 daily, till 9 Friday, and noon–5 Sunday.

Quakertown Farmers' Market, 201 Station Rd, 536–4115. Produce, poultry, cheese, and homemade baked goods are among the delectable products for sale in the 100 stalls of this busy market. Hours are 10–10 Friday and Saturday, 11–5 Sunday.

 DINING OUT. The price categories are based on a three-course dinner for one person, not including beverages, tax, or tip. *Inexpensive,* under $8.00; *Moderate,* $8 to $15; *Expensive,* $15 to $25; *Deluxe,* over $25. For information on credit card and meal abbreviations used below see "Dining Out," in *Practical Information for Philadelphia.*

DOYLESTOWN

Conti's Cross Keys Inn. *Expensive.* Rtes. 611 and 313; 348–3539. This historical landmark is a Bucks County institution specializing in Continental cuisine that can be inconsistent but is frequently very good. L, D Monday–Friday; D only, Saturday. AE, DC, MC, V.

West Side Bistro. *Moderate.* 57 W. State; 348–7293. The atmosphere is cozy and simple, and the fare is an interesting combination of French, American, and Oriental. They have no liquor license, but you can bring your own wine. L, Monday–Saturday; D, Wednesday–Saturday. MC, V.

ERWINNA

Golden Pheasant. *Expensive.* Route 32, 15 miles north of New Hope on River Road; 294–9595. A favorite retreat for romantics, this inn has a Victorian atmosphere and a lovely location on the Delaware Canal. The candlelit solarium is a favorite spot for dining, or you can sit in the cozy parlor. Food is international with a menu that changes seasonally. D, Tuesday–Sunday. AE, MC, V.

FEASTERVILLE

Angelo's. *Moderate.* Feasterville Plaza, Bustleton Pike; 355–6266. Good homemade pasta is the attraction at this popular Italian restaurant. L, D Monday–Saturday. All major cards.

El Sombrero. *Moderate.* 1046 Bustleton Pike; 347–3337. It's a long way from Tijuana, but the homemade Mexican food in this unassuming little restaurant is first rate. A good selection of tortilla dishes is available, as well as a variety of unusual authentic Mexican specialties. L, D Monday–Friday; D only, Saturday and Sunday. AE, MC, V.

LAHASKA

Animal Crackers. *Inexpensive.* Peddler's Village; 794–3311. An upscale, fast-food sandwich-and-salad spot that's a pleasant and convenient place to take a break from shopping. B, L, D daily. No cards.

Jenny's. *Expensive.* The Yard, Rt. 202; 794–5605. Despite the homespun name, this is a sleek, sophisticated restaurant all gussied up in velvet, mirrors, brass, and stained glass. The food is Continental with a bias toward nouvelle. L, Monday–Saturday; D, Tuesday–Sunday. SB. AE, MC, V.

NEW HOPE

Chez Odette. *Expensive.* S. River Road, 4 miles south of New Hope; 862–2432. The atmosphere here is French country bistro, with a Continental menu of old favorites. L, D Tuesday–Saturday; D only, Sunday. SB. AE, DC, MC, V.

Havana. *Moderate.* 105 S. Main; 862–9897. This isn't a fancy place, but the kitchen cares about what it's doing. The menu is eclectic and the view overlooking New Hope's Main Street is great for people-watching. L, D daily. No cards.

Hotel du Village. *Expensive.* Phillips Mill and N. River Rds. (north of New Hope); 862–5164. French cuisine served in a Tudor-style dining room or on the sun porch. It's a lovely setting. D, Wednesday–Sunday. AE.

Karla's. *Expensive.* 5 W. Mechanic; 862–2612. The atmosphere will remind you of a European cafe, and the menu is similarly international. L daily; D, Monday–Saturday. All major cards.

QUAKERTOWN

Sign of the Sorrel Horse. *Expensive.* Old Bethlehem Rd.; 536–4651. This quaint building used to be a pre-Revolutionary tavern. The food is ultra-modern these days, with a French-accented menu that changes with the season. D, Wednesday–Sunday. SB. No cards.

WASHINGTON CROSSING.

Fife and Drum Cafe. *Expensive.* River Road; 943–1725. The kitchen is small and the blackboard menu short, but the quality of the food is excellent. No liquor, so bring your own wine. L, D Wednesday–Saturday; L only, Tuesday. SB. No cards.

 NIGHT LIFE. In **Doylestown,** try the *Doylestown Inn,* 18 W. State St.; 345–6610. Live jazz Wednesday–Saturday 9 P.M.–1 A.M., Sunday 8 P.M.–midnight. No cover, no minimum, and food is available.

In **New Hope,** *The Baron,* Rt. 202; 862–9431. Piano entertainment nightly, with disco Wednesday–Sunday, 9 P.M.–2 A.M., and live cabaret Mondays at 10 P.M.

Chez Odette, S. River Road; 862–2432. Live jazz Friday and Saturday 8 P.M. –midnight in this French country bistro.

Havana, 105 S. Main; 862–9897. Sip on a Kiss in the Dark, an irresistible drink, and listen to live entertainment Wednesday–Sunday nights.

John and Peter's Place, 96 S. Main; 862–5981. A variety of live bands, mainly rock, keep this popular spot hopping every night and Saturday and Sunday afternoon.

EXPLORING VALLEY FORGE AND READING

Valley Forge and Reading are two major Pennsylvania visitor attractions—for very different reasons.

Valley Forge

In American minds Valley Forge is most affiliated with the Revolution and with the patriots who struggled to oust the King from his seat of control over the Colonies. It is an area rich in history, offering an awesome beauty that seems to whisper of the past. It wouldn't be incongruous for the area's inns and lodges to sport signs boasting: "Washington Slept Here." He did have to sleep somewhere.

But it is doubtful that Washington had many peaceful nights as he struggled with the war and the morale problems that beset his troops in Valley Forge. Valley Forge is where Washington and his Continental Army spent a ragged winter of discontent back in December 1777. Thousands of soldiers were forced to endure horrid conditions—blizzards, insufficient clothing, poor housing, and meals of doubtful taste. "Fire cakes" (made in outdoor ovens) would pose no threat to Betty Crocker. Gastronomically, however, one good item did come out of those hard times. Washington's cook, ordered to concoct a satisfying meal for the ravished soldiers, mixed tripe, food scraps, and peppercorns for a new taste sensation—Philadelphia pepperpot soup.

In June 1778, Washington and his troops, by then hardened by the rough winter, left Valley Forge in search of the British. If there is a legacy left by the winter of '77 at Valley Forge, it is that of a war of wills won by the soldiers. But remaining behind were the thousands unfit to continue. A single grave marks the site at which the many soldiers died.

Circumstances are far better for those visiting the area today. Much awaits the daytripper interested in unearthing a part of the past. A visit to Valley Forge National Historical Park, just twenty-five miles west of Center City Philadelphia, is not something to be rushed through. If the weather's fine (there aren't many Decembers like the one in 1777), consider packing a lunch and picnicking in the park. Your first stop should be the Visitor Center at the intersection of Routes 23 and 363. Here you can pick up a map of the whole area, of individual tour routes and bicycle paths.

A self-guided tour route visits the Muhlenberg Brigade. Reconstructed huts have been placed throughout the area and hosts attired in garb of the era depict what it was like to be one of General Peter Muhlenberg's soldiers. Then it's on to the National Memorial Arch, an impressive structure that pays tribute to those soldiers who suffered through the infamous winter. Other sites include the Wayne statue in honor of the spot where General Anthony Wayne and his band of men were encamped; Washington's Headquarters with its Revolutionary furnishings; and the Artillery Park, where the soldiers stored their cannons. A stop at the Washington Memorial Chapel rounds out the trip; to serenade you on your way out is the chapel's bell tower, featuring a 58-bell carillon.

Reading

After enjoying the richness of Valley Forge's past, you may want to hop onto the Pennsylvania Turnpike and continue north to Reading (Red-ing), a city of 81,000 residents, but one which swells considerably thanks to the tourist trade. Founded by Thomas and Richard Penn, sons of William Penn, Reading was known as an industrial city by the 1800s. By then, it was generally conceded that its greatest accomplishment was the building of the Reading Railroad.

Much has happened to the city since then. In 1974, the Reading Center City Development Fund was established with the purpose of putting life back into the downtown area. The fund helped establish Penn Square Center. And right now, Reading is undergoing subtle, useful changes such as the Callowhill Restoration area, meant to be to Reading what the Society Hill redevelopment was to Philadelphia.

Many visitors to Reading arrive by chartered buses—some from as far away as Maryland—to take advantage of the city's reputation as the Factory Outlet Capital of the world. Not for nothing does the city have such a reputation: there are outlets for clothing, pretzels, candy, luggage, jewelry, shoes, pet food—even tropical fish!

Most shoppers hop off the bus right onto Moss Street, site of the Great Factory Outlet Store and many other shops. Once you've had your fill of shopping, and filled your shopping bags with the bargains, Reading has a lot more to offer.

There's the Pagoda, sitting prettily atop Mount Penn on Skyline Drive. A seven-story building of Japanese design, the Pagoda is a favorite haunt for those who want a great view of the city. The Skyline Drive is a meandering road, itself offering drivers miles of unspoiled vistas. It is one of the loveliest attractions of the city. Close by is Penn's Common, a public park deeded by the Penns to the city. As pretty as it is, the grounds once served as the backdrop for public hangings.

Nearby, about nine miles east on Route 422, is the Daniel Boone Homestead. It is an interesting renovation of the frontiersman's home. Just go another mile east on 422 and you'll happen onto the Mary Merritt Doll Museum, housing dolls dating back to 1725. Also, the Merritt's Museum of Pennsylvania Dutch Country (Reading is located in the Pennsylvania Dutch region) offers a sweeping view of our country's rural past.

PRACTICAL INFORMATION FOR VALLEY FORGE AND READING

HOW TO GET THERE. For more information on getting to Philadelphia see *Practical Information for Philadelphia*. The Schuylkill Expressway (I-76 west) goes directly to Valley Forge from Center City Philadelphia. *Trailways* (215–569–3100) has daily service to Valley Forge; *Greyhound Bus Lines* (215–568–4800) goes to nearby King of Prussia. To get to Reading by car, take the Pennsylvania Turnpike to exit 22 or 21. *Trailways* also provides bus service here.

TELEPHONES. The area code for both Valley Forge and Reading is 215. From Philadelphia you must dial "1" before dialing the local Reading number. For directory assistance in the area, dial 1–555–1212; from outside the area dial 1–215–555–1212. Operator assistance is available by first dialing "0" before your number. For information about toll-free numbers for both regions, dial 1–800–555–1212.

 **HOTELS AND MOTELS.** Both Valley Forge and Reading offer a wide variety of choices for lodgings. Accommodations are grouped here by area and categorized by price: *Deluxe*, $80 to $100; *Expensive*, $70 to $79; *Moderate*, $60 to $69; *Inexpensive*, $50 to $59; and *Budget*, under $50.

READING

(Wyomissing)

Sheraton Berkshire Inn. *Moderate.* Route 422 West on Paper Mill Rd.; (215) 376–3811. 200 rooms. Heated indoor pool.

Reading Motor Inn. *Inexpensive.* 1040 Park Rd.; (215) 372–7811. A very pretty, well-kept, and classy complex with more than 200 rooms. Pool. Nicely landscaped to give a resort effect.

Luxury Budget Inn. *Budget.* Spring and Paper Mill Rds.; (215)378–5105. 84 rooms. Convenient to Reading attractions.

VALLEY FORGE

(King of Prussia)

Sheraton-Valley Forge Hotel. *Deluxe.* Route 363, north of turnpike exit 24; (215)337–2000. A lavish, spacious hotel with more than 300 rooms. Fine dining, dinner theater, disco.

Stouffers Valley Forge Hotel. *Deluxe.* 480 N. Gulph Rd.; (215)337–1800. Lovely, tasteful complex. 290 rooms. Steambaths offered. Heated pool, entertainment.

Valley Forge Hilton. *Expensive.* 251 W. Dekalb Pike; (215)337–1200. Handsome surroundings; more than 200 richly decorated rooms.

Holiday Inn of Valley Forge. *Moderate.* Goddard Blvd.; (215)265–7500. More than 300 units, with two pools and a whirlpool.

Howard Johnson's Motor Lodge. *Moderate.* Route 202 North at 363; (215) 265–4500. Rooms offer balconies and patios. Pool.

George Washington Lodge. *Budget.* 202 South at Warner Rd.; (215)265–6100. Close to 400 rooms. Convenient to Valley Forge attractions.

 TOURIST INFORMATION. There is a *Visitor Center* inside the *Freedoms Foundation at Valley Forge* on Route 23 (215–933–8825), and at the *Valley Forge National Historical Park,* at the junction of Routes 23 and 363 (215–783–7700), open daily in summer 8:30 A.M.–6 P.M., to 5 P.M. the rest of the year. Or, write to the *Valley Forge Country Convention and Visitors Bureau,* Box 311, Norristown, PA 19404 (215–278–3558). Information about Reading is available from the *Berks County Pennsylvania Dutch Travel Association,* in the Sheraton Berkshire Inn, 422 West on Papermill Rd., Reading, PA 19610 (215–375–4085).

SEASONAL EVENTS. In the Reading area, the *Kutztown Folk Festival* (Kutztown is between Reading and Allentown) is staged in **July.** Examples of Pennsylvania Dutch lifestyles, including demonstrations of wood whittling and sheep shearing, and lots and lots of food, are featured. The *Reading Fair* is held every **September** at the Fairgrounds. The *Gemutlichkeit Bier Fest,* an **Oktoberfest** of German specialties including beer, sausage, and fun, is a big event every year in nearby Adamstown.

TOURS. In the *Valley Forge National Historical Park,* visitors can enjoy taking the self-guided auto tape tours, which recount Washington's winter of 1777. The tapes are rented mid-May to October at the Visitor Center. A 45-minute bus tour originates at the Visitor Center three times a day from April to October. *Gray Line Tours* (215–568–6111) offers trips from Philadelphia both to Reading and Valley Forge. *SEPTA Bus Rambles* make the trip from Philadelphia to Valley Forge (215–574–7800).

SPECIAL INTEREST SIGHTSEEING The Pagoda. Atop Mount Penn in Reading, reached from City Park via Skyline Blvd.; 372–0553. A seven-story Japanese house attached to the top of this mountain by 10 tons of bolts offers a panoramic view of the area. Open Monday–Friday, 11 A.M. to 9 P.M.; Saturday–Sunday, 10 A.M. to 9 P.M. Admission: 25 cents.

STATE AND NATIONAL PARKS. The 2,500 acre *Valley Forge National Historical Park* is open daily 8:30 A.M. to 5 P.M., til 6 P.M. during the summer; it closes only on Dec. 25. For information, call the Superintendent at 787–7700. (See "Historic Sites," below.)

HISTORIC SITES. *Valley Forge National Historic Park* will bring you back to the winter of 1777. There are reconstructed soldier huts; the National Memorial Arch, honoring the soldiers; Washington's Headquarters; Artillery Park, where the cannons were stored—and more. The Visitor Center phone number is 783–7700. (See "Tourist Information," above.) Besides the attractions in the park, the *Freedoms Foundation* on Route 23 (933–8825) offers a wonderful sense of history on its campus with its Patriots Hall of Fame, Independence Garden, and Medal of Honor Grove. The purpose of the foundation is to generate interest in this country's landmarks and foster an appreciation of freedom.

MUSEUMS. Daniel Boone Homestead. Boone Rd. off Route 422, 9 miles east of Reading; 582–4900. The homestead, situated on 600 acres, shows the way the great frontiersman lived during his early years. Open Tuesday–Saturday, 9 A.M. to 5 P.M.; Sunday, noon to 5 P.M. Adults $1.50; seniors $1; children 50 cents.

Harriton House. 500 Harriton Rd., Bryn Mawr; 525–0201. This is the restored home of Charles Thomson, secretary of the Continental Congress. Open Wednesday–Saturday, 10 A.M. to 4 P.M. Adults $1.50; students and children free.

Mary Merritt Doll Museum, Route 422, Douglassville; 385–3809. Rare dolls dating from 1725 to 1900. **Merritt's Museum of Pennsylvania Dutch Country,** same location; 385–3408. Pottery, quilts, antique toys, William Penn's papers, and more on display here. Open Monday–Saturday, 10 A.M. to 5 P.M., Sundays and holidays, 1 P.M. to 5 P.M. Single admission for both: Adults $1.50; seniors $1; children 5 to 12, 75 cents.

Mill Grove. Audubon; 665–5593. The home of John James Audubon, prominent naturalist and artist, plus acres of natural park and a wildlife sanctuary. Open Tuesday–Sunday, 10 A.M. to 2 P.M. Free admission.

The Reading Public Museum and Art Gallery. Museum Park; 371–5850. Beautiful botanical garden open for the public's inspection, art and science exhibits, planetarium. Museum open daily except Saturdays in the summer. Call for hours. Adults $1.50; children under 19, $1.

SHOPPING. To list all of Reading's outlets would require a separate section. Various outlets are scattered throughout the city, but the two prime destinations for those shoppers crowded on chartered buses are the Vanity Fair Complex and Moss Street.

The *Vanity Fair Complex,* Hill Ave. and Park Rd. (378–0408), offers up to 50 percent off on cosmetics, coats, leather goods, hats, china, glass, and of course, Vanity Fair label products, including lingerie.

The *Great Factory Store Outlet Mall,* 1130 Moss St. (378–1681), showcases bargains in housewares, toys, luggage, and clocks, among other items. Call for hours.

In the Valley Forge area, the *Court and Plaza* at King of Prussia, with some 300 shops, make up the country's largest shopping center.

STAGE. The *Valley Forge Music Fair,* Route 202, Devon (644–5000), is a 3,000 seat theater-in-the-round featuring the top names in the entertainment business. The Music Fair, part of a successful chain owned by Lee Guber and Shelly Gross, also stages Broadway musical fare. *Lily Langtry's* (337–LILY), situated in the Sheraton Valley Forge Hotel, has lavish Las Vegas-style entertainment.

DINING OUT. Valley Forge and Reading serve up an impressive array of restaurants with varied prices. The following restaurants are described according to the cost of an average three-course meal for one person, not including drinks, tax, or tips: *Deluxe,* $20 and up; *Expensive,* $15 to $20; *Moderate,* $8 to $15; and *Inexpensive,* under $8. For explanation of credit card and meal abbreviations used here, see "Dining Out," in *Practical Information for Philadelphia.*

OLEY

Inn at Oley. *Expensive.* Main St., 7 miles south of Reading on Route 73; 987–3459. French cuisine in a nice country inn atmosphere. D Tuesday–Saturday. AE, MC, V.

READING

(Wyomissing)

Joe's. *Deluxe.* 450 S. 7th St.; 373–6794. Joe's has mushroomed over the years (indeed mushrooms are a popular item on the menu). Elegant Continental cuisine served here. D Tuesday–Saturday. All major cards.

Red Lobster. *Moderate.* 945 Woodland Rd.; 376–2905. Nice nautical atmosphere and good, fresh seafood. L, D daily. All major cards.

Arner's. *Inexpensive.* 9th and Exeter sts., Reading; 929–9795. Howard Blvd., Mount Penn; 779–6555. Good, quality food in a friendly atmosphere. Also a bountiful salad bar. Specials makes this a real hard-to-beat bargain. B, L, D daily. No cards.

VALLEY FORGE

(King of Prussia)

Lily Langtry's. *Deluxe.* Sheraton Valley Forge Hotel, Route 363 north of turnpike exit 24; 337–LILY. Ornate decor which enhances a cabaret/club show. Well-prepared American and Continental dishes. L with matinee, Wednesday, Friday, Saturday; D and show Tuesday–Sunday. All major cards.

EXPLORING LANCASTER COUNTY

The plain and the fancy live alongside each other in Pennsylvania Dutch country, where rolling hills are sometimes clogged as horse-drawn buggies and horn-tooting cars vie for position.

The Plain People, as the old orders of the Pennsylvania Dutch are called, have made a life out of shunning the amenities of modern civilization—using kerosene or gas lamps instead of electricity and heating by coal or oil or wood. Ironically, in turning their backs on the modern world, they have attracted that world's attention in record numbers.

Lancaster

Nowhere is the worldly interest in the Amish more evident than in Lancaster, the seat of Lancaster County, some 65 miles from Philadelphia. It is an area where weekend visitors crowd the highways, looking, often gawking, at the Amish—one of the more conservative Pennsylvania Dutch sects, whose men wear wide-brimmed hats while the women wear bonnets. Then its on to the barn shops and souvenir stores for miniature Hex signs—ornate designs originally (and erroneously) thought to be used to ward off evil; and then to the restaurants for some shoofly pie.

The term Pennsylvania Dutch is a catch-phrase for several sects. And, despite the name, the Pennsylvania Dutch aren't Dutch at all. Rather, they are descendants of German and Swiss immigrants who clustered mainly in the Lancaster area starting in the late 1600s. The "Dutch" comes from "Deutsch," meaning German.

The sects are varied within a surprisingly wide framework. Best known are probably the Old Order Amish, who keep mainly to themselves. Children are sent to one-room schoolhouses, with eight grades covered in that one room, rather than to larger schools where the parents worry they would be exposed to the influence of "outsiders." By a Supreme Court ruling these children need not attend school beyond eighth grade.

On the other end of the spectrum are the "gay" or "fancy" Dutch, more colorful in appearance and in lifestyle. They are the ones who use as decoration the Hex signs that seem to abound on every nearby barn.

Much can be learned about the Plain People on what should be the first stop of any tour of Pennsylvania Dutch country—the Pennsylvania Dutch Visitors Bureau, at Route 30 and Hempstead Road in Lancaster. A thirty-minute movie (not a touristy production but one with Hollywood-style value) is a good introduction to the area. The bureau is practically flooded with pamphlets and maps and people willing to answer questions.

While the Amish are a prime attraction, they are by far not the only lure. Lancaster itself is an intriguing city to explore. Very residential, with blocks of charming row houses, its claim to fame during the American Revolution was that it served as the nation's capital—for one day, Sept. 27, 1977—as Congress scurried away from Philadelphia after the Battle of Brandywine. Philadelphians who want to flee the city still head here for the peace and pleasure.

Wheatland, on Route 23, is the home of Pennsylvania's only contribution to the White House—James Buchanan (also the only unmarried president). The restored home contains much of Buchanan's furnishings arranged as they were during his lifetime.

Farmers markets are as much a part of the scenery as buggies. The Central Market of Penn Square (open Tuesdays and Fridays—or the day before if a holiday falls on either day—6 A.M. to 2 P.M.) offers a cornucopia of fruit, vegetables, cheeses, meats (try the Lebanon bologna), and baked goods such as sticky buns and the famous shoofly pie. Come for lunch. If you haven't gotten your fill, try the Southern Market, 102 S. Queen St. (Saturdays, 6 A.M. to 2 P.M.) or the Meadowbrook Market, on Pa. 23, just a few blocks from Leola (open Fridays, 9 A.M. to 8 P.M.; Saturdays, 8 A.M. to 4 P.M.).

East downtown, on Route 30, are the Amish Farm and House. Built in 1805, this site features a lecture tour (about 1½ hours long) through ten rooms filled with Amish furniture. On the grounds are barns and farm animals.

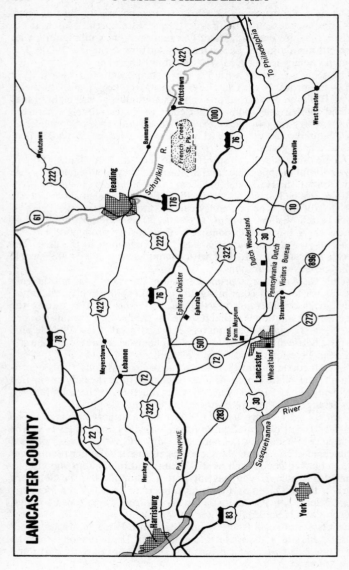

Countryside around Lancaster

Farther east, in Strasburg, on Route 30 and then south on Route 896, is the Amish Village. You can visit the Amish house, blacksmith shop, smokehouse, and a school furnished in the Amish style of today.

Proceed south a bit more on Route 896 and look skyward: for an aerial view of Pennsylvania Dutch Country, try one of the balloon excursions offered by the Great Adventure Balloon Club. Advance reservations are needed.

Down to earth again. If you prefer trains, the Strasburg Rail Road awaits you. Billed as "America's oldest short line," the train chugs its way through some nine beautiful miles of Pennsylvania Dutch country-side. To get to the train, head south on route 896, turn left on 741. The Railroad Museum of Pennsylvania, which traces the history of rail-roads in the state and displays restored locomotives, is here as well.

At this point, head back to Route 30 and stop at Mill Bridge Village, just a half-mile south of 30 on South Ronks Rd. The village is a handsomely restored Pennsylvania Dutch business area, circa 1700, with a hearth broom shop and hand-dipped candle shop. Funnel cakes and shoofly pies are available during the summer. An Amish Quilt Cabin is a popular attraction as are the scheduled festivals.

Then continue to Route 30, heading west to Dutch Wonderland, whose 44 acres of rides, shows, and gardens are popular with children. The gift shop next door rents and sells tapes for a self-guided auto tour.

Hershey

If you've come as far as Lancaster, you may want to extend your stay and travel north to Hershey, the "Chocolate Town" founded by Milton S. Hershey in 1903. Here, the street lights are shaped like giant Hershey Kisses. The number one attraction is Hershey Park, a 76-acre theme park with kiddie rides and roller coasters, theaters and live shows. Also, Hershey's Chocolate World offers tours (visitors sit on little moving cars) into the simulated world of chocolate production, from the deep jungles where cocoa plantations flourish to a modern choco-late factory.

PRACTICAL INFORMATION FOR LANCASTER
COUNTY

HOW TO GET THERE. For information on getting to Philadelphia, the gateway to Lancaster County, see "How to Get There" in *Practical Information for Philadelphia.* From Philadelphia, take the Pennsylvania Turnpike to exit 20, 21, or 22; then proceed to Lancaster. It's about 65 miles; allow 1½ hours. *Greyhound Bus Lines* (215–568–4800) provides two runs daily from Philadelphia to the RCS Bus Terminal, 22 W. Clay St., in Lancaster. *Amtrak* (215–824–1600) covers the route in 90 minutes with frequent train service from Philadelphia's 30th St. Station.

TELEPHONES. The area code for the Pennsylvania Dutch region is 717. Directory assistance is available by dialing 1–555–1212. Operator assistance is available by first dialing "0" before your number. For directory information from outside the 717 area, use the number "1," then 717–555–1212. To determine if a place you want to reach has a toll-free number, call 1–800–555–1212 for information.

HOTELS AND MOTELS. The lodgings available are much like the people themselves—plain and fancy. One can take advantage of the many campgrounds in the area, cut back on some expenses, or truly indulge in a resort with all the trimmings. Some choose to stay with a family of farmers and discover that eggs are not delivered in cardboard boxes. Depending on the type of lodging, you may be in for some real home cooking or gourmet cuisine.

Hotel rates listed below are based on double occupancy. Accommodations are described by price: *Super Deluxe:* $100 and up; *Deluxe,* $80 to $100; *Expensive,* $70 to $79; *Moderate,* $60 to $69; *Inexpensive,* $50 to $59; and *Budget,* under $50. If you travel off-season (anytime but summer) you'll find reduced rates at many hotels.

DENVER

Colonial Lodge and Banquet Center. *Budget.* On Route 272 at Pennsylvania Turnpike Exit 21; (215) 267–5501. 102 rooms, pool, restaurant.

HERSHEY

Hotel Hershey. *Super Deluxe.* On a hill 1½ miles north of the town; (717) 533–2171. Gracious, Spanish-design hotel surrounded by golf course and gardens. American Plan. Complete resort with swimming, tennis, riding, fine dining.

Hershey Lodge & Convention Center. *Deluxe.* W. Chocolate Ave. and University Drive; (717) 533–3311. Full resort with extensive recreational facilities, live entertainment.

LANCASTER

Americana Host Farm Resort and Corral. *Super Deluxe.* 2300 Lincoln Highway East (Route 30); (717) 299–5500. A vast resort with something for everyone. Available are 12 tennis courts, four pools, ice skating, rental bikes. All this and 508 rooms. Top name entertainment appears in the nightclub. Dinner theater is also offered.

Treadway Resort Inn. *Moderate.* 222 Eden Rd.; (717) 569–6444. 230 rooms, two pools, sauna. Entertainment available.

Willow Valley Inn. *Moderate.* 2416 Willow Street Pike; (717) 464–2711. A stylish atmosphere. Nine-hole golf course, two pools, sauna.

Americana's Host Town. *Inexpensive.* 30 Keller Ave.; (717) 299–5700. 193 rooms. Three tennis courts, playground. Lots of recreational facilities at a good price.

Howard Johnson's Motor Lodge. *Inexpensive.* 2100 Lincoln Highway East; (717) 397–7781. 112 rooms, indoor pool, restaurant.

MOUNT JOY

Cameron Estate Inn. *Moderate.* Donegal Springs Rd.; (717) 653–1773. Commodious, historic country inn with 18 rooms, some appointed with canopied beds and fireplaces. Fine restaurant on premises.

STRASBURG

Historic Strasburg Inn. *Moderate.* Route 896 south of Route 30; (717) 687–7691. Fifty-eight acres with 103 rooms. Entertainment in the Washington House. Christmastime celebrated with the "12 Days of Christmas," featuring minstrels, choirs, and gingerbread houses.

BED AND BREAKFASTS. See reservation services under *Practical Information for Philadelphia.*

 FARM VACATIONS. If a day in the country just isn't enough, don't despair. There are plenty of opportunities to extend your trip in a down-to-earth manner. Pennsylvania Dutch Country is rich in farm vacations.

The Verdant View Farm, one mile east of Strasburg on Route 741 (717–687–7353), offers 94 acres of dairy and crop farming. Accommodations are available in an 1896 farm house, as are homegrown breakfasts.

The Mennonite Farm Home, R.D. 3, Mount Joy (717–653–4449), offers lodging in a 200-year-old stone farm house. Breakfast included every day but Sunday.

Rayba Acres is a 100-acre working dairy farm on Black Horse Rd. in Paradise (717–687–6729). The owners invite guests to not miss milking time.

Jonde Lane Farm, on Route 7 in Manheim (717–665–4231), offers a family room that can sleep up to seven.

SEASONAL EVENTS. **May** is the month for the annual *Fire Expo,* a firefighting equipment display, at Dutch Wonderland in Lancaster. In **July** is the annual *Kutztown Folk Festival,* a country fair with handmade items and local foods. Buggies and sleighs are on the block each **August** and **October** at *Martin's Carriage and Sleigh Auction,* held in Intercourse. The **August** *Old Threshermen's Reunion* features antique steam and gas engines on display at the Rough and Tumble Museum, Route 30, Lancaster. Also in August is the *Pennsylvania Guild of Craftsmen State Fair* at beautiful Franklin and Marshall College in Lancaster. **October's** chief event is the *Antique Car Show* at Dutch Wonderland. In **December,** the Historic Strasburg Inn offers its *12 Days of Christmas* with music and holiday entertainment. There are *candlelight tours* at Mt. Hope Estate and Winery; at Wheatland, James Buchanan's Lancaster home; and at Ephrata Cloisters, in Ephrata.

TOURIST INFORMATION. The *Pennsylvania Dutch Visitors Bureau,* 1799 Hempstead Rd., Lancaster, PA 17601 (717–299–8901) offers a wide variety of information. So does the *Mennonite Information Center,* located at 2209 Millstream Rd., Lancaster, PA 17602–1494 (717–299–0954).

TOURS. You can rent or purchase a tape for a self-guided auto tour (tape recorders are supplied, deposits are required). They are available at Dutch Wonderland, Holiday Inn East, the Old Mill Stream Camping Manor and National Wax Museum. Tape rentals are $8.50. Also available are private car tours ($18 per car) with *Rutt's Tours,* nine miles east of Lancaster on Route 340. The *Historic Lancaster Walking Tour* offers 90-minute trips. It is located at 15 West King St. (717–392–1776). The *Gray Line* offers Amish tours in conjunction with *Conestoga Tours Inc.* at 825 E. Chestnut St. (717–299–6666). Gray Line Tours (215–568–6111), also offers trips to Hershey and Pennsylvania Dutch Country from Philadelphia.

SPECIAL INTEREST TOURS. *Great Adventure Balloon Club,* Box 1172, Lancaster 17608 (Rte. 896); 397–3623. A three-hour, bird's-eye view of Pennsylvania Dutch Country. $85 per person; advance reservations required.

The *Strasburg Rail Road,* SR 741, Strasburg (687–7522), provides a scenic 9-mile trip through Amish country on what's called "America's oldest short line." Hours and admission fees vary.

THEME PARKS AND AMUSEMENTS. *Dutch Wonderland,* Route 30; 291–1888. This is a wonderland, indeed. With 44 acres of fun and games—and rides—the amusement park is ideally suited for families. Admission with five rides included is $5.80; children under 4 free. Package tickets with unlimited rides are $8.80. Open daily 10 to 7, Memorial Day to Labor Day. Open weekends only Easter to Memorial Day and after Labor Day to Oct. 31.

Hershey's Chocolate World, Park Blvd.; 534–4927. Tours into a simulated world of chocolate, from a cacao plantation to a chocolate factory. Open Monday–Thursday, 9 A.M.–4:45 P.M.; Friday–Sunday, 9 A.M.–8:45 P.M. Shorter hours in winter. Call for times. Free admission.

Hershey Park, SR 743 and US 422; 534–3900. A dream come true for chocaholics who love rides. Who could pass up a towering Hershey Kiss and a Hershey Bar that walks? In addition to the many rides, there are five theaters, a zoo, and crafts shows. All-inclusive admission, with ZooAmerica, is $13.95. Special rates for children and adults over 62 as well as reduced mid-day and evening rates. Opens 10:30 A.M. daily mid-May to Labor Day plus 3 weekends in September. Closing hours vary.

 HISTORIC SITES. The land itself is a testimonial to hundreds of years of care and hard work. But Lancaster County also offers formal tributes to its people. (See also "Museums," below.)

The Ephrata Cloisters. Routes 272 and 322, Ephrata; 733–6600. Twelve restored buildings reflect the religious communal society that existed in the 1700s. Open Tuesday to Saturday, 9 A.M. to 5 P.M.; Sunday, noon to 5 P.M. Adults $2.50; seniors $1.75; children $1.

The *Hans Herr House.* 1849 Hans Herr Drive; 464–4438. A restored 1719 sandstone building that once served as a meeting place for area Mennonites. The house is the topic of several art works by Andrew Wyeth, whose ancestors were members of the Herr family. Open Monday–Saturday, March to December; Saturdays only rest of the year. Hours vary. Adults, $2; children ages 7 to 12, $1.

Wheatland. 1120 Marietta Ave., Lancaster; (392–8721). A must-see for those who have a fix on President James Buchanan, Pennsylvania's only citizen ever to become President. This is the 1828 mansion in which he lived. Open daily April to November, 10 A.M. to 4:15 P.M. Adults $3; students $1.75; under 12, 75 cents.

 MUSEUMS. *Amish Farm and House.* US 30, Lancaster; 394–6185. Lecture tours are conducted through this ten-room house furnished in the old-order Amish style. Open daily 8:30 A.M. to 8 P.M. in the summer; til 5 P.M. fall and spring; til 4 P.M. in winter. Adults $3.50; children 6 to 11, $1.25.

Amish Village. 2 miles north on SR 896, 1 mile south of US 30, Strasburg; 687–8511. See an Amish home and other buildings furnished in the Amish styles of today. Open daily 9 A.M. to 5 P.M., spring and fall; 9 A.M. to 7 P.M. summer. Adults, $3; children 6 to 12, $1. Discount for seniors.

Mill Bridge Village. US 30 and South Ronks Rd.; 687–8181. A restored 18th-century Pennsylvania Dutch trading center with shops and a covered bridge. Open daily April to October; Friday to Sunday, November and December. Adults, $3.50; children 6 to 12, $1.50.

The *Pennsylvania Farm Museum of Landis Valley,* on Oregon Pike (569–0401), offers displays examining country living before 1900. Open Tuesday–Saturday, 9 A.M. to 5 P.M.; Sunday, noon to 5 P.M. Adults, $3; children ages 6 to 11, $1.

Rock Ford Plantation and Kauffman Museum. Lancaster County Park at 881 Rock Ford Rd.; 392–7223. A preserved 1792 plantation once owned by Edward Hand, an officer in the American Revolution. Pewter and utensils of Zoe and Henry Kauffman are displayed in the barn. Open April 1 to November 30. Hours Tuesday to Saturday, 10 A.M. to 4 P.M., Sunday, noon to 4 P.M. Adults, $2.50; children ages 6 to 18, $1.

Toy Train Museum. SR 741, Strasburg; 687–8976. Antique and 20th-century model trains are displayed not far from *The Railroad Museum of Pennsylvania*

(687–8628), which features restored versions of the real things, and the *Strasburg Rail Road* which gives visitors a scenic 9-mile trip through Amish country.

THEATER. *The Fulton Opera House.* 12 N. Prince St. (Box 1865), Lancaster 17603; 397–7425. Year-round entertainment in a restored 19th-century Victorian theater. The company produces its own children's theater and presents a music, dance, and theater series including ballet, Broadway shows, and big bands. This is the America's oldest theater in continuous use.

DINING OUT. Pennsylvania Dutch dinners are "good and plenty"; tables groaning with food await eager diners. Area restaurants are known for their "seven sweets and seven sours" and homemade sausage and apple butter and fried potatoes and—don't worry, there will be enough for everybody. For the restaurants recommended below, the price categories are based on the tab for a three-course dinner for one person, not including drinks, tax, or tips: *Expensive,* $15 to $20; *Moderate,* $8 to $15; and *Inexpensive,* under $8. For the key to credit card and meal abbreviations see "Dining Out" in *Practical Information for Philadelphia.*

BIRD-IN-HAND

Plain and Fancy Restaurant. *Moderate.* SR 340; 768–8281. Family-style without menu. L, D Monday-Saturday. Open for breakfast in the summer. MC, V.

LANCASTER

Hoar House. *Moderate.* 10 S. Prince St.; 397–0110. Victorian decor. Fresh fish is a specialty. L, D Tuesday–Friday; D, Saturday and Sunday; SB. All major cards.

The Lemon Tree. *Moderate.* 1766 Columbia Ave.; 394–0441. Fine dining in a refined farmhouse-turned-restaurant. Specialties include Canard au Citron Lemon Tree. L, D Monday–Friday; D, Saturday and Sunday; SB. AE, DC, MC, V.

Leola Family Restaurant. *Inexpensive.* 2491 New Holland Pike; 656–2311. Informal. B, L, D Monday–Saturday. No cards.

MOUNT JOY

Cameron Estate Inn. *Expensive.* Donegal Springs Rd.; 653–1773. Country French cuisine in a country inn setting. L, D Monday–Saturday; SB. MC, V.

Groff's Farm. *Moderate.* Pinkerton Rd.; 653–2048. House specialty is Chicken Stoltzfus. Dinner begins with chocolate cake. Nationally know for good, hearty meals. L, D Tuesday–Saturday. Dinner seatings at 5 P.M. and 7:30 P.M. MC, V.

PARADISE

Miller's Smorgasbord. *Moderate.* 2811 Lincoln Highway East; 687–6621. A lavish buffet. L, D daily; B Saturday and Sunday. MC, V.

INDEX

The letter H indicates hotels, motels & other accommodations. The letter R indicates restaurants & other eating facilities.

GENERAL INFORMATION

PHILADELPHIA
Geographical and Practical Information